# GEORGE TOOKER

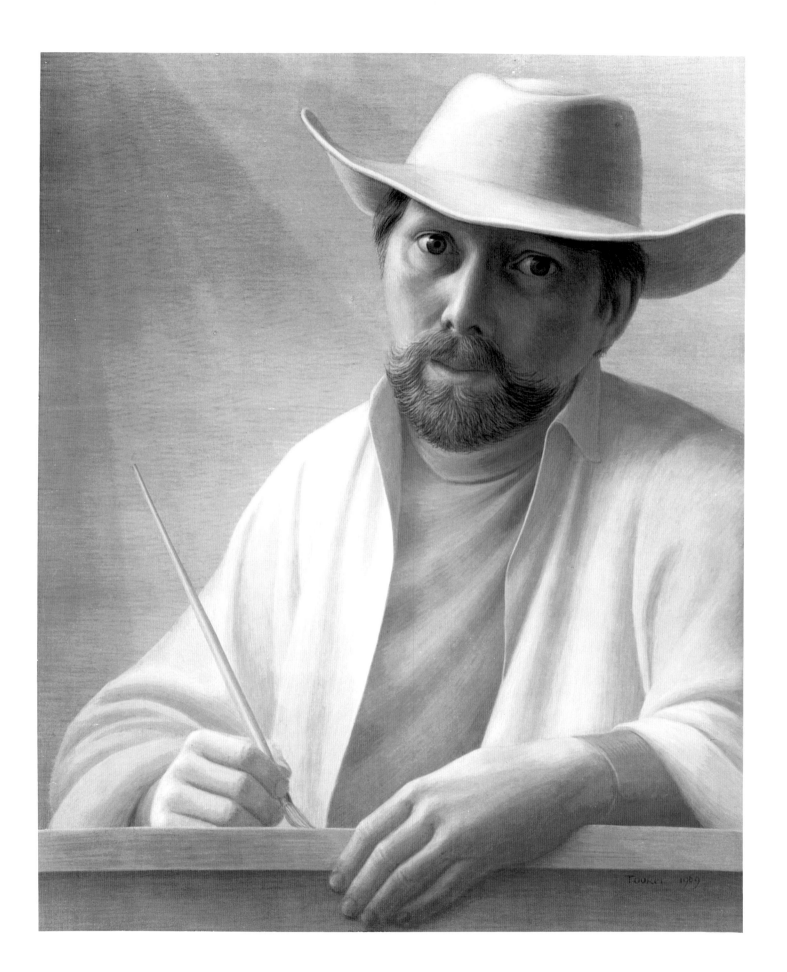

A CHAMELEON BOOK

# GEORGE TOOKER by Thomas H. Garver

*Pomegranate*

SAN FRANCISCO

A CHAMELEON BOOK

Published by
Pomegranate Communications, Inc.
Box 6099,
Rohnert Park, CA 94927
800 227 1428; www.pomegranate.com

Pomegranate Europe Ltd.
Fullbridge House, Fullbridge
Maldon, Essex CM9 4LE, England
44 1621 851646

Produced by
Chameleon Books, Inc.
31 Smith Road
Chesterfield MA 01012

Creative director/designer: Arnold Skolnick
Design associate: KC Scott
Copyeditor: Jamie Nan Thaman

Printed in China

Pomegranate Catalog No. A633

Library of Congress Cataloging-in-Publication Data
Garver, Thomas H.
    George Tooker/by Thomas H. Garver
      p.    cm.
    Includes bibliographical references and index.
    ISBN 1-56640–069-4. – ISBN 1-56640-068-(pbk.)
    1. Tooker, George–Criticism and interpretation.    I. Title.
    ND237.T585G37      1992
    759.13 – dc20                                              92-17056
                                                                    CIP

10 9 8 7 6 5 4 3 2 1

*Frontispiece:*

**SELF PORTRAIT** 1969
Egg tempera on gesso panel,
24 x 19¼ in.

## A NOTE ABOUT THIS REVISED EDITION

This revised edition of the original 1985 and 1992 monographs ful-
fills a promise made to George Tooker that the book remain in print
and be brought current. His complete ouevre of 165 paintings is
included, 105 of which are now in full color. Thomas H. Garver's
text has been preserved, and the catalogue raisonné and bibliography have been brought up to date.

## ACKNOWLEDGMENTS

Chameleon Books would like to thank Thomas F. Burke, president
of Pomegranate Communications, whose interest and support of
American art has made this reprint possible.

We also wish to express our gratitude to all the public and private
collectors, art galleries, and auction houses, notably Skinner,
Sotheby's, and Christie's, who supplied us with images and information for the first two publications and this second revised version.

Thanks are also owed to Nancy Crompton, who did the original
proofreading and created the index; Carl Sesar, who did the editing;
Jamie Nan Thaman, who copyedited this updated edition; and
Cynthia Meyer, whose creative presence is felt throughout the book.

Finally, my very special thanks to George Tooker, who always
shares with me his valuable time and insights, which has helped
make these books truly his.

ARNOLD SKOLNICK

## AUTHOR'S ACKNOWLEDGMENTS

I met George Tooker for the first time in September, 1973, while
preparing the exhibition of his work which took place the following
year at the Fine Arts Museums of San Francisco. He and I have
remained friends for almost twenty years, and I have had the pleasure of writing about his paintings on several occasions. Each experience has been both a pleasure and a revelation, and I am very
appreciative of his support and cooperation.

I also wish to thank Loni Hayman and Carl Sesar for their
thoughtful and insightful assistance in editing and Priscilla Greene
for research into the artist's exhibition history.

*FOR NATASHA*

## CONTENTS

## PREFACE:
## THE ARTIST IN HIS STUDIO
*Photographs by Arnold Skolnick*

It is a day in late August 1983, near the end of an unusually warm summer. The landscape drowses in the voluptuous heat and humidity of northern New England, and cicadas buzz in the long grass. George Tooker's house, located on a dirt road a few miles north of Hartland, Vermont, nestles easily into the land. Recently constructed, it butts up against the road, making use of the cellar of a building long gone, and only a few trees and the remnants of a stone wall separate the house from the road.

The house has no identifiable style, but it looks remarkably comfortable. The exterior is of shingle and old wood with a metal standing-seam roof, all common enough in these parts, but each room within has its own character and flavor. The low entryway facing north that formerly served as Tooker's studio, the living-dining room with a sleeping loft above, and a minuscule study comprise the original structure built as a summer and weekend retreat. Constructed of hand-hewn timbers and siding from an early nineteenth-century barn purchased in the late 1950s for $50, this section of the house is low-ceilinged, but not dark, for a row of windows faces south into a sunny, overgrown vegetable garden.

The first addition, an east wing, was built in a functional (but not particularly historical) style a few years later, with a large kitchen, bath, sleeping attic, and a separate studio for Tooker's friend, William Christopher. The next and last addition, a west wing, expanded the original study into a handsome, comfortable library where large windows opposite the fireplace open onto a New England vista – a small flower garden luxuriantly going to seed in

the foreground that gives way to pastures and woodlands. It is a scene that is suggested emotionally (even though it does not actually appear) in many of Tooker's paintings.

The nineteenth- and early twentieth-century furnishings in the library, as in the rest of the house, are simple and warmly complement the space. A Shaker rocker on one side of the fireplace is balanced by a Biedermeier chair on the other. A wing chair, writing table, and early Victorian sofa complete the furnishings. In the living-dining room, an old grain container made from a single hollow log has been transformed into a deep tub chair, and the dining room table was made from three large slabs of Honduras mahogany. Baskets, copper, pewter and china ware, a nineteenth-century painting of a sailing ship (a family memento), and drawings by Paul Cadmus, Reginald Marsh, and William Christopher (all gifts from the artists to Tooker) decorate the room. There are no works by Tooker to be seen.

George Tooker's studio occupies the northwest corner of the house. By any standards, it is not a large room and is certainly a small studio. A partition running part of the way down the center separates a lower-ceilinged anteroom that serves as a storage and shelf area (part of the original structure) from the painting space itself, which is perhaps ten by eighteen feet with a nine- or ten-foot ceiling.

The furnishings not used for painting are minimal: a stand-up desk, a dropleaf table, a closed counter-height cupboard and next to it several cardboard storage boxes. These boxes contain all the final drawings for Tooker's paintings and constitute the only complete record the artist has retained of his work. The drawings are treasured private documents as well as a major source of images continually drawn upon for new works.

The easel, facing the windows in the center of the space, is rarely used for painting but is used instead to hold a work in progress when the artist wishes to study it at a distance. Tooker paints in the northwest corner of the studio sitting at a small, low, slant-top desk that he himself built some years ago. The taboret is an unassuming white enamel tray perhaps twelve by eighteen inches perched on top of an old stool. Several mirrors, used to study hands or to answer the artist's questions about the articulation of the body, hang on the wall or sit on the floor.

External time – the time of clocks – seems redundant here. Tooker's own internal flow of energy sets the pace of his life. A typical day finds George Tooker attending morning prayer and early Mass at St. Francis of Assisi Church in nearby Windsor, Vermont. When he returns, mid-morning, he goes to the kitchen where he artfully cracks an egg, separates the white from the yolk, and gently transfers the yolk from the shell to the palm of his hand. After removing the few remaining flecks of white, he punctures the yolk and drains it into a small plastic cup in which he stirs enough cool water to approximately double the volume. In the studio, Tooker decides which areas of the painting he will work on that day and for the next day or two, and he then prepares his palette

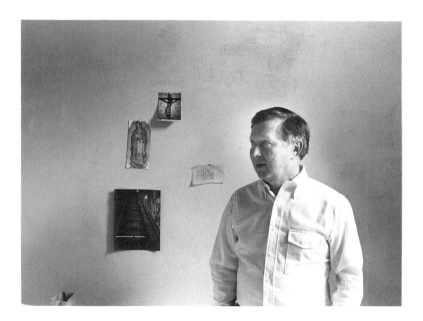

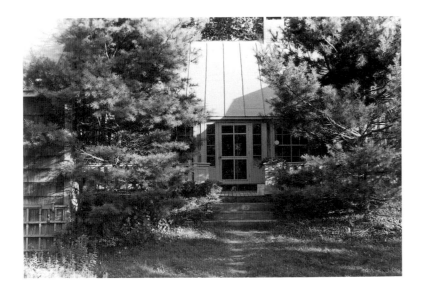

accordingly.

On this late August day, Tooker is at work on a painting now entitled *Corporate Decision*, which he has been painting for perhaps two and a half months. The work is well along and the image (illustrated on page 45) is yet another variation on a theme he so often explores. One of Tooker's political or public paintings, it is a vivid commentary on the unequal struggle between the individual and a faceless secular bureaucracy. In the lower left foreground a woman, apparently Hispanic, cradles the supine, nude body of a man. Behind this modern Pietà, another woman envelops a child in her arms so completely that just a tiny sliver of head shows. In the upper right, in contrast to the penumbral light of the foreground, a tribunal of seven figures is gathered in an alcove, bathed in the cool, white, shadowless light Tooker reserves for those aspects of a mechanical, distanced society that he most dislikes. The figures all wear black suits and their heads and faces resemble skulls. It is apparent that an unmerciful judgment has just been passed.

Today, Tooker is working on the dress worn by the woman cradling the male figure. It is a dark blue-green, but he shades its contours and folds with a deep reddish color that seems to glow darkly. After studying the figure for several minutes, Tooker begins to mix colors. Using powdered pigments, he takes two parts of ultramarine blue, two parts of ivory black ("mars black is too cold"), and one part of titanium white and puts them on a white, glazed tile on the taboret tray to mix the color for the dress. A few drops of water are sprinkled on the pigment and the colors are rubbed together into a paste. The paste is then transferred into one of the thirty-six deep round depressions – or "pots"– of a porcelain watercolor palette. Using an old sable brush ("one that doesn't hold a point anymore") Tooker adds several brushes full of the thinned egg yolk, swirling the egg and pigment together until the mixture is the texture of thin cream. In this section of the painting, completely muted by shadow, the ultramarine is too intense, so another little

pot is filled with raw umber mixed with a bit of yellow ochre and terra vert to make the color greener and more transparent. For the highlights, he has invented his own Naples yellow – titanium white with a little yellow ochre and cadmium lemon – because real Naples yellow, a lead-based pigment, is unsuitable for use with a water-based medium. A fourth pot is filled with burnt sienna, to paint the shadows.

In addition to the pots of ultramarine, raw umber, Naples yellow, and burnt sienna, Tooker fills eight more, first mixing equal parts of blue and umber in each pot as a base color, then adding increasing amounts of burnt umber to four of the pots for the darks; he repeats the process in four more pots with increasing amounts of Naples yellow for the highlights. As each color is mixed, Tooker paints a test swatch on the mixing tile, which verifies the proper relationship of one color to the next. The eight-color scale is only an index, and many more variations are made as the painting progresses.

All but one painting George Tooker has done since 1945 have been executed in egg-yolk tempera on untempered pressed-wood board that has been previously brushed all over with five or six coats of gesso, a fine, white, plaster-like ground layer made of whiting (powdered chalk) mixed with thin rabbit-skin glue.

To begin, the outlines of the drawing for a painting are transferred to the panel by placing a sheet of paper that has been coated with red pigment mixed with water or alcohol between the original drawing (which is full-size) and the prepared panel. The artist then traces the original drawing, transferring the image from drawing to panel. Following the transfer, he applies a transparent medium-tone wash across the surface of the entire panel. This wash, perhaps a gray-green or soft brown, eliminates the brilliancy of the gesso, making color development easier, but it does not obscure the under drawing.

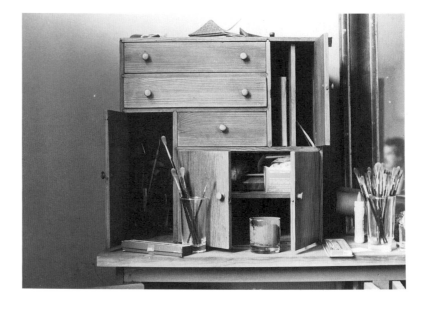

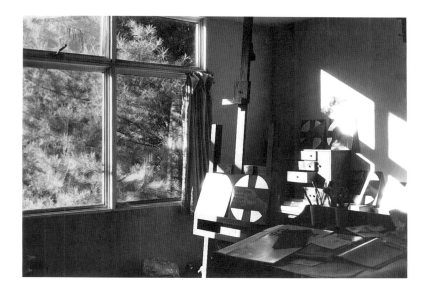

The act of painting, after the careful ritual of mixing, is deceptively simple. Tooker paints from back to front – that is, from the most distant part of the image to the foreground. Changing and modifying forms, he goes over the panel again and again, adding subtle textures to otherwise uninflected areas of the painting by hatching his brushstrokes and refining highlights and shadows as the forms take on bulk and dimension. Observing the development of a Tooker painting has been compared to "watching the fog roll in." Changes are taking place, but they are almost imperceptible from one moment to the next.

The soft brush is dipped into color, wiped against an absorbent tissue to remove the excess and applied in a few gentle strokes. Intermediate shades are mixed from the color scale in the eight little pots, and gradually the other openings in the palette fill up with other color variations. To build luminosity and transparency, extra egg is added to the color, and, as he works on the blue dress, building and modeling its forms, he continually measures the quality of the area he is working on against the tonality of the whole piece. Tooker now decides that the tribunal of seven figures is too stark – too present – and plans to put a transparent wash across them in a day or two to soften the figures' obvious angularity and the stark contrast between their black suits and white, death-mask faces.

Thus, the painting proceeds. Six days a week, pigment is mixed and applied, and the image grows in density, richness, and depth. Egg tempera painting is slow work and there are no shortcuts. Layer after layer of color is laid down in order to achieve the luminosity characteristic of George Tooker's work. This painting will require two more months of intense effort before it is finished.

A query to Tooker about the difficulty of painting with egg tempera brings a laugh. "Tempera isn't hard at all. It's a very easy, plodding medium. It's slow, and since I'm slow in knowing just what I want to do, it suits me well." And so it does. Painting as Tooker paints, a color put down today may be modified or painted out tomorrow. Painstakingly, the artist builds and models layer upon layer of the translucent and opaque colors that give his paintings, no matter what their subject, their physical presence and structure.

The day wears on into mid-afternoon. Painting requiring this intensity and focus cannot be carried on for more than four to six hours a day. Tooker stops working and wraps the palette, takes it to the kitchen, and puts it into the refrigerator. Kept cold, his palette is usable for a day or two longer.

After Tooker finishes painting for the day, he does household chores or reads or thinks about ideas for new works, making tiny sketches on scraps of tracing paper. Some days Tooker looks through painting and sculpture books that reproduce the works of the old masters or of twentieth century artists, not necessarily seeking specific references, but enriching his own vision that merges the artistic traditions of past and present.

George Tooker is a wonderful cook, and as the light begins to fade, he returns to the kitchen to prepare a simple evening meal, one often influenced by the cuisine of Spain where for some years he spent the winters.

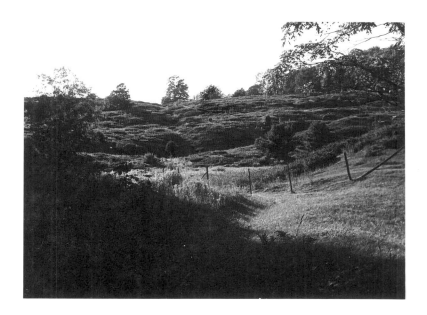

*I have visited George Tooker several times in Hartland, in the winter as well as the summer, and the routine continues. In the winter Tooker plans the garden he will plant and tend the following summer. Potted plants, outside during the summer, have been brought in and provide the touch of growth he needs around him. Yet the wellsprings of life come not from plants or a garden but from within. In these last few years, George Tooker has found peace, order and harmony in this tiny community, a solace and nourishment that eluded him for so long.*

# INTRODUCTION

In the last fifteen years, the tradition of illusionistic painting has been recognized once again as belonging to the mainstream of modern art. This newfound legitimacy of "art with content"– as opposed to abstract art, which for many years had eclipsed all other kinds of art – has been part of a wider acceptance of multiple forms of expression in today's art, with no single style predominating. Along with this more eclectic point of view has come a renewed curiosity about artists whose work may have been overlooked in the rush from one style to another during the middle decades of this century. Certainly among the most prominent of these is George Tooker, whose one-person show at the Marisa del Re Gallery in February 1985 was his first exhibition in New York City in almost twenty years.[1]

For almost fifty years, Tooker has painted as though the art world has not existed, and, for him, it really has not. Although his work became widely known in the late 1940s and early 1950s, relative obscurity came in the wake of the tidal wave of Abstract Expressionism and with it an avant-garde sensibility that sought out and valued the new, often at the expense of art produced within established traditions. While many artists of Tooker's generation responded to early success and later eclipse with anger and bitterness, Tooker did not. In Tooker's world art has nothing to do with fashion or popularity. A deeply spiritual man, Tooker does not regard himself as "creating" his paintings in the latter twentieth-century sense of the word. When he says, "I don't really think I'm a creator. I feel that I'm a passive vessel, a receptor or translator," he speaks without any self-consciousness or false modesty. "The fascinating thing about painting is the discovery. I don't want to explain in words what I'm about. I can't explain it. I don't think about it. I don't examine it myself and I don't want to." He admits that he may be superstitious in this regard, and acknowledges a fear of losing works by "explaining them away" before he paints them. This is the quiet and self-renewing sense of wonder that has sustained and nourished his work for five decades. Through the years George Tooker has continued to paint, producing one to three pictures a year, which have been immediately acquired by faithful and appreciative collectors.

Tooker's painting style has undergone only slight stylistic changes since 1945. "The Classicist is concerned with being rather than becoming . . . and the power of his art lies only partially in his mode of execution."[2] By this definition, originally applied to Edward Hopper, George Tooker is a Classicist. He is an individual trained to the virtues of intellection and the benefits derived from a knowledge of history. He uses a quotation, "Art comes from other art," which he attributes to Thomas Aquinas, to explain his need to draw upon many stylistic sources.

Tooker acknowledges his debt to the sculptors of classical antiquity, to the Flemish and Italian painters and sculptors of the fourteenth and fifteenth centuries – particularly Uccello and Piero della Francesca – and to Dutch and French seventeenth-century painters as well. In the twentieth century, the *Neue Sachlichkeit* artists of Germany and Mexican painters of the 1920s and '30s have been important to him. American painters of a more recent vintage, as disparate as Jared French, Henry Koerner, Paul Cadmus, Alton Pickens, Honore Sharer, and Edward Hopper, have also had an influence.

In Tooker's paintings content determines the visual forms, techniques and subject matter. Tooker quotes his painter friend, the late Jared French, to stress this point. "The design of a picture must come out of its meaning. There is no such thing as 'good design' unless it comes out of the meaning that the artist intends." This idea, simply stated but deeply embedded in the artist's ethical sensibilities, along with the artist's never ending sense of wonder and discovery, propels the act of painting.

Tooker began to study painting at the Art Students League in 1943 under Reginald Marsh, with whom he studied until the summer of 1945. During this time he also worked briefly with two other artists at the League. One was Kenneth Hayes Miller, a close friend of Marsh's and a respected lecturer on art. Tooker, however, felt him to be indifferent to his art, and there was little personal contact. Harry Sternberg, like Marsh, was more sympathetic to Tooker's paintings. Tooker regarded Sternberg as a good teacher and critic who asked simple yet very pointed questions that challenged a number of Tooker's developing mannerisms. It was Miller, however, who in the long run may have had the greatest influence of the three on Tooker. Although he was not directly responsive to Tooker as a student, his lectures, laced with aphorisms such as "The artist should pack the picture plane as carefully as he packs a suitcase," or "A hole in a composition is as serious as a hole in a teakettle," had a strong effect. Furthermore, Miller used Renaissance figural prototypes for his images, although he painted them in modern dress and set them in scenes drawn from life observed on Fourteenth Street. It was Miller, too, who encouraged his students to develop a particular type of figure without the use of a model and to emphasize form and mass at the expense of specific emotions.

In late 1944, Tooker developed a friendship with the painter Paul Cadmus, who, though not a student at the League, came to Saturday drawing classes there. Tooker was at that time painting in a technique developed by Reginald Marsh. A wonderfully facile draftsman with a baroque dash, Marsh used well-thinned egg tempera as a wash, drawing as much as painting with the brush, flicking in outline forms, then washing a transparent body color over the drawn outlines. It was a bravura high-speed painting style with which Tooker was not very comfortable. Cadmus, an equally facile draftsman, albeit more "Renaissance" by persuasion, encouraged Tooker to read Daniel V. Thompson's book *The Practice of Tempera Painting* and to try painting in tempera in the traditional Renaissance manner. Tooker subsequently adopted this method and found that it suited him perfectly. Paintings done in egg tempera require substantial forethought, and it was just the right medium for Tooker's contemplative sensibilities, which demanded that his works of art be as well considered intellectually as they were carefully executed.

In Tooker's paintings, many of the images are mysterious, complex, and, in the final analysis, ambiguous. But if there is one touchstone to the paintings of George Tooker, it is the utter simplicity of his themes. His paintings often rely on literary references or imagery from the past, but these come into effect only after the idea of the work has been formed. They are made in homage to the medium in which he works, to the richness and density of the history of art. But little is to be gained by the search for these historic references in Tooker's painting. George Tooker's particular genius lies not in the selection of his sources, which are many and varied, but in the way he has used them to develop and express his ideas.

Lincoln Kirstein, an early champion of Tooker's work, identified a group of artists who were working outside the Abstract Expressionist mainstream of American postwar art as "symbolic realists." In a critical introduction to the exhibition "Symbolic Realism in American Painting, 1940–50," Kirstein stated that symbolic realism ". . . takes painting for an intellectual . . . more than an emotional or manual profession or responsibility. It assumes the durable products of this art are expressions of ideas rather than a craft or the demonstrations of self-love or self-pity. It accepts painting as a triumph of the orderly, the intelligent, and the achieved, rather than as a victim of the decorative, the fragmentary, or the improvised. It assumes the human mind is obligated toward synthesis, and that, at its most interesting, establishes order rather than disorder, from infinities of observable phenomena. . . .These pictures are essential rather than anecdotal. They attempt to define qualities and conditions independently of their designers' appetites. . . . Their reference moves outward toward a universal legibility rather than inward toward a limited correspondence."[3]

Tooker strips away detail to probe the similarities beneath the individual surfaces. Society as he envisions it becomes a melting pot of individual characteristics and personalities, and differences as basic as sex and race are frequently blurred and obscured in the construction of the universal from the fragmentary vision. Tooker's work, embodying Kirstein's sense of "universal legibility," has developed in several parallel sensibilities or themes, each interlocked stylistically but stressing different aspects of the artist's basic concerns.

The best known of Tooker's *oeuvre* are his paintings of strong social comment, sometimes described as his "public" or "political" pictures. In these, psychological observation has been placed at the service of a collective vision to intensify the expression of numbing isolation and anonymity Tooker finds in modern life. Several of these works are in public collections – among them *The Subway*

(1950), *Government Bureau* (1956), and *The Waiting Room* (1959) – and thus are widely known and reproduced.

As a foil to these paintings and, indeed, comprising a much larger part of his output, is another group of paintings more intimate in subject matter. These pictures deal with transcending the harshness of life, divine and carnal love, the struggle of communication, and a meditative state of being somewhere between death and life, sleep and wakefulness, when ideas enter the soul in the most unexpected forms. These interests of the painter's have been joined more recently by another. With his conversion to the Roman Catholic faith, a singular group of paintings, culminating in the radiant *Seven Sacraments* (1980), has ascended from a deep personal despair to glowing triumph. This body of work reveals Tooker's belief in the perfectibility of humanity possible under divine guidance.

Tooker has described himself as "rather didactic. In one kind of painting I'm trying to say 'this is what we are forced to suffer in life,' while in other paintings I say, 'this is what we should be.' I oscillate between the earthly state and a concept of paradise." Given this didacticism and desire for perfection, it is not surprising that Tooker returns repeatedly to his themes. Like the gardener who carefully prunes his vines, Tooker constantly refines his imagery, working within his chosen set of themes to make them "stronger and more solid."

As the appearance of his paintings has resisted change over the years, so, too, they resist precise dating. George Tooker has neither dated his paintings, nor has he maintained records of their creation beyond his archive of carefully preserved cartoon drawings and preliminary studies, which are also undated. The dates given here have been based on exhibition records and other data. Tooker has traditionally painted between two and four pictures per year and has never painted two variations of the same subject in succession.

In his mature work he has melded history and contemporary life in a way that has been neither excessively historicist nor amusingly *au courant*. Unlike many of his peers, among them Koerner, Cadmus, Marsh, and Ben Shahn, Tooker rarely paints specific events or artifacts of a period (often documented by these other artists through the use of crumpled newspapers with their headlines visible, fashionable clothing, or objects popular at the moment the painting was executed). Neither is he interested in overt surrealism. "I am after painting reality impressed on the mind so hard that it returns as a dream," Tooker has stated, "but I am not after painting dreams as such, or fantasy."[4] Tooker's paintings, perhaps even more than Edward Hopper's, look at contemporary life in the long view. They examine issues removed from specific events and pose questions about ourselves and our lives in the context of the larger universe.

———

**AUDIENCE** 1945.
Egg tempera on gesso panel,
9 x 12 in.

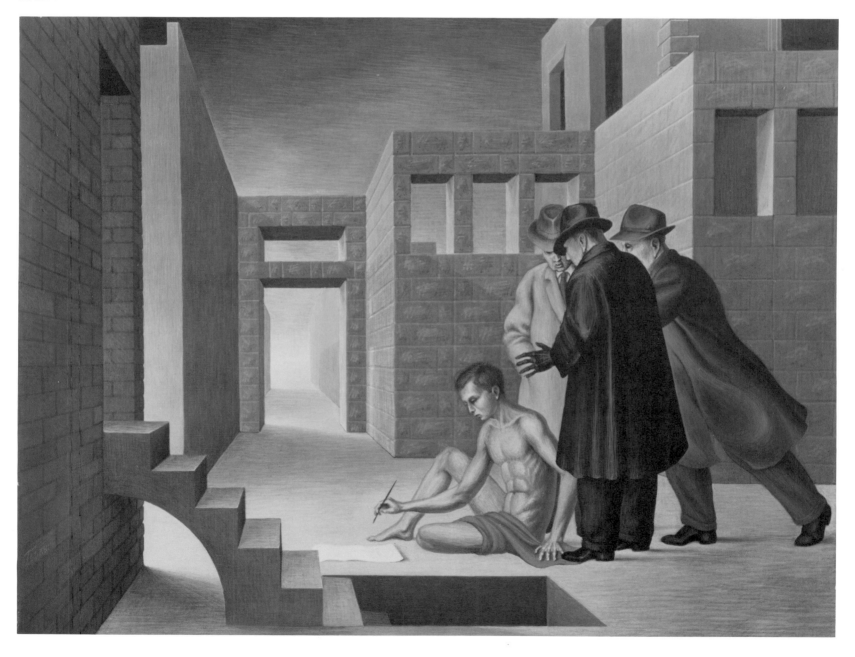

In *Audience* (1945), the painting that George Tooker regards as his first mature work, a seated, semi-nude male figure is working intently on an architectural drawing, apparently unaware of his "audience." Three men dressed in overcoats, hats, and gloves appear ready to seize the highly vulnerable artist, who is oblivious to everything but his task at hand. At the heart of the scene is the imminent threat of a sinister or violent act, but, characteristically, no overt violence is shown. With rare exception, Tooker's paintings bring us into the drama moments before–or occasionally after–any action takes place. In *Audience*, as in much of his later work, Tooker depicts clothed and unclothed figures in juxtaposition, where nudity may symbolize visionary truth opposed by the agents of obstruction, doubt, and conventionality. The artist portrayed is surely the young Tooker (compare the face to the self-portrait of 1947). Indeed, many of the figures he portrays throughout his work are the artist himself in one guise or another.

The compositional stratagems Tooker uses here are also those he has employed throughout his career. The architectural setting and the classical manipulation of perspective stress the formal goals of order and containment, and show the influence of the fifteenth-century Italian primitives in the Johnson collection at the Philadelphia Museum of Art. Also typical of his work is the use of deep and shallow spaces played against one another. Many of the paintings created in the ten-year period from 1945 to 1955 use the same sort of spatial arrangement: deep open space to the left, rapidly compressed by strong diagonal or step forms to a much shallower space at the right-hand side of the panel. This composition is given an added twist of complexity in the use of the curious little stairway at the left front. It is a device that shapes the space and stops it just inside the picture plane but also suggests the illusion of breaking out of the picture plane through openings below grade level and off to the left.

*Audience* was a composition on which Tooker worked very hard. According to the artist, the image developed by "trial and error," and there were a lot of "preliminary scribbles until I sensed what I wanted." In this case, he developed the composition completely in a pencil drawing on pale blue paper heightened with white. The completeness and finish of the drawing was a mistake that he has not repeated since. "I've found it is better to work things out less thoroughly in the preliminary drawing because then there is more discovery when you get to the actual painting," he asserts. In its use of light, too, this painting prefigures much of Tooker's later work. The light is soft, and the precise angle of the sun is indicated by a triangular shadow thrown against the wall in the middle ground. The shadows are remarkably light and open, almost glowing with their own internal phosphorescence. The shadows, and the space which simply disappears at the end of the long opening to the left, suggest light refracted by fine dust in the air, a quality of atmosphere incongruous with the clarity of detail in the foreground. Yet this softness of light, so suffused into the atmosphere as to appear to be bent through it, is a quality that is a constant

throughout all his work. It is this diffusion of light that forms the roundness and volume of the figures and that often gives these paintings the illusion of transcending the harshness of real life.

Tooker's next painting, *Dance* (1946), was much more dependent on his contemporaries for its sources and style of execution than was *Audience*. At that time, he was rapidly absorbing ideas and eager to try them out, and this painting was strongly influenced by Paul Cadmus and Jared French. Tooker's acquaintance with Cadmus, begun in 1944, had blossomed into warm friendship by 1946, and it was through Cadmus that he met Jared French and his wife, Margaret. French, a remarkable painter of almost reclusive nature, was at that time living in New York, where he shared a studio with Cadmus. While both French and Cadmus painted with tempera and often used the nude or semi-nude figure in their work, the results were quite different. Cadmus was devoted to meticulously rendered views of New York street or beach scenes, filled with well-muscled sailors, half-naked boys, and firm-busted women, and sprinkled with newspapers and other common street litter, all observed with a curious, distancing irony. Jared French, on the other hand, was much influenced by Carl Jung's hypothesis of the collective unconscious, a racial memory of sorts, which is inherent in the mind of all human beings. French used figures outside of a specific time or place, abstracted into a type that resembled the *kouros* form of pre-classic Greek sculpture, to transmit images of emotional or mental states. Tooker admired French's ability to shape emotional intensity without having to define specific characters within a painting.

*Dance* is a modern-day variation on a favorite late medieval and early-Renaissance theme, "The Dance of Death," the moment when death takes its victims, who, no matter what their station in life, cannot save themselves. Tooker was aware of Hans Holbein's woodcut series depicting the dance of death and knew the intense activity and close observation that marks the work of the Flemish fifteenth-century painters. It is activity and observation rather than the geometric order of the Italian early-Renaissance masters that is evident here. *Dance* is set at the intersection of two busy city streets, with people crowding the sidewalk in front of a tiny hamburger stand at the corner. The tiny building's castellations and grid of steel interior panels establish a theatrical space and echo the long recessive lines of the sidewalk's grid pattern. It is a windy evening, and a few crumpled sheets of newspaper, one bearing the artist's signature, are being blown about near a chasm that is about to open up in the sidewalk in the immediate foreground–a reference perhaps to the eternal life below. Death, dressed in a black cape, his diaphanous skin stretched over the skeleton frame, has arrived to carry off his victims, a wealthy older man and his younger female companion; while at the same time, in the right background, another death figure is claiming two more victims. Marching in from the right is a trio of young women–improbably dressed in red, white, and blue outfits and complete with Rosie-the-Riveter hairdos–who, though they are heading directly toward the

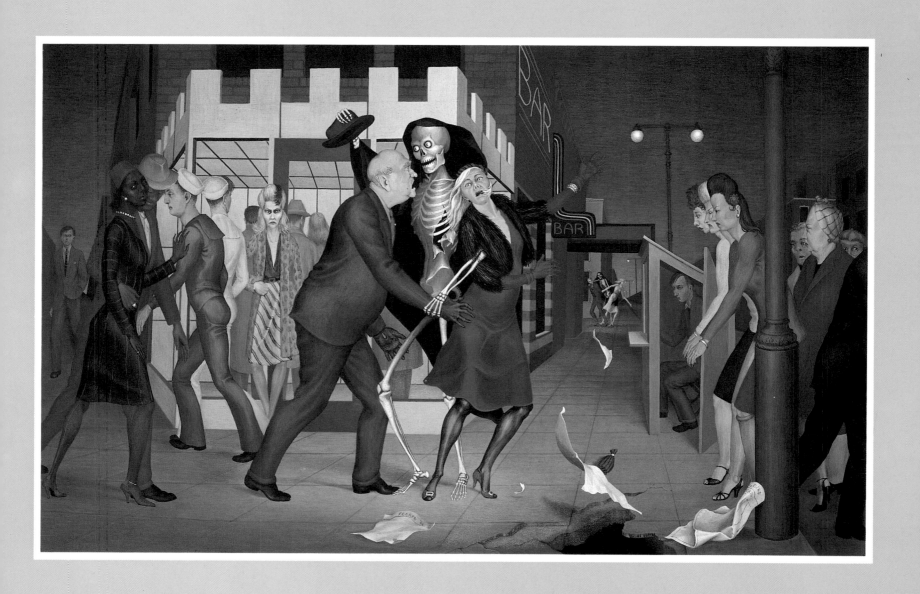

**DANCE** 1946.
Egg tempera on gesso panel,
13 x 20½ in.

**THE CHESS GAME** 1947.
Egg tempera on gesso panel,
30 x 15 in.
(Opposite)

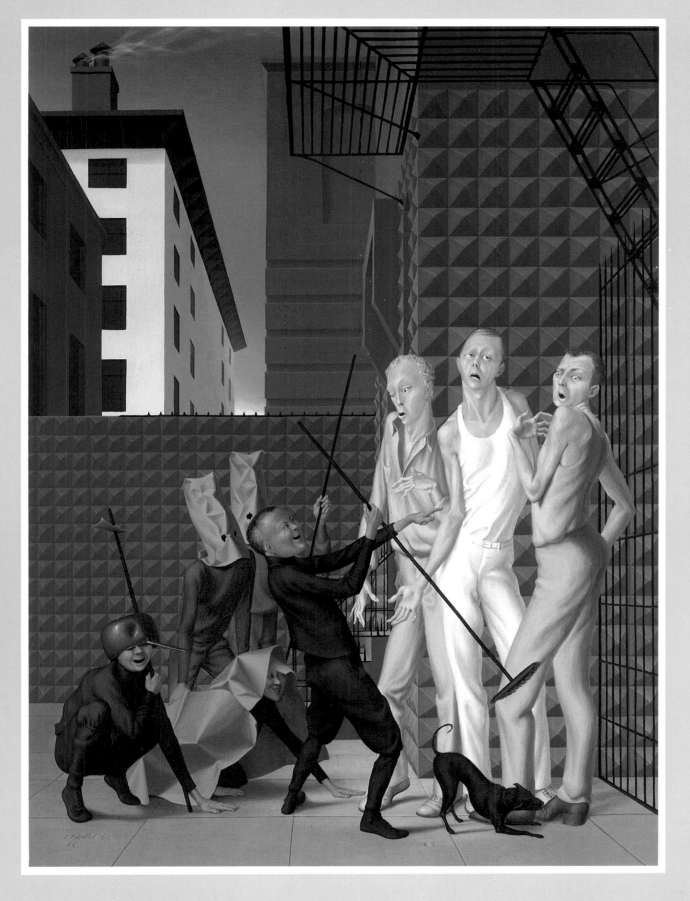

**CHILDREN AND SPASTICS** 1946.
Egg tempera on gesso panel,
24½ x 18½ in.

impending tragedy, seem totally unaware of it. In fact, only two of the other figures that populate this street scene – including a sour-faced hooker, a newspaper vendor lost in thought, and the other standard street types found in paintings by Marsh and Cadmus – seem aware of anything amiss. One of them is a black woman at the left who suddenly seems aware of the hideous visitor in their midst. She raises her hand in warning, but it is too late. The work parallels the ideas of Tooker's friends and teachers in its pointedly contemporary treatment of a traditional theme and even in certain details (such as the rip in the translucent "flesh" of the skeleton, which is similar to the treatment of torn flesh in a series of panels depicting the Seven Deadly Sins on which Paul Cadmus was working at the time). One other figure notices what is happening and appears not to be happy about it. It is the young man walking into the scene at the extreme left. It is George Tooker. It is apt that he should arrive thus, for, in Tooker's best paintings, no matter what the subject, his presence is always felt, not only as an observer, but as an empathizer and often as a principal character (or sometimes even several at once). There is no distancing of the artist from his subject, through irony or amusement, and Tooker always holds the focus directly on that subject.

His next painting, *Children and Spastics* (1946), is also about the threat of violence, but this time it is of a more common sort. Set against a boldly patterned architectural background, five children dressed in black costumes and their small black dog are tormenting three pale young men. They are grouped in front of a russet wall of pyramidal-cut stone, in the style of a Renaissance palazzo, a fanciful image that contrasts strongly with the tenement-style fire escape visible just above them. (The white building with the deep black cornice in the background was modeled after the former Mills Hotel on Bleecker Street, which Tooker could see from his apartment.)

The "children" are not children at all but rather pygmies, grotesques, embodiments of an anonymous, cruel society. They are dressed in black to offset their victims' pale figures, whose clothes somehow heighten their vulnerability rather than protect them. "The painting wasn't meant to be about physical violence, but about spiritual violence," says Tooker. As originally composed, the three "spastic" figures, whose gestures also suggest the mannerisms of homosexual stereotypes, were more centrally located in the composition and were much less exaggerated in their gestures. The source of this image was the painting of the martyrdom of St. Sebastian by Pollaiuolo in which the central figure of the saint, bound to a stake, is surrounded by bowmen in various poses, a lesson in figure anatomy rendered from every angle. It is an image that will appear again and again in Tooker's work.

*The Chess Game* (1947), an autobiographical painting, was a watershed work of the early years. The setting is Tooker's Bleecker Street cold-water flat, three rooms in a row with a shared toilet in the hallway. The twisting figure at the lower right, hand raised as though to ward off disaster, is the artist himself. The game is an

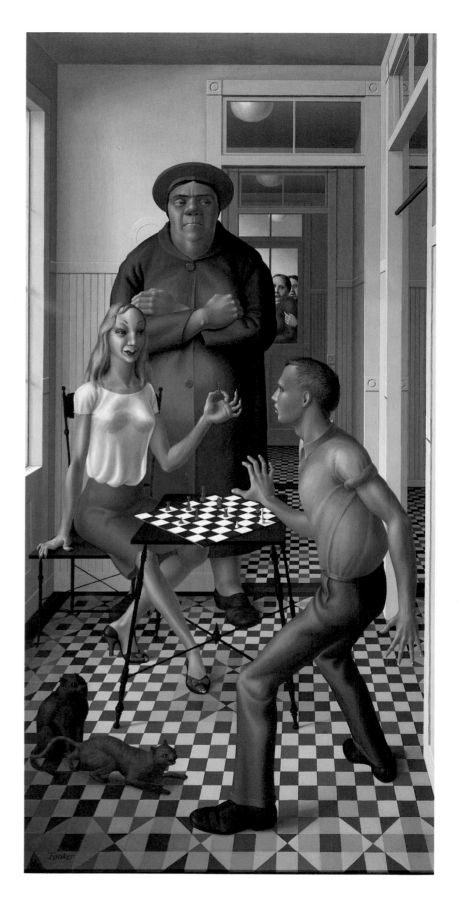

uneven match, and Tooker is losing. It is a visual allegory of an internal struggle that pitted Tooker unequally against a society that expected him to mature, settle down, establish a family, and be socially correct and productive. The physical allure of his chess partner, the young woman in her loosely fitted and revealing blouse, is countered by the frowning, heavy-set duenna standing like a fortress behind her, there perhaps not only for protection but as a suggestion of the future as well. The young woman appears to be offering Tooker a chess piece. The gesture, a modern parallel of the flower offering in Renaissance betrothal portraits, will probably remain uncompleted, hindered by the stern gaze and formidable bulk of the massive guardian. At the end of the hallway, the silent watchers – the rest of us – stand as witnesses at the window. The painting is a document of one of the major decisions of Tooker's life. He did not marry, nor did he conduct his life as he anticipated society thought he should.

In *The Chess Game*, Tooker still relies on a dense geometry to underscore his dramatic scene. The flow of space through the interconnected rooms is emphasized by the tessellated Renaissance floor, certainly not a standard feature of a New York old-law tenement, and by the alternating light and dark patterns of walls and openings. The angularity of the two opposing figures, set at forty-five degrees to the major axis, breaks the right-angle construction; the chess board too is set on the diagonal, just as aggressive a pattern as the floor but a bit self-conscious, perhaps.

Tooker does not often directly acknowledge himself as one of the protagonists in his paintings but has described the content of this painting as being "a little heavy-handed." He was also somewhat unhappy with the style; he found the figures to be too attenuated and lacking in volume. The furniture, in particular, came to annoy him, and, after completing *The Chess Game*, he made a conscious effort to reshape his forms more volumetrically.

In the spring of 1947 Tooker began one of the most extraordinary paintings of his early career. *Self-Portrait* is a tondo of modest dimensions which sprang from a modest source. He had bought a round, black frame, not very old, but the profile of its molding was reminiscent of seventeenth-century Dutch frames. Inspired by the shape, Tooker sought to create a series of variations of circular volumes in a plane. He also wanted to work from a model and "if you want to work from a model, a mirror image gives you a model whenever you're ready to paint." He began the portrait in his Bleecker Street studio (the details of the molding in the background of the painting are taken from the woodwork there).

He carried the painting with him to Provincetown that summer, which was spent with Paul Cadmus and Jared and Margaret French. He had his hair cut while he was there, and, by mistake, the barber cut the hair on the sides of his head so short that he simply had all of it cut to the same length. That haircut was a fortuitous mistake, however, for the short hair emphasized the structure and volume of Tooker's head, contributing to the success of the painting's composition. This Tooker portrait is the first fully-

formed embodiment of the "Tooker man," a physical form loosely modeled after the artist's own face which appears again and again in his work. Tooker admits to using his own head shape, round and with symmetrical features, repeatedly, but not as a deliberate or even extended portrait of himself. One must speculate, however, that the use of his facial type, no matter how it may be modified, is strong evidence of the desire of the artist to place his persona within his paintings as a participant.

Tooker here uses a motif that will appear in a number of future works, the sweater draped over the shoulders, with the sleeves tied under the neck. It gives greater definition to the volume of the neck as support for the head. It is a device which serves as a stylistic flourish and an element which here suggests the hood of a monk's robe. Clearly its use is other than a casual form of dress; the artist is already wearing a sweater.

The polished nautilus shell was an inspired addition. It is a variation on the circular form, of which there are three in the painting: the architectural detail in the woodwork behind the hand and the two natural variations of shell and head. This simple, small painting contains variations not only on the circle but on subtle surface textures and luminosity as well, with the artist's flesh taking on elements from the flat stony background and the gloss of the shell with its touch of iridescent highlights.

Returning to Bleecker Street in the autumn of 1947, and perhaps inspired by a summer spent at the beach, Tooker began work on *Coney Island* (1947–48), a painting that establishes the physical structure of his mature work. Although Tooker here takes on a subject and location that were particular favorites of Reginald Marsh, the sensibilities that motivated the two artists were very different. Tooker's painting, while wonderfully organized, does not possess the fluid, music-hall choreography of Marsh's best beach paintings. This work is a series of individual compositional elements, each rather static in isolation but given vitality by their juxtaposition and ordering. Tooker himself felt that this painting showed his affinity for the work of Julio Castellanos, a Mexican-American painter who, regrettably, has never received much notice. Tooker admired Castellanos's work for its "quality of the celebration of life," particularly the painting *St. John's Day* (1940), in which many figures are set around a great urban public swimming pool surrounded by large apartment blocks.

Both Tooker and Castellanos framed their compositions as if placed on a stage. In *Coney Island*, the heavy decking and posts of the pier literally form a proscenium. The painting is centered on an inverted triangle of sunlit space, delimited by stairs and figures to the left, and the strong diagonal of the stairway to the right. However, this sunny, open space filled with a variety of small figures cannot compete in mass or compositional power with the foreground's strong dark triangle of five figures to the left or the half triangle of the two bulky women to the right. Shaped and defined in the penumbral glow of light (reflected from the sand and filtered through the sheets and towels set up as impromptu

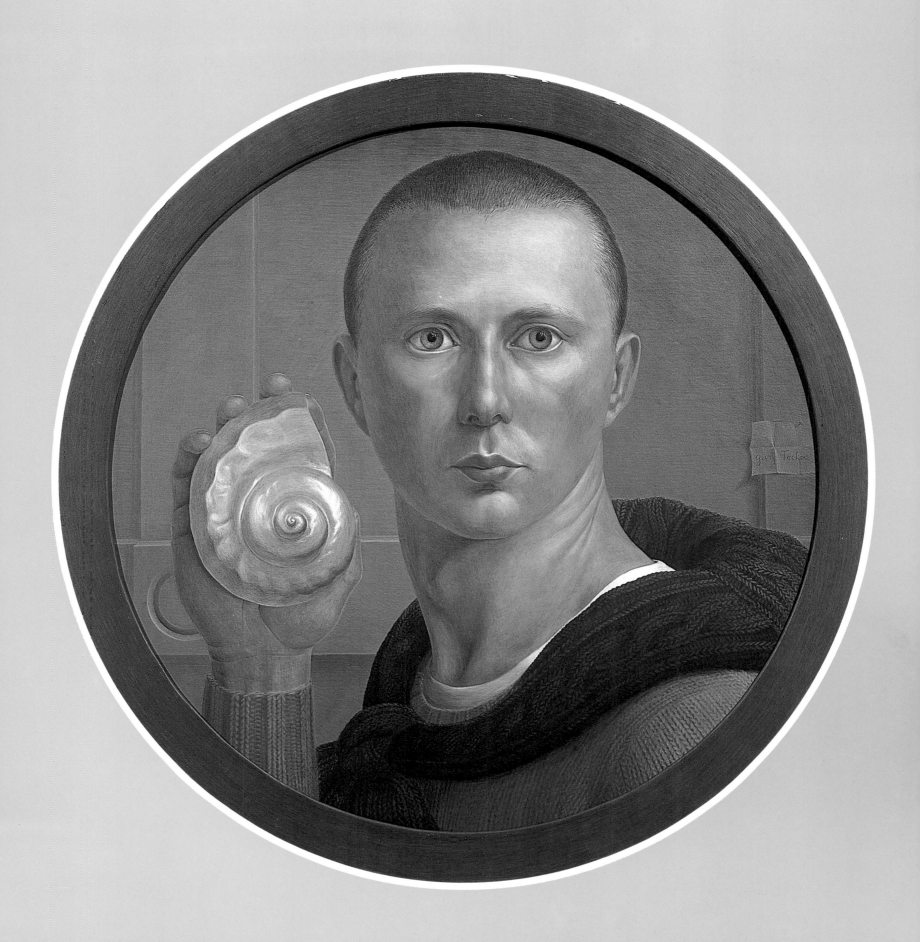

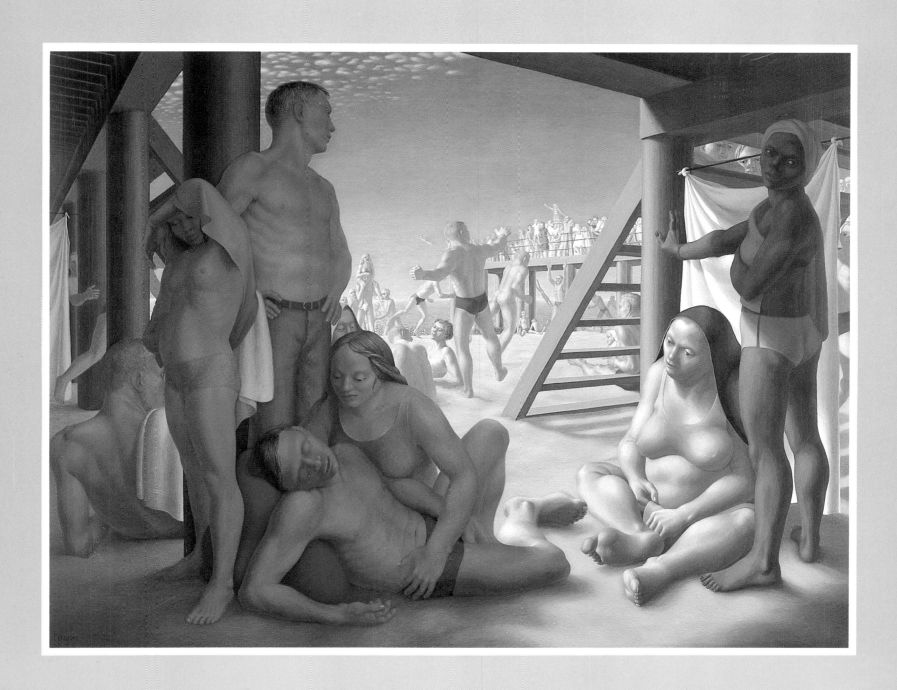

**CONEY ISLAND** 1948.
Egg tempera on gesso panel,
19 x 26 in.

(Detail opposite)

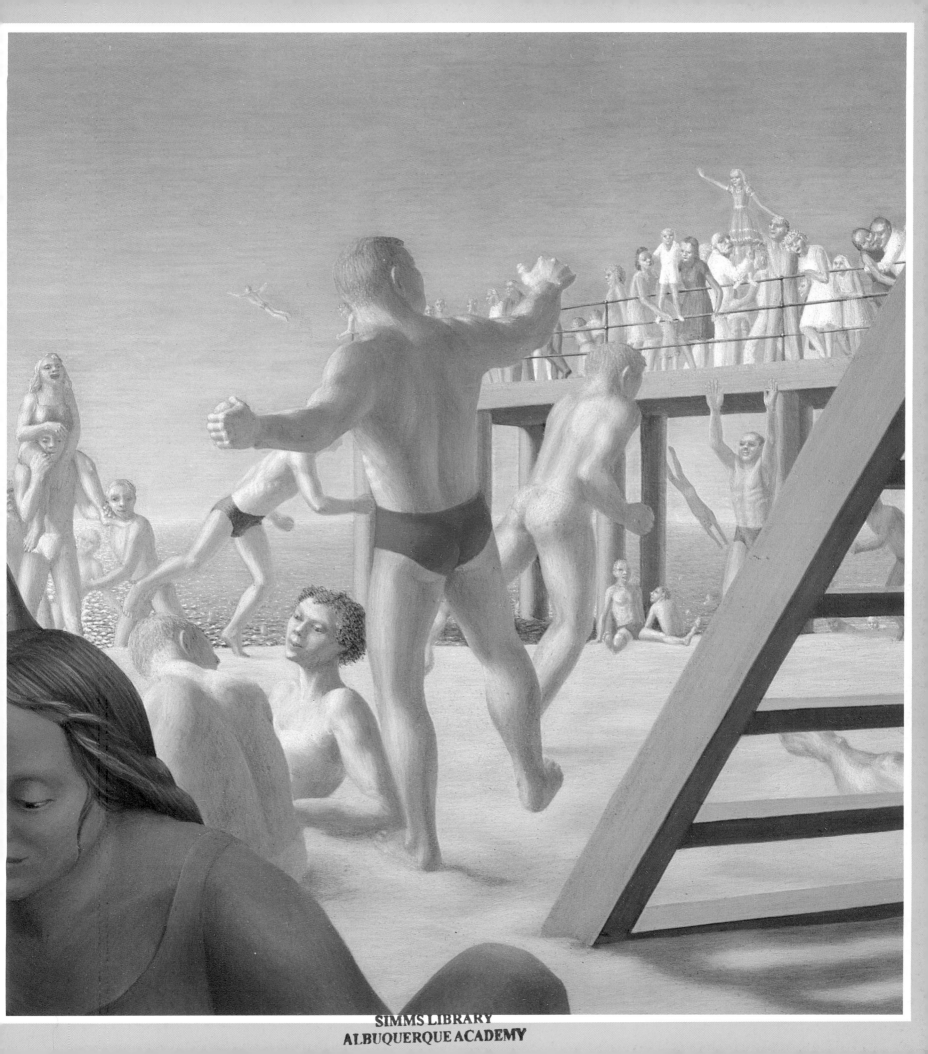

changing booths), the figure group to the left is a magnificent example in Tooker's early work of his ability to model figures. Tooker declares that he "intended this to be a happy picture," but the figures in this group appear to be rather more distracted or lost in thought than happy. They are forms of compact flesh, dominated by shadow, in sharp contrast to the sunlit parade of bodies further out on the beach. The couple in the lower part of this group even resembles a modern pietà, an image that recurs in several of Tooker's works. Yet there are little jokes and gestures of affection here. Tooker has placed his friend Reginald Marsh in the crowd on the pier, and the faces of the two boys seen back at the extreme right and left sides of the painting look startlingly like the young George Tooker.

*Coney Island* contains an interesting sensual charge, less obvious but far more powerful here than in Reginald Marsh's works. The bathing suits are startlingly skimpy for the time and are not so much articles of clothing as bands of color, somehow attached to flesh. Most importantly, these figures are aware of their corporeality and sexual identity, even if they are not always models of stylish form. Although this painting is successful, the beach as a source of imagery is really less suited to Tooker's contemplative style than it is to the work of Marsh or Cadmus.

*Bird Watchers* (1948) combines the new, more volumetric figure forms with a subject more static and monumental and better suited to Tooker's style. Tooker, the son of a churchgoing Episcopalian father and raised in a believing family, stopped attending church when he went to art school. Yet the religious art of the past affected him deeply, both in its formal esthetic and in the unselfconscious way in which the artists had expressed their beliefs. "I wanted to paint a positive picture," he recalls, "a religious picture without religious subject matter. I thought watching birds was a good subject which could get close to a religious picture, but I was not yet ready to make a painting with a religious subject." The painting was based on quattrocento Italian prototypes, but the faces are, for the most part, modeled on Tooker himself, his friends, and his family. His sister posed for two figures (the woman on the bridge and in the red-cowled coat), and his mother is seen in the slate-blue coat and hat, a figure partially hidden by the tree to the right. Paul Cadmus and other friends also posed. The faces were not, however, specific portraits, but rather included Tooker's day-to-day observations of "the types who lived around me on Bleecker Street."

Even though the painting is clearly set in an obviously urban park (Manhattan's Central Park), Tooker has muted the "modern city" aspect of the work. Even the attire of his subjects has been modified to impart a more universal simplicity to the scene. The raglan-sleeve topcoat, for instance, stripped of its buttons and buttonholes, appears to be a loose robe of indeterminate period.

If the scene is Central Park, the construction of the painting suggests the Crucifixion, with the figures of Mary, Mary Magdalene, and the apostles and soldiers at the foot of the cross. The panel's intended if covert religious reference is emphasized by the use of an

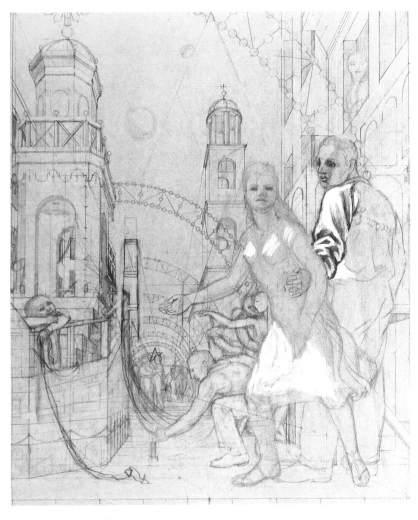

Study for FESTA, 1948.
Pencil heightened with white on toned paper,
19½ x 15 in.

**FESTA** 1948.
Egg tempera on gesso panel,
21½ x 17¼ in.

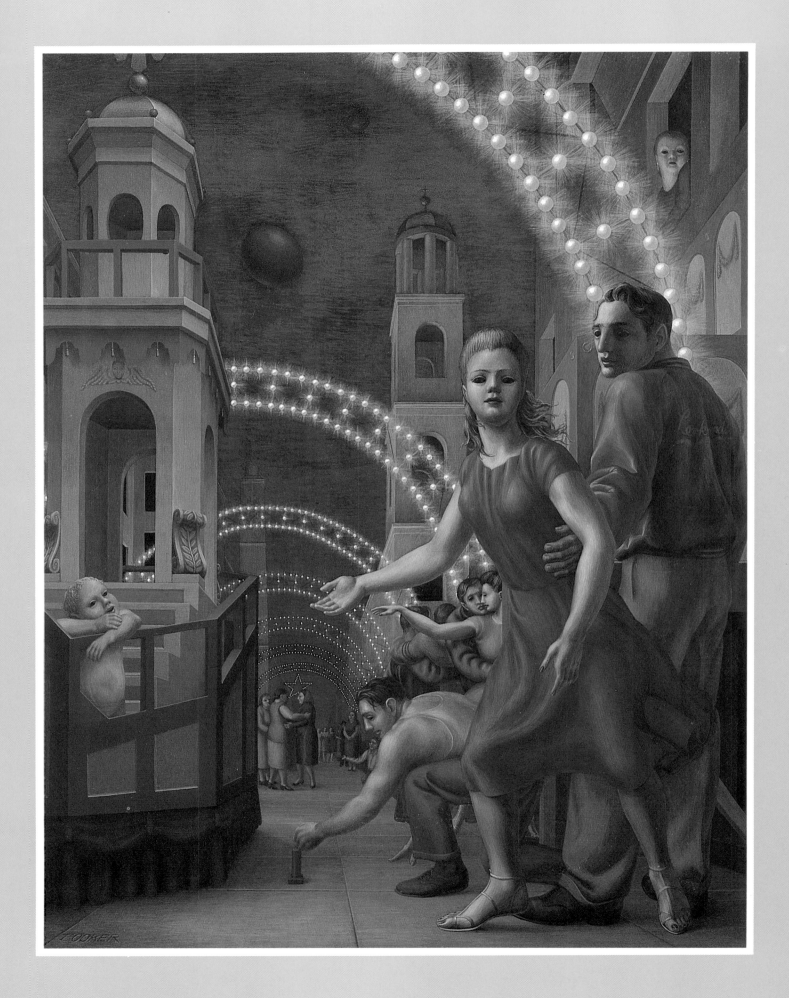

**BIRD WATCHERS** 1948.
Egg tempera on gesso panel,
26½ x 32½ in.

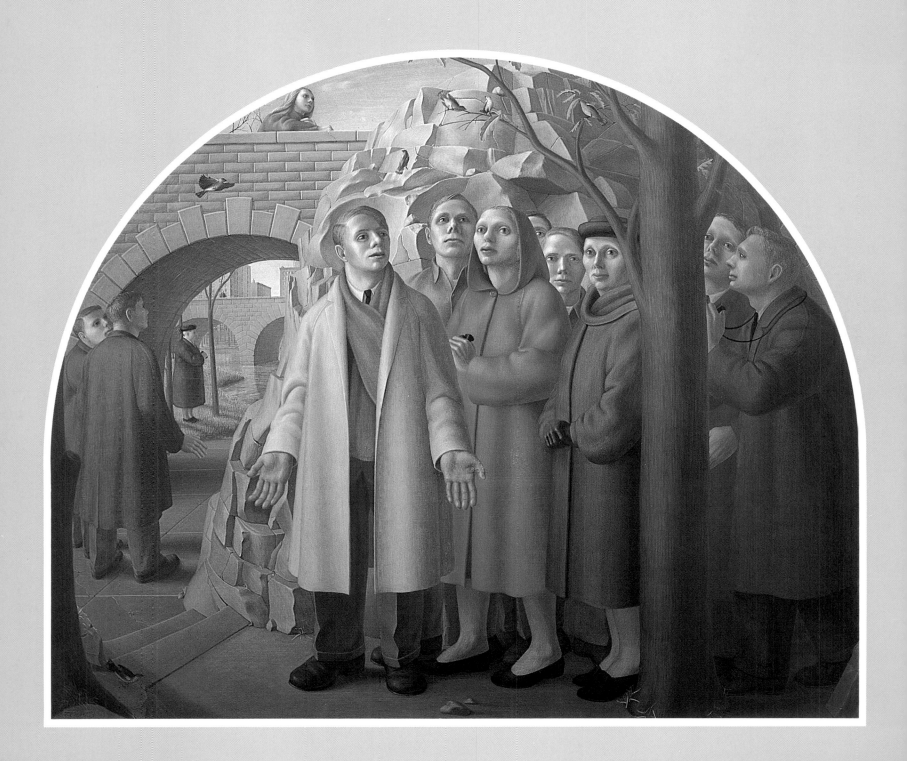

arched top, selected because of its strong association with Renaissance altarpieces. The tree to the right (representing the cross) is balanced by an opening to the left in the line of figures that form the foreground, offering a vignette of deep space in a painting which is otherwise rather compressed into the shallow foreground.

As in many of Tooker's works, the space opens deeply to the left and is brought up abruptly at the right. Light, too, flows in from the left and diminishes into shadow toward the lower right corner, a frequently used Tooker device. The strong push and pull of space and shifting light, working one against the other, activates the painted surface of the panel.

In the summer of 1948, Tooker did not join his friends in Provincetown, but decided to stay in New York to concentrate on

Study for BIRD WATCHERS, 1948.
Pencil, 13 x 16 in.

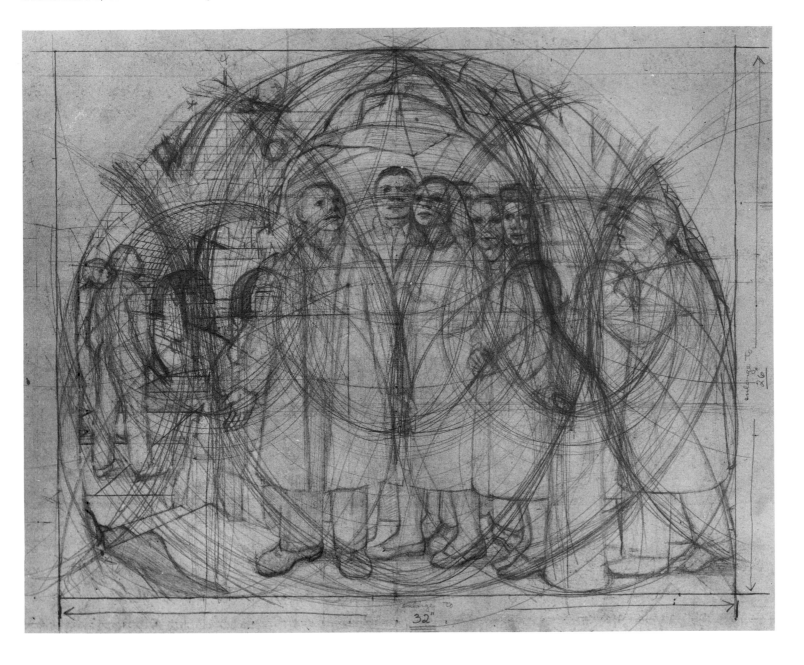

painting. *Festa* was produced that summer. Its iconography is curious; it is a Christian religious procession turned inside out and put to the service of the gods of classical mythology. The source of *Festa* was one of the Italian street festivals that take place every summer in Little Italy just south of Tooker's Greenwich Village apartment. The festival portrayed was one honoring Our Lady of Pompeii. It was not a large festival, but the several small blocks of Carmine Street were brightly decorated with arches of lights for a week or so, and the event featured booths for games and food, along with nightly processions in honor of Our Lady of Pompeii.

Tooker had been reading extensively about Greek and Roman mythology and transposed this festival into a Priapean ritual to Aphrodite and Dionysus. Aphrodite, brought into the twentieth century, is seen here as a young girl in a red dress of a brightness Tooker often reserves for portraying carnal passion or the threat of violence. She beckons to us to join in the fun, but her consort, Dionysus, the young man in his "Leopards" jacket, reaches his hand protectively about her waist and is obviously much more interested in her than in encouraging spectators to the event. Hands form an important element in this painting. The hands of each figure – Aphrodite, Dionysus, the spectator about to light a Roman candle, and others pointing and gesturing – draw us deeper into the space which has been shaped so robustly by the lighted arches overhead. Each arm emphasizes a strong diagonal that sweeps across the work, ending so abruptly at the curious and elaborate processional car to the extreme left. The geometry of this little wagon repeats the architecture of the church tower behind it, but this is a vehicle not of sacred but of profane love. It is the tower of Priapus, the youthful god of male love, seen smiling demurely as his car, a glorious column of soft pink and rose, moves slowly from the scene to the left.

Tooker derived the head of Aphrodite, and the head of the woman in the window to the right as well, from a small bisque china doll's head someone had given him. The glass eyes which opened and closed when the head was moved up and down had disappeared, and the artist maintained that strange, blank, empty-socketed stare in all the faces visible within the painting. *Festa*, like the several paintings that preceded it, evokes a strange feeling of melancholy, but not one of horror or depression or even sadness. Tooker may use places of fun and casual relaxation – the beach, a park, a street party – as a stage on which to set his scenes, but he always probes beneath the surface gaiety. He portrays his figures – common folks – in quiet and intense moments of personal contemplation and reflection, even as mindless excitement and activity swirl around them.

In March 1949, George Tooker and Paul Cadmus sailed for Europe on the *Queen Elizabeth*. They spent four months there, most of it in Italy, with a few weeks in France and a week in England. It was Tooker's first trip to Europe.

*Market* (1949) was the first painting Tooker completed upon his return from Europe. It was modeled after a small open-air market on Bleecker Street, but its construction is straight from the Italian

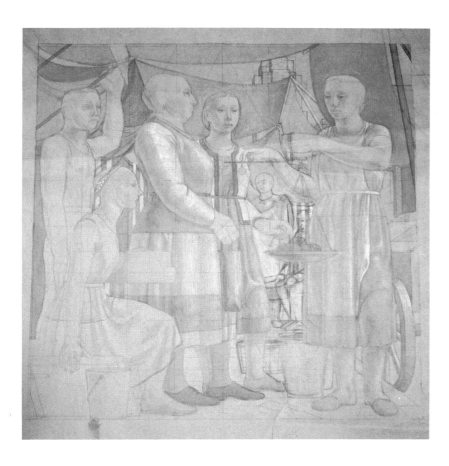

Study for MARKET, 1949
Pencil and wash on toned paper, 22 x 22 in.

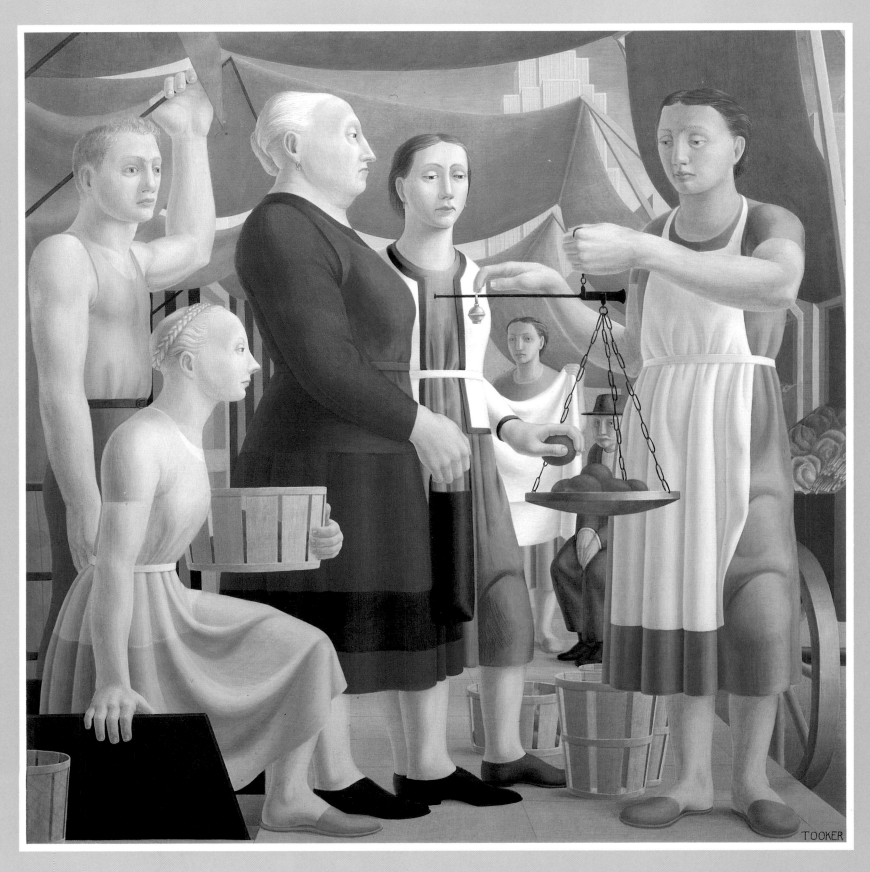

**MARKET** 1949.
Egg tempera on gesso panel,
22 x 22 in.

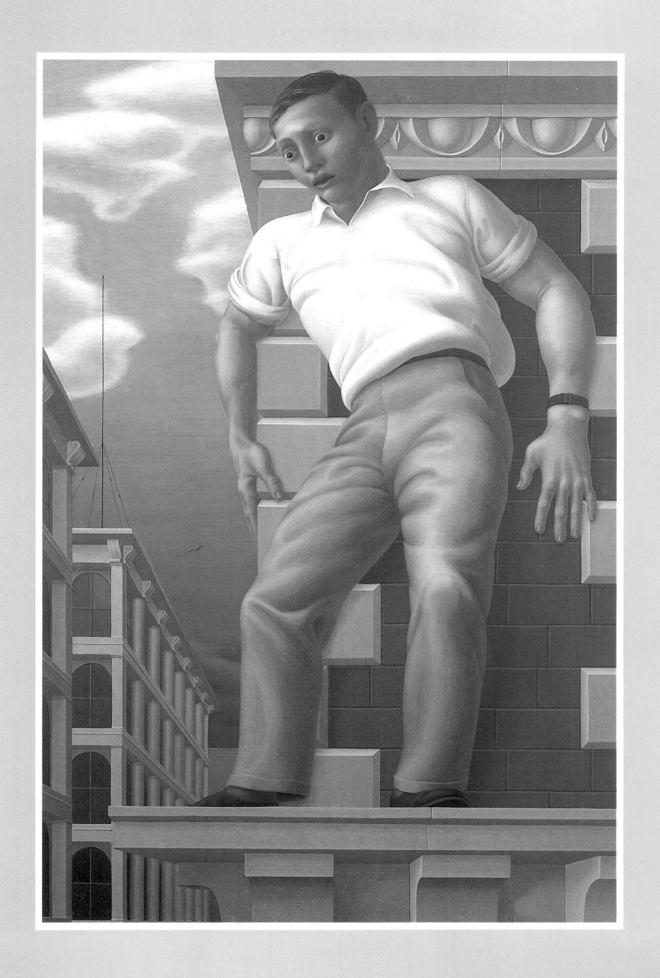

quattrocento. Tooker had been much taken by the frescoes of Cosimo Tura in the Palazzo Sciffenoia in Ferrara. The strong profiles, intense, clear blue, and the treatment of the canvas sunscreens as architecture also show the influence of Piero della Francesca. *Market* is Tooker's most obviously geometrically composed painting, and the architectonic power of its construction has mitigated those qualities of compressed portraiture and the suggestion of events-at-the-edge-of-occurrence that inform and energize so much of his best work.

*Cornice* (1949) is a work directly inspired by literature, in this case W. H. Auden's long poem in verse and prose, "The Sea and the Mirror: A Commentary on Shakespeare's *The Tempest*". The genesis for the painting is drawn from a monologue by Caliban, Prospero's brutish slave, who addresses the audience in a long epilogue.

> *Now it is over. No, we have not dreamt it. Here we really stand, downstage with red faces and no applause; no effect, however simple, no piece of business, however unimportant, came off; there was not a single aspect of our production, not even the huge stuffed bird of happiness, for which a kind word could, however, patronizingly, be said.*

> *Yet, at this very moment when we do at last see ourselves as we are, neither cozy nor playful, but swaying out on the ultimate wind-whipped cornice that overhangs the unabiding void – we have never stood anywhere else – when our reasons are silenced in the heavy huge derision, – There is nothing to say.*[5]

Caliban speaks prophetic words here, words that strongly resonated with Tooker, who, in his art, has always felt suspended above that "unabiding void."

The general presumption is that *Cornice* deals thematically with suicide, the moment of paralysis before making the final leap. In fact, taking the literary source of the painting into consideration, *Cornice* is about the exposure of artifice and the realization that even if artifice achieves only bombast, complacency and dullness will achieve nothing. The leap contemplated here is not a leap to oblivion, but a leap of faith, and such a leap – of either sort – is surely preceded by a moment of stark terror. The figure is that of the younger "Tooker man," and the painting is again a visual embodiment of the artist's own feelings at that moment in his life. The figure has a generous volume and physicality that supports the emotional intensity of the image. The architectural setting, fragments of lower Manhattan's nineteenth-century cast-iron buildings, has been simplified and emboldened in detail as well.

By the end of 1949, George Tooker had been painting in his chosen style for almost five years, and he had been included in several of the important annual group exhibitions at major American museums. These were the modern "salons" through which so much new work was first seen at a time when there were few commercial galleries available to the contemporary artist. In that year, too, Tooker met William Christopher. A few years younger than Tooker, Christopher was a painter and cabinet maker. They cast their lot together and shortly thereafter took a space over a garage, an illegal loft on West Eighteenth Street, where they lived and worked for the next several years, painting by need and making custom furniture to survive.

**CORNICE** 1949.
Egg tempera on gesso panel,
24 x 16 in.

## THE PAINTINGS OF SOCIAL CONCERN

The best known of Tooker's paintings, although they form only a small part of his *oeuvre*, are those which represent public concerns in a very public way. Intended as an anguished response to a specific contemporary problem, each of these works addresses the condition of the individual in society by compounding the individual sense of anxiety, terror, or resignation, suggesting that what we see is perhaps a universal fate. This condition affects everyone, so it seems, and few appear to be willing or able to challenge it.

*The Subway* (1950) is perhaps Tooker's best-known painting. Acquired by the Whitney Museum of American Art shortly after it was painted, it has been widely reproduced (more often in psychology and sociology texts than in books on art). Compositionally, it is one of Tooker's most elaborate paintings, exploiting as it does the complexity of the New York City subway's underground passages in which it is set. With corridors running straight ahead and diagonally off to the left and to the right, and stairways leading up and down out of the picture plane, *The Subway* displays Tooker's preoccupations with intricate pictorial structure, oblique angles, and complex light sources. In one of his rare public comments on a specific painting, Tooker described the reason for selecting the

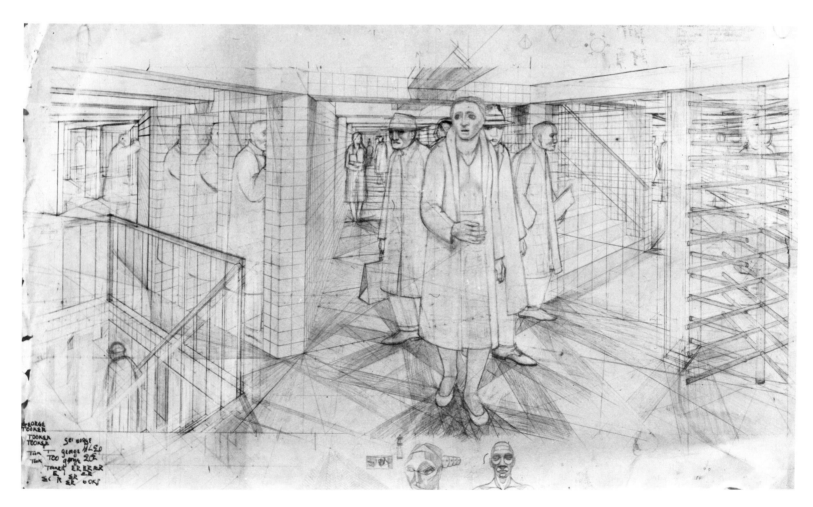

Study for THE SUBWAY, 1950.
Pencil, 18 x 36 in.

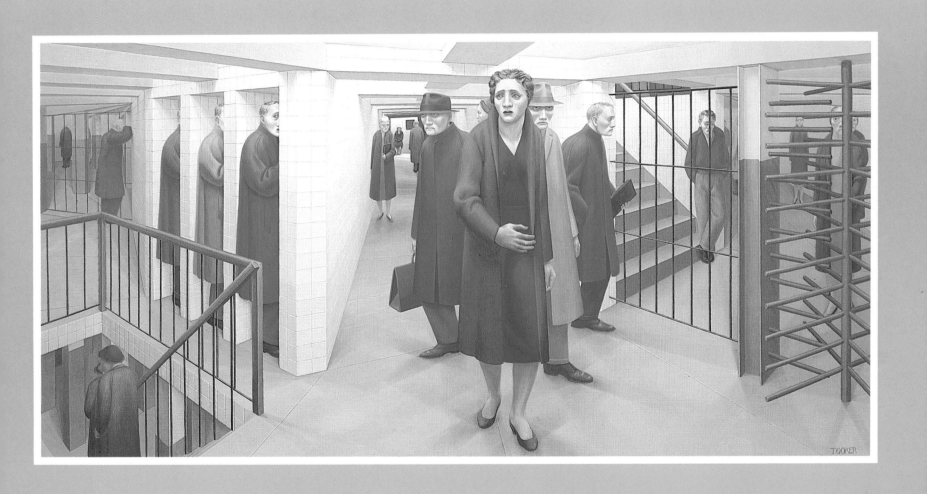

**THE SUBWAY** 1950.
Egg tempera on gesso panel,
18 x 36 in.

(Detail overleaf)

locale of this work: "I was thinking of the large modern city as a kind of limbo. The subway seemed a good place to represent a denial of the senses and a negation of life itself. Its being underground with great weight overhead was important."[6]

The figures are all swathed in layers of clothing, and every face that Tooker shows us is wearing an expression of nameless dread. It is as if these people are frozen in place, unable to extricate themselves from the seemingly endless maze of white-tiled corridors and dim gray stairways in which they are trapped; even the figures that Tooker has painted in motion seem paralyzed. These are human beings who have been robbed of humanity, isolated from one another by the exigencies of modern life. Each exists as an island of terror, fearful of what the invisible but everpresent "They" will do. The central figure is both weary and terrified; her fear can be seen not only in her face, but in the gesture of her hand which covers her abdomen in unconscious self-protection. The two men who are following so closely behind her, however, are obviously far more fatigued than sinister. But the feeling of fear dominates everyone in the subways, whether the threat is real or imagined. One can see it on the face of the first of the three men in the old-fashioned telephone niches at the left, the shallow hollows of which can provide little protection from whatever it is they are afraid of.

Tooker has been criticized for his seeming lack of interest in delineating the individual personality, yet, clearly, if the artist does not portray the individual psyche of each figure, he does construct works filled with a powerful social drama, in which an archetype replaces the individual. Psychological observation has been placed at the service of a collective vision to intensify the expression of numbing isolation and anonymity Tooker finds in contemporary society.

Several years after painting *The Subway*, Tooker produced two other remarkable paintings: *Government Bureau* (1955–56) and *The Waiting Room* (1956–57). *Government Bureau* is a document of anonymous processing, a dumbshow of conditioned response to Kafkaesque bureaucratic demands beyond either the comprehension or control of the participants. It has as its source an actual experience of the artist. Having bought an old house in Brooklyn Heights, Tooker and Christopher had to go to Brooklyn's Borough Hall to get the permits necessary to convert the building from a rooming house into two apartments, and spent several frustrating weeks on their mission caught up in the maze of their local bureaucracy.

The architectural setting of this painting is oppressive in its rectilinear order and sameness, as are the bureaucrats – visible only as hands, eyes, and ears through openings in the textured glass partitions – and the supplicants who have come to transact their business. Everyone has the same business, and they are, quite literally, the same individual – the anonymous Tooker protagonist – who, younger in some works and older in others, has been described as a metaphysical self-portrait. No business is actually being

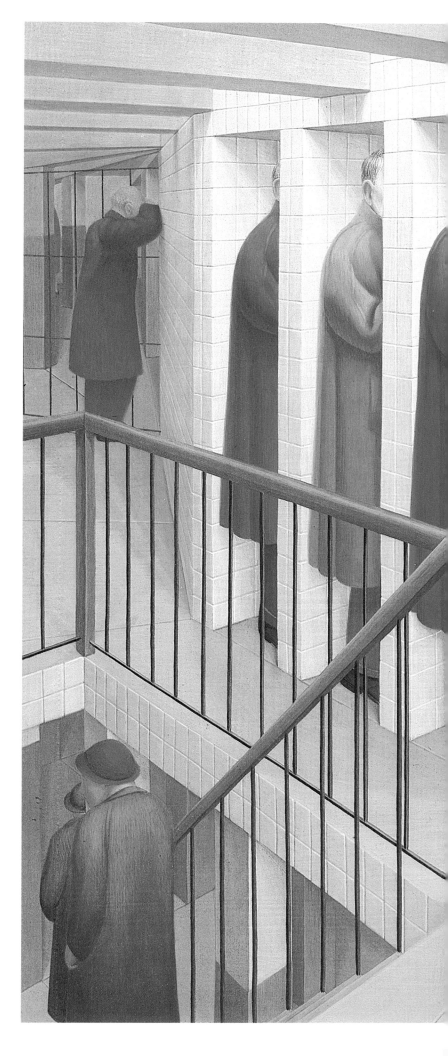

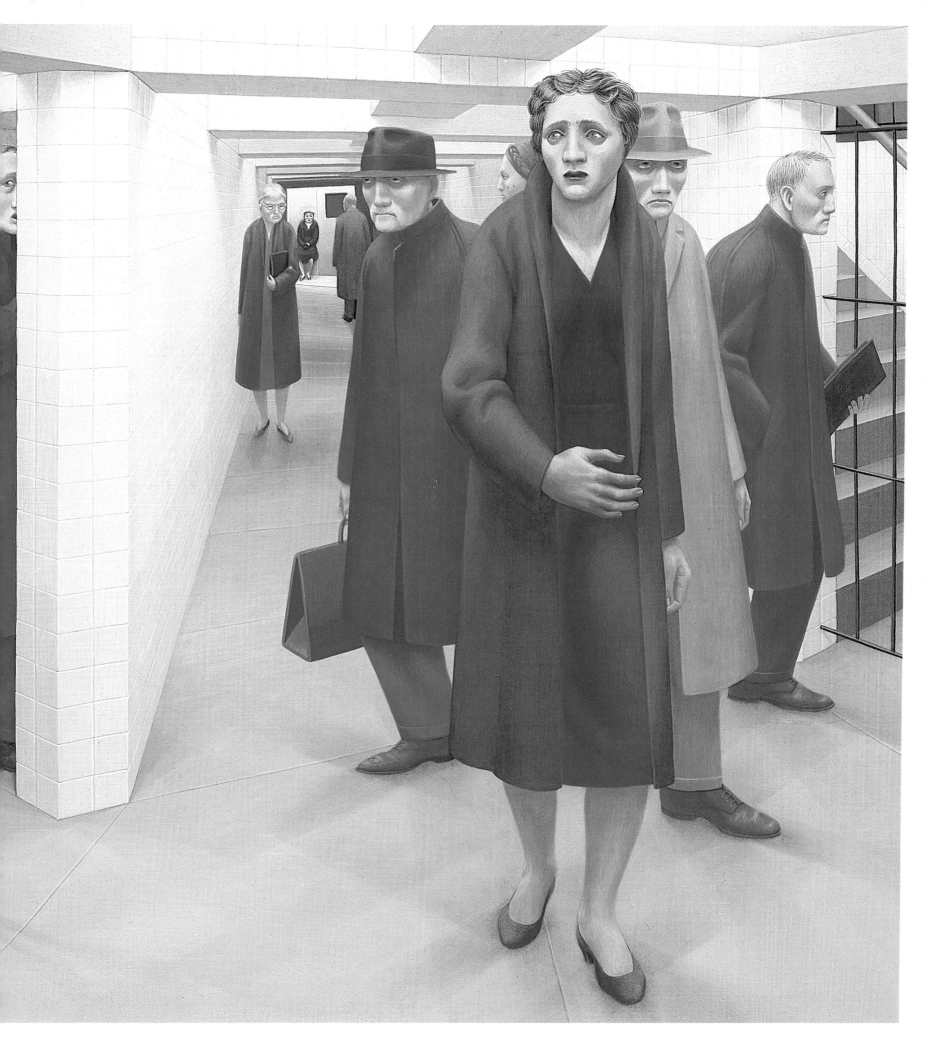

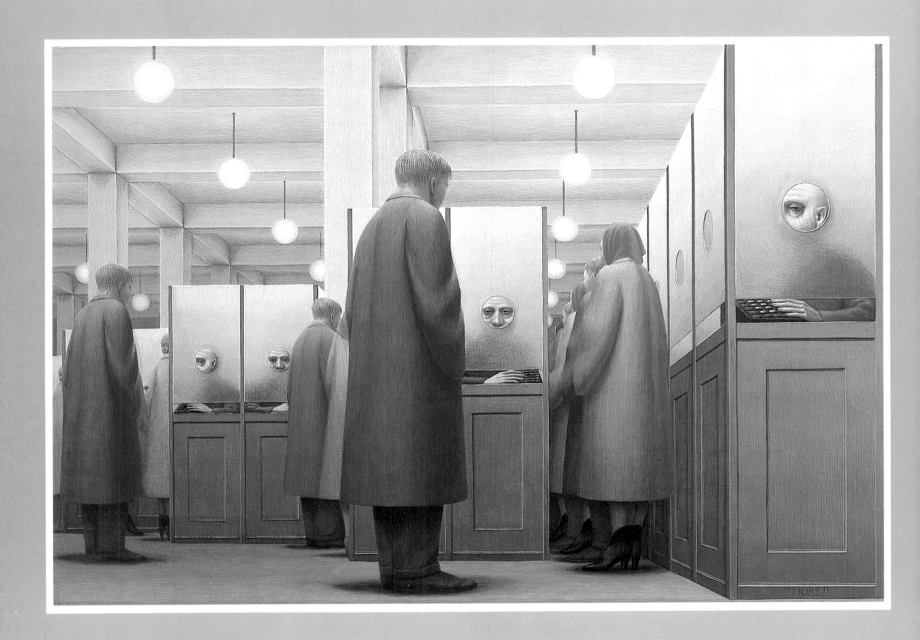

**GOVERNMENT BUREAU** 1956.
Egg tempera on gesso panel,
20 x 30 in.

**THE WAITING ROOM** 1959.
Egg tempera on gesso panel,
24 x 30 in.

(Opposite)

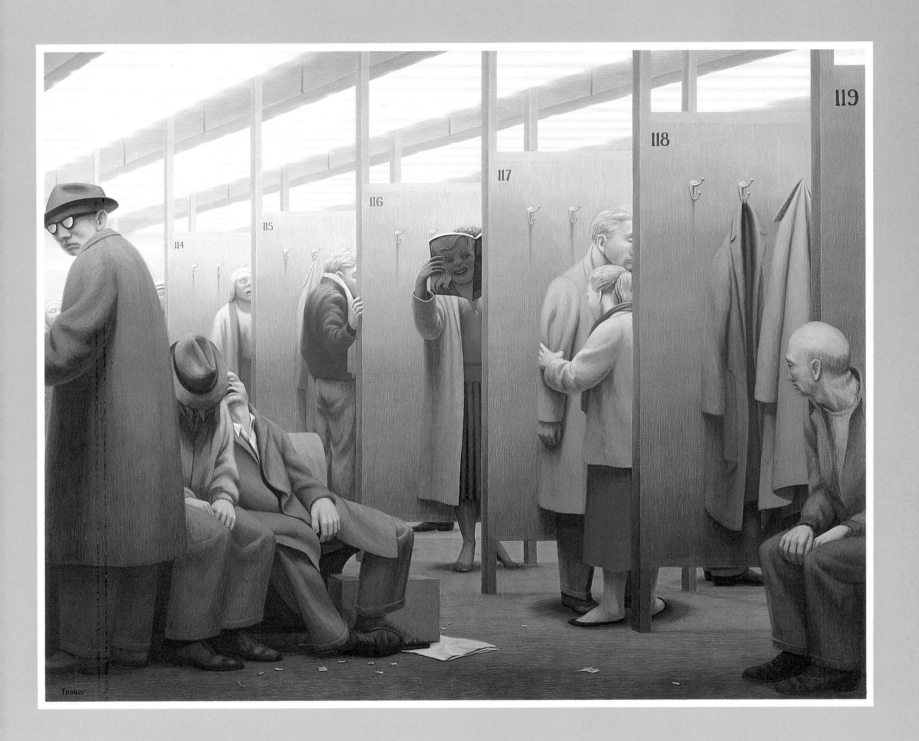

transacted, however, for they are all waiting for "instructions," for approval to proceed that must come from "authorized personnel." The painting's subject is the conflict between the processors and the processed, the misuse of authority without responsibility.

The purpose of the wait in *The Waiting Room* is completely obscure. Like the characters in Sartre's play *No Exit*, the figures that animate the waiting room are just there, seemingly without reason, but, unlike *No Exit*, they do not interrelate. They simply exist as if in suspended animation, neither happy nor unhappy. The setting has no identifiable function or character; it is not a clinic, police station, or customs office. Tooker's vision of hell is not the same as Sartre's – "other people" – it is not conflict with others, but rather it is being alone with others – sequestered in some form of data bank, in blank, unthinking suspension, available if needed, ignored if not. And no one makes an effort to share the wait or change the experience. As Tooker himself describes it, *"The Waiting Room* is a kind of purgatory – people just waiting, waiting to wait. It is not living. It is a matter of waiting – not being one's self. Not enjoying life, not being happy, waiting, always waiting for something that might be better – which never comes. Why can't they just enjoy the moment?"

Study for GOVERNMENT BUREAU, 1956.
Pencil heightened with white, 20 x 30 in.

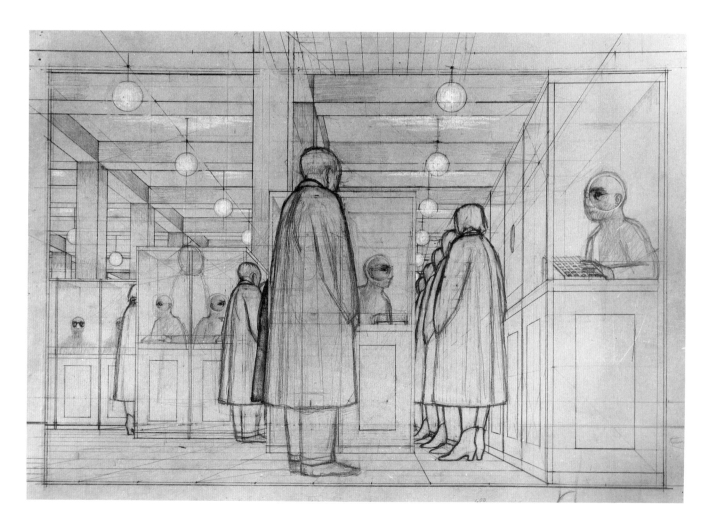

All three of these major political works – *The Subway, Government Bureau*, and *The Waiting Room* – share Tooker's love of precise geometric order as an intellectual and physical construct against which his protagonists, almost always shrouded with heavy coats and hats, are completely intimidated by the very structures built to serve them. About ten years after *The Waiting Room*, Tooker created *Landscape with Figures* (1966), another painting equal to it in power and mystery, and equally haunting in its unresolved implications. *Landscape with Figures* is the first of three pictures of widely variant points of view that bear this title. This painting is one of Tooker's most inventive and socially demanding works. The figures, within their little learning/work/living cells, stare out with little emotion and only the slightest curiosity about the world beyond them. Man's isolation from himself through the creation of faceless architecture, urban anonymity, and soulless ritual, is now codified and complete. Tooker's light, rarely natural and always obscure in source, here dramatically removes the last vestiges of the real world. One responds silently and ironically, for these young faces, trapped within their cells, are either unconscious of their condition or unwilling to acknowledge it.

This was a painting produced by an angry man, not a cool-headed observer. In 1968, shortly after the painting was reproduced in a national magazine, Tooker was asked by an advertising agency for permission to use the work as an illustration for a steel company's employee recruiting poster. Tooker's response, a draft of which has been preserved in the Archives of American Art, was short and emphatic: "I cannot give my permission for the use of *Landscape with Figures* for any steel company since the subject of the picture is the victimization of our youth by the military-industrial complex and its servant, advertising."

In 1983, *Landscape with Figures* was included in a large exhibition entitled "1984" at a New York gallery. The exhibition examined the problems and promises of that notorious year (made famous by Orwell's novel written thirty-five years earlier), and shortly after the show closed a book documenting the exhibition was prepared. Tooker was asked to produce a statement about the painting. The artist is still clear about his point in creating the work. "*Landscape with Figures* is not about the future – it is about the present. It is about people being trapped in a society that places no value on spiritual life."

The painting took longer than usual to create. Tooker was meticulous in producing the proper gradations of color, which took a great deal of time to bring to the required density. The work underwent significant, if subtle, alterations in its planning as well. An early drawing for the work has been substantially transformed in the final painting. The scanning angle over these isolation booths has been lowered, thus providing a much longer vista of this landscape of little cells. Moreover, the faces originally sketched into the drawing were individual and curious, perhaps even a little angry, but are emotionally deadened in the final work. Their intellect, their passion, has been drained away. They are no longer thinking beings.

In *Supermarket* (1973) the shoppers shuffle as if in a trance through numbered aisles of geometrically arranged products, carefully processed, packaged and brand-named, clutching only at the colors and labels they have been conditioned to want. This is another work that expresses Tooker's strong surreal sensibility. There is even a moment of dark humor here, as though the best industrial designer in the world ran amok in the supermarket, redesigning everything, but leaving the shoppers – regrettably – as the only thing that could not be repackaged in a stylish and up-to-date manner. The shoppers, of indeterminate age, are as uniformly bland as the packaging is assertive. They are demographic ciphers and wander through this maze of shouting colors and forms as if in a pre-programmed trance, moving and buying by instruction without individual will or identity. Even the managers who operate the store (visible in a window at the upper right) are caught in the same trance as the shoppers themselves, for they too have been preprogrammed: programmed to "give the shoppers what they want," and what they all want has already been determined – elsewhere.

*Highway* (1953) is one of the most overtly surreal and aggressive paintings Tooker has ever created. Lunging down an expressway at twilight, the sharp-fanged cars resemble late 1940s Buicks and DeSotos. The adjacent buildings are seen at cornice level, for the roadway is elevated. The atmosphere, fading from blue-gray to smog beige, is leaden and airless, while the streetlights overhead do not illuminate so much as they merely trace the path above these monstrous vehicles as they roar toward us. This stretch of road is under construction, and the traffic is jammed between partitions of black-and-white-striped plywood. In the foreground, a triangular area is blocked off by silver, arrow-topped road markers to divert the lanes of traffic around an obstacle. The figure dressed in black standing in the traffic lane with his hand up is not intimidated by the onrushing mass of machines. It is his job to stop traffic; he *will* stop traffic. His identity remains a mystery, his face completely hidden by the red reflector he holds in front of him; his function – that of traffic controller – is as mindless and faceless as the streetlights behind him.

Tooker compresses so many compositional elements into the pictorial space that the painting induces a feeling of claustrophobia in the viewer, a feeling that is reinforced by the repetition and juxtaposition of contrasting shapes and patterns (such as the silver arrows and red reflectors against the striped partitions). It was an opportunity for Tooker to express "how much I hated highways." Yet for all its snarling energy, the painting does not contain the same power found in so many other of his paintings where the oppression of anonymity and isolation takes precedence over direct aggression.

Direct aggression, however, is the theme of *Men and Women Fighting* (1958). It is about the passionate struggle of adult family

**LANDSCAPE WITH FIGURES** 1966.
Egg tempera on gesso panel,
26 x 30 in.

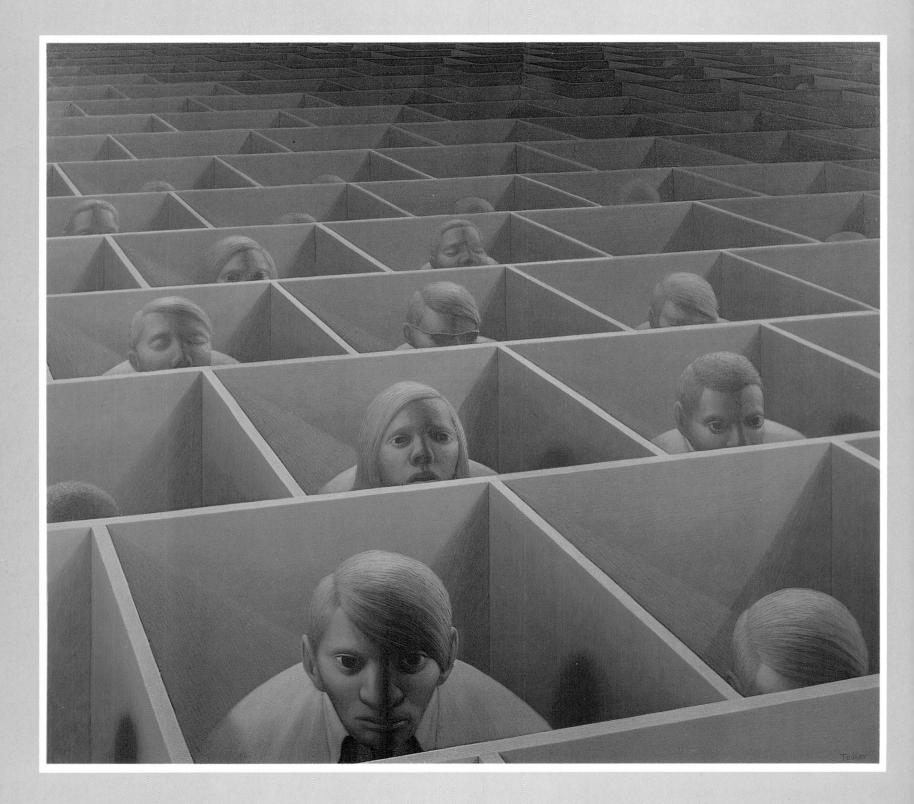

**SUPERMARKET** 1973.
Egg tempera on gesso panel,
23 x 17¼ in.

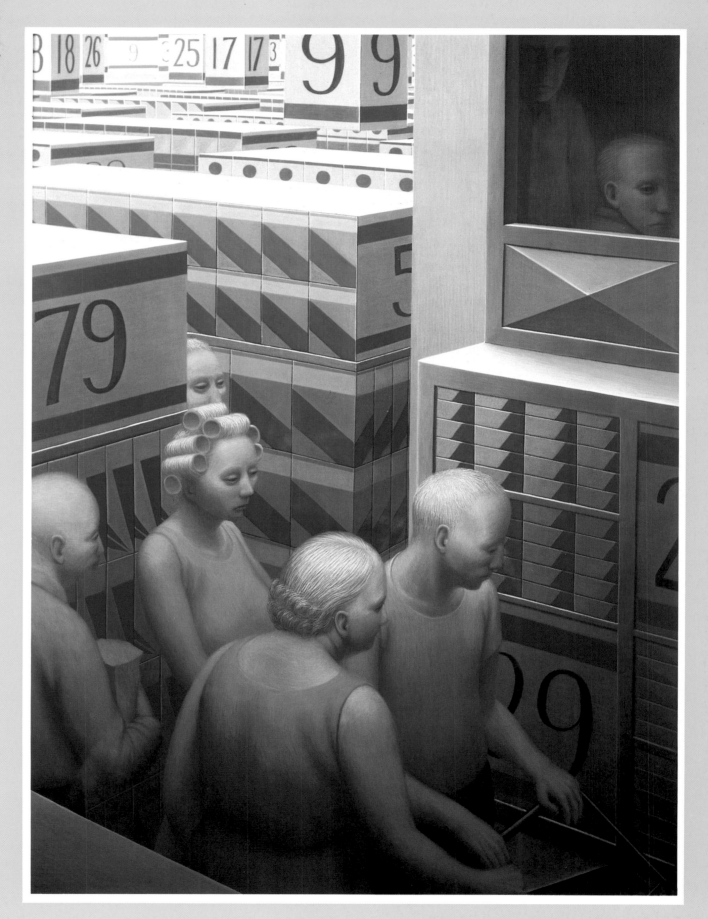

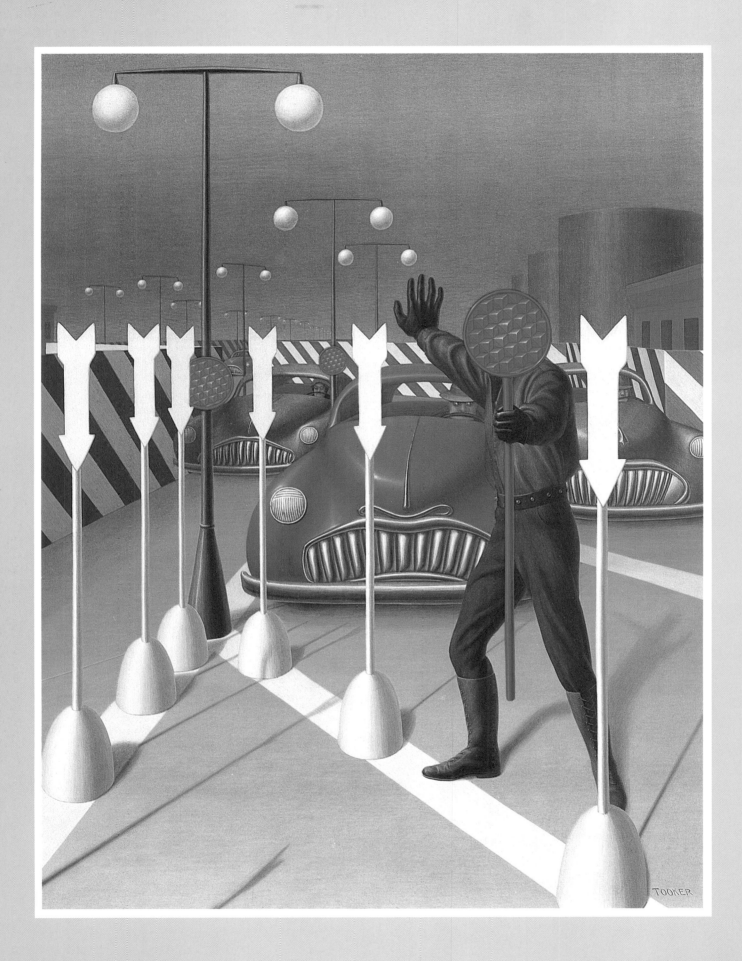

**HIGHWAY** 1953.
Egg tempera on gesso panel,
23 x 18 in.

(Opposite)

**MEN AND WOMEN FIGHTING** 1958.
Egg tempera on gesso panel,
24 x 30 in.

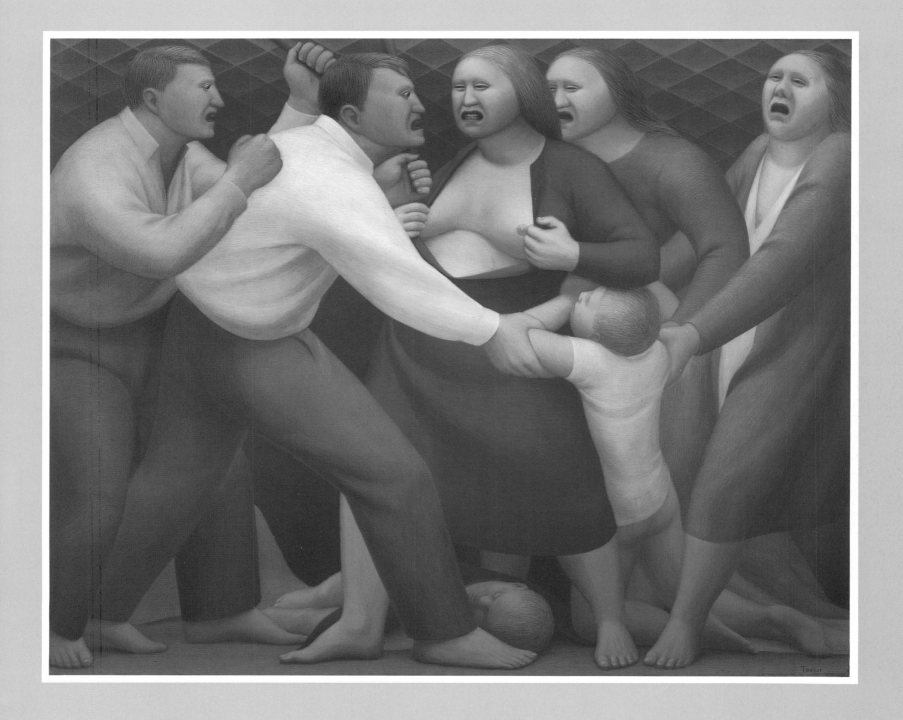

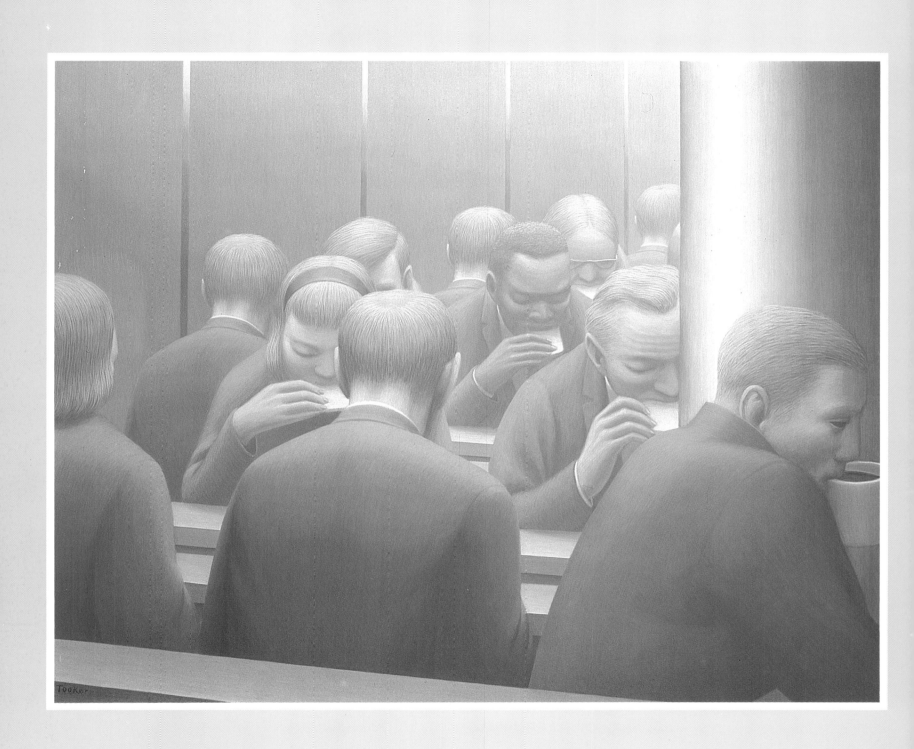

**LUNCH** 1964.
Egg tempera on gesso panel,
20 x 26 in.

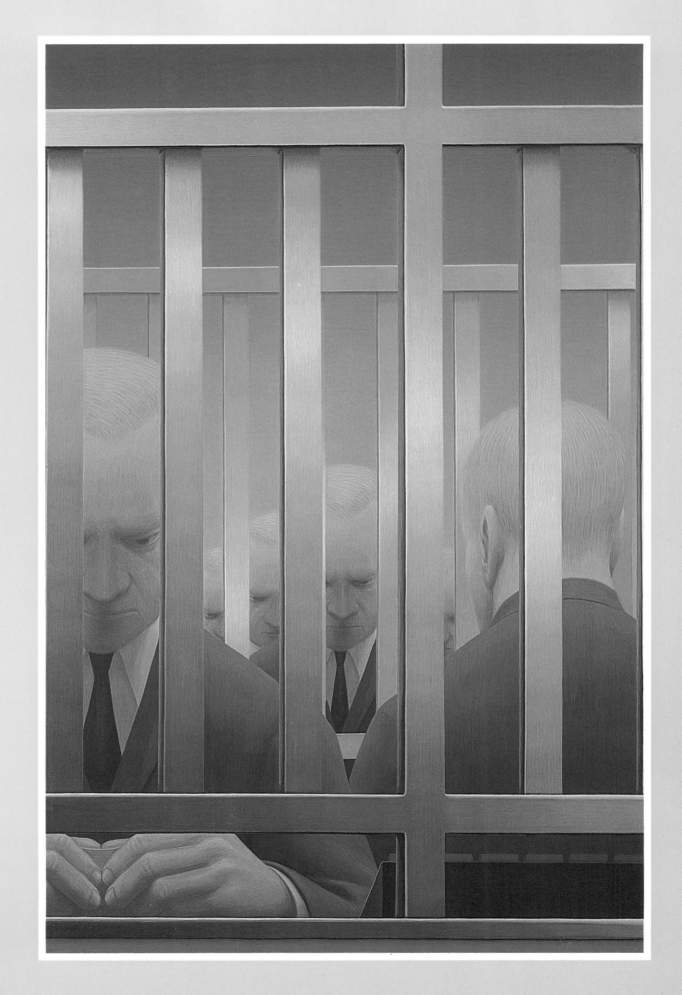

**TELLER** 1967.
Egg tempera on gesso panel,
23½ x 15½ in.

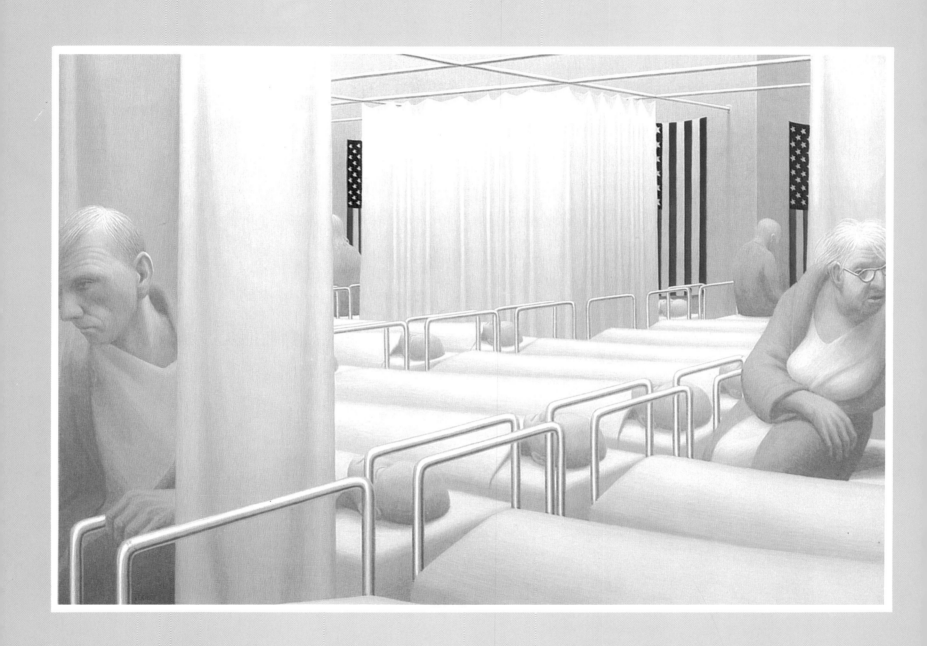

**WARD** 1970-71.
Egg tempera on gesso panel,
19¾ x 29½ in.

members for custody of the children. The work is unique in Tooker's *oeuvre* in its direct depiction of physical violence. Clubs have struck flesh, and one of the children lies underfoot – knocked senseless, or perhaps even dead. Another, half naked, is being pulled by both arms as the men and women battle over possession of him.

The use of children incapable of defending themselves as pawns in the battle of adult egos infuriated Tooker as had little else. This is an elemental struggle with no room for architectural niceties, although Tooker recalled that he used passages from Giotto for the massing of the figures in a shallow space. The setting has been reduced to a single blood-red wall, with a diaper pattern reminiscent of stamped tin ceilings. Red of this intensity over such a large area almost always connotes carnal or physical passion in Tooker's work. The shallow space and violent color aggressively press the intention of the painting and emphasize the struggle of the figures. The men and the women have taken sides against each other in the age-old battle, the men with clubs, the women with taunts, weeping, and baring of breasts. It is of course the children who suffer most, a modern-day massacre of the innocents.

Pervasive silence is much more common in Tooker's work than violence. The people he portrays – whether at work, having a meal, performing their toilette, or even making love – seem so often to be lost within themselves. At times this pensive state may be quietly supportive, but in such works as *Lunch* (1964) or *Teller* (1967), the isolation is chilling.

In *Lunch*, office workers on their lunch break are shown sitting shoulder-to-shoulder, row after row, in a nearly featureless room of a fast-food restaurant. Almost identical in dress and appearance, they raise identical right hands to bite into identical white-bread sandwiches. All eyes are cast down; no one makes contact with anyone else. Tooker has collapsed the perspective of this crowded lunch room as though looking at the scene from afar through a telephoto lens, and has bathed it in that cool wash of shadowless fluorescent light he so despises, bleaching the life out of everything it illuminates. A woman's rose headband is the only color note, a pale echo of Tooker's usual emphatic red highlights.

*Teller*, although painted a few years later, is closely related in feeling and structure to *Lunch*. Here, we are in a bank, looking directly into a teller's cage. The same man, pale-faced and sandy-haired, eyes cast down, appears six times (once from the back), compressed as neatly into his teller's cage as he is into his dull, conventional suit. The top of the painting is the blue of the sky, but it is not sky. We are once again in an anonymous institution, without feature or distinction. The only color seen against the sheen of steel, dark suit and pale flesh are the buttons of the posting machine, cheerless, red mechanical blossoms. We can see the bank teller at the left counting money with the same mechanical precision, but otherwise showing no signs of life. He is almost back-to-back with another teller, who must be performing the same routine. Just on the other side of that teller's cage are the other men, absolutely identical in dress and appearance, lined up as if they were a series

of infinitely reflected images of the teller himself. Are they bank tellers, too, or are they customers? And if they are customers, visual logic dictates that we, the spectators of this scene, are on a line in front of the first teller, and that they are our own mirror image.

*Ward* (1970–71) was created at the height of the Vietnam War and might, at first, be read simply as a direct polemic against that war. It is a painting that Tooker acknowledges as a great favorite of his. "I was striking out in a number of directions, and it was intended to shock and jolt people, not depress them." The work dealt as much with the treatment of the old as well as the wounded; it documents the surrender of power, individuality, and identity to the ritual and standardized convenience of a mechanized process.

Here Tooker uses several devices often found in his large-scale, more dramatic works. The bold grid pattern directly rendered in *Landscape with Figures* is strongly implied in *Ward* by the organization of the beds. The effect is numbing. This space is the structural equivalent of "the Tooker man," shaped to fit the Procrustean bed of a society that does not admit elements of individuality or spirit. The only intense color is the red in the American flag, but it is not a true flag red but rather, as Tooker has suggested, that of "dried blood."

*Waiting Room II* (1982) and *Corporate Decision* (1983) are paintings that document a twentieth-century voyage of life in which isolation, fear, and, above all, endless waiting for dull processing become one's lot. *Waiting Room II* is a vastly different work from its namesake. The composition is analogous to that of *Subway*; the physical space depicted, however, is a futuristic combination of catacomb and columbarium. The walls and floors are perforated with openings that might almost be mistaken for ornamental paving, save that a few have their true use revealed by the figures contained within them, just their heads visible. The other figures in the composition are of two clearly marked types. The lower left and right foreground of the panel each contain small groups of seated figures. They are the dispossessed and despised, the have-nots, children and old people, just waiting. They are offset by five groups of standing figures, who are of a different class, each comprising the same four people – the army officer in uniform, diplomat in his claw-hammer coat, businessman in dark overcoat and hat, and fashion-able lady in red, fur-collared coat. Each group is identical, each gesture within the group is identical, and each member of the group is "just doing his or her job."

There is complete separation between these two classes. Neither seems to recognize the other, and the scene is tightly ordered within the tyranny of silence. Interestingly, however, though there are two classes depicted, and one is clearly the ruling class, there is nothing here that would suggest that their life is happier or more fulfilled than that of the underclass. Within this labyrinthine structure the rulers are as devoid of joy and pleasure as those who have nothing.

*Corporate Decision* is one of the few Tooker paintings of social

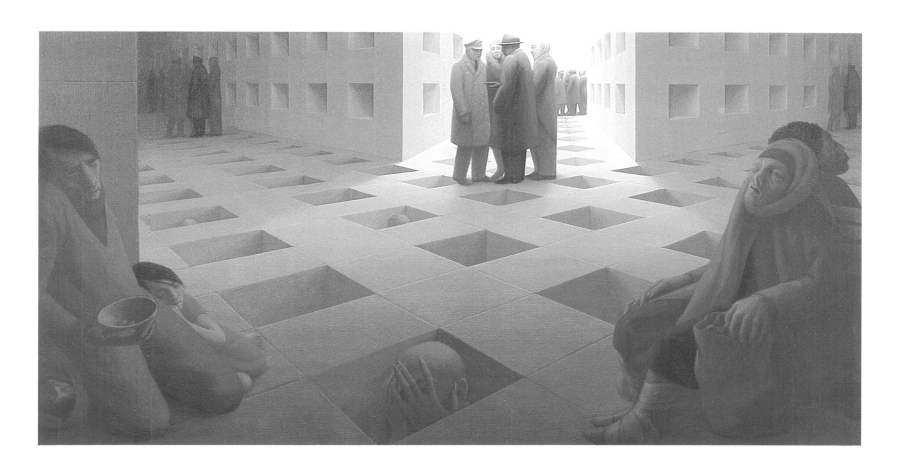

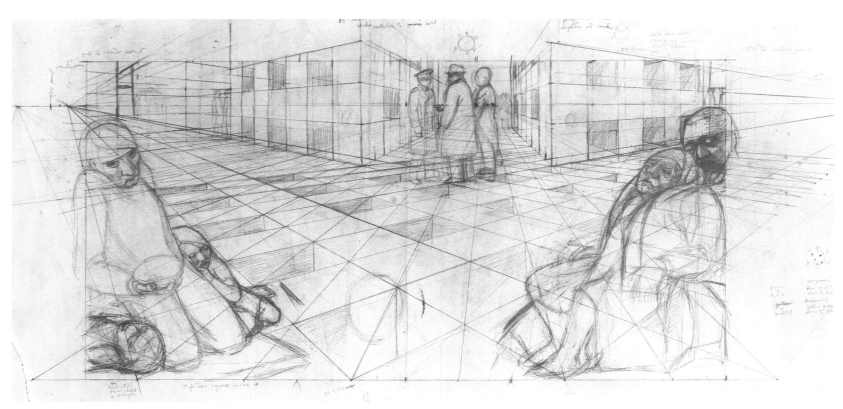

Study for WAITING ROOM II, 1982.
Pencil, 18 x 36 in.

**WAITING ROOM II** 1982.
Egg tempera on gesso panel,
19 x 37 in.

(Opposite)

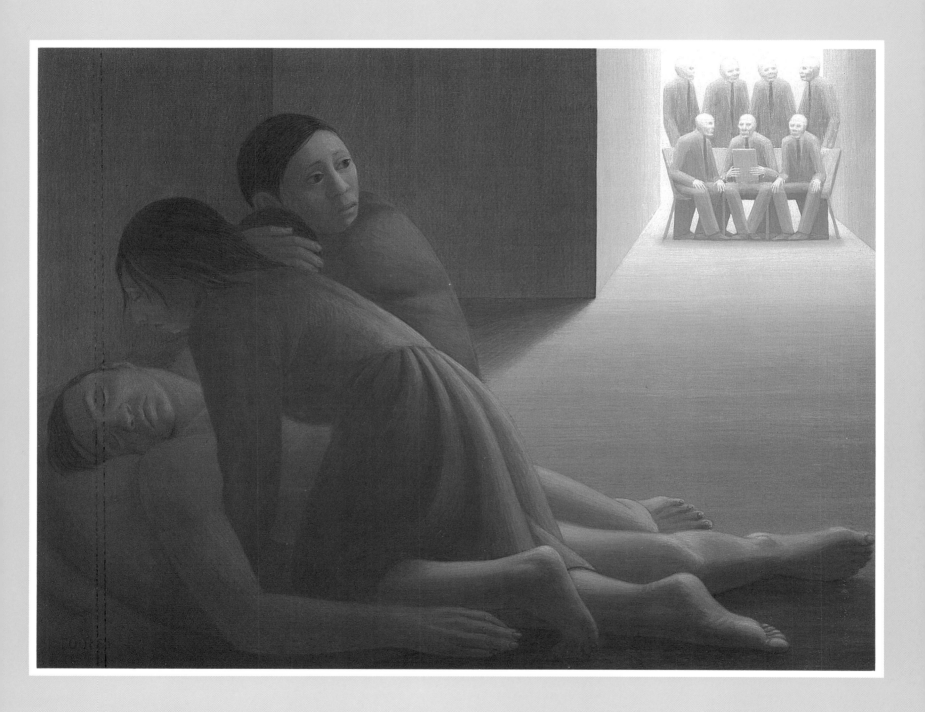

**CORPORATE DECISION** 1983.
Egg tempera on gesso panel,
18 x 24 in.

protest and outrage in which there is not a pervasive, overall visual pattern. It is a painting that the artist warns might seem "corny – if seen too fast" and one that shows the utter loathing he holds for decisions based on "operating conveniences" without regard for the needs of the spirit. It is a work which shows the influence of his conversion to Roman Catholicism. His passion is now stated much more directly and without oblique references to offstage forces. The masterful control of his technique does keep the subject from becoming "corny," because he has separated the "pietà" group in the foreground from the tribunal in the background through the use of light and space alone. He has conspicuously underlighted the foreground, and that subtlety of lighting, which almost obscures the principal figures, saves it from being either self-conscious or maudlin.

Tooker waited more than 35 years to produce the pendant to *The Subway. Terminal*, painted in 1986, is surely one of the artist's strongest expressions of social outrage. *Terminal* and *The Subway* are almost the same size and share the same general compositional structure. In both a wide hallway in the center is flanked by subsidiary openings angling off diagonally at each side. That nasty, cool fluorescent glow that Tooker reserves for subjects that deeply disturb him illuminates both pictures. Its chill is particularly marked in *Terminal* because it is mixed with the warmer daylight which filters in from the entrance. Any resemblance between the two stops there. If *The Subway* is a statement of urban *angst*, the figures and the interior itself are nevertheless well tended, even clinical. Its rendering of anxiety and sterile anonymity, so upsetting when it was painted, now seems, if not friendly, than at least bearable by comparison to Tooker's statement on the present day conditions of life below ground. In *Terminal*, the lights have all but gone out. The side passages are almost invisible in the penumbral gloom, just enough light remaining to reveal several supine figures that all but block the openings. The spiky energy found in *The Subway* has sagged into a lethargic hopelessness, and the architecture, inhuman but orderly in the earlier work, is now just crushing.

The central composition of two figures is a variant of the Renaissance triangle, a timeless form, but one which here has lost its vivacity and gone sadly out of plumb. The figures, a secular, modern-day pietà, twist and collapse into a lumpy foreboding mass silhouetted against the fading daylight from the entrance – the doorway to a contemporary Hell. The woman, slumped to the floor, is in a huge bag. Is she dead? The artist responds to this question only by repeating the painting's title. The male figure hovering over her (friend? mugger?) is startled by a presence in the corridor and looks up warily. Is he concerned about the woman's welfare or has he been caught in the act? We shall never know. *The Subway* is frequently illustrated in social science texts as a visual rendering of the anxieties and soullessness of our cities. *Terminal*, unfortunately should replace it.

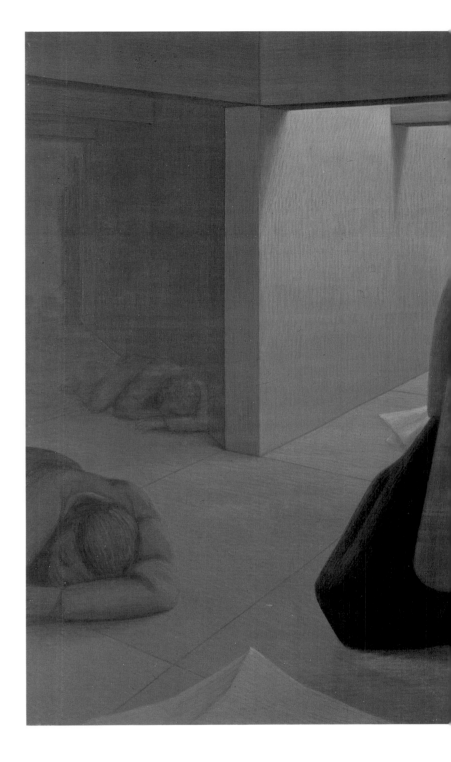

**TERMINAL** 1986.
Egg tempera on gesso panel,
21 x 39 in.

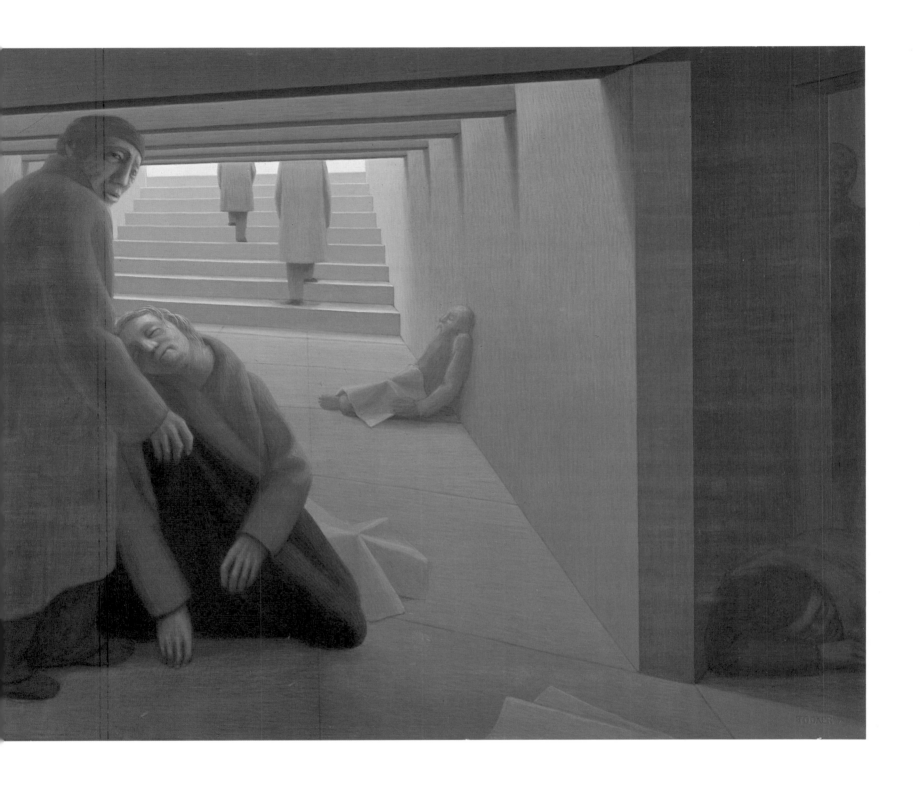

# WINDOWS, MIRRORS, AND THE ARCHITECTURE OF THE MIND

If the progression of paintings that marks the "public" side of Tooker's work is solemn, there is also a more "private" side of his work that is more intimate in its subject matter and perhaps more positive in the tone it conveys. These constitute the majority of his works, consisting for the most part of variations on a few relatively simple themes.

Tooker develops ideas slowly and refines them patiently. Each painting may take from two to four months to design and complete, but the idea itself often requires more than a single painting for the artist to achieve the expression of that idea. It is the composite of all the variations on a single theme – the numerous explorations of a subject within the confines of a particular form – that can be said to capture the whole idea for him.

The theme of figures in a window has been the subject of a series of nine numbered variations that Tooker painted between 1954 and 1987. There are also eleven paintings of various titles devoted to that same theme, and several other paintings not explicitly identified with the theme but strongly associated with it. The window as a "natural" framing device draws the viewer into a closer involvement – a kind of complicity – with the figures in these paintings. Some of them stare right back at our inquiring gaze; most, however, are exposed to our view without any apparent awareness of our visual "eavesdropping." Either way, our voyeuristic impulse is being appealed to quite frankly, if with a certain degree of subtlety or detachment. Often there is a strong visceral, sensual quality to the figures. These paintings rarely focus on direct sexual relationships, but are certainly erotic in the very best sense of that misused word – erotic because they extend themselves so powerfully into the realm of sensual fantasy, and in that regard might well be compared to the best work of Balthus.

Many of Tooker's works mix racial and sexual features of his figures in a manner that suggests not only a certain homogeneity, but an androgynous quality as well. He is very conscious that he himself is a mixture of Latin and northern European roots, and he regards the softening and blurring of any specific racial type to be a device for "showing the beauty of different people." His ambition is to make "things as clear as I can, visually," but his "sharp, focused painting," to use James Soby's phrase, is filled with ambiguity. Unlike the camera, which generally presents the surface of things by recording the most minute details, Tooker's art strips away detail to probe the similarities beneath the individual surfaces. What Lloyd Goodrich wrote about Georgia O'Keeffe applies equally to the work of George Tooker, who is also concerned "not with the mere visual appearance of things, but with their essential life, their being, their identity. The thing-in-itself is what matters. Photographic illusionism is disregarded in favor of basic form . . . the forms of nature are translated into the forms of art."[7]

In Tooker's earliest window paintings, the framing device of the window is implied rather than included as part of the actual pictorial space. Tooker painted *Gypsy* (1951) shortly after he and William Christopher moved into their loft on West Eighteenth Street. Some of the storefronts had been converted to gypsy fortune-telling parlors and, while Tooker acknowledges that the specific image in the painting is imaginary, it is based on scenes he witnessed in his new neighborhood.

*Gypsy* introduces a number of elements characteristic to this body of work, including the strong framing that vigorously contains the space and the translucent drapery that defines and obscures that space as it presses the principal figure of the gypsy woman closer to the picture plane. This translucent curtain is imprinted with the shadow of a figure standing behind it in profile. The only light source filters through the faded fabric, illuminating the foreground figure from the back with a deep, warm glow. The interior of the room, bare of furniture save for the two chairs on which the gypsy reclines, as much at her ease as Jacques-Louis David's *Madame Recamier*, is nevertheless crowded with detail. Tooker provides a variety of textures, especially with the crisply formed, sharply foreshortened surface patternings of embossed wall and ceiling (derived from pressed tin work), and the contrasting patterns of the rugs hung on the wall to the left.

Tooker, having not yet perfected all of the elements of these images, has set the bulk of the foreground figure in nervous contrast to the spidery bentwood chairs on which she rests (as in *The Chess Game*). The woman's face is the first of a type that hints at that mix of Anglo-Latin and black characteristics that people so many of his paintings. A reprise of this painting, *Gypsies* (1968), is similar in basic structure, but with the addition of a standing figure, who leans on the back of the chair behind the original seated figure, and with the elements pared down to the basics. The (male) figure behind the translucent curtain in this later picture has turned forward and is apparently about to make an appearance as his hand begins to draw back the curtain. There is less detail here to distract one's attention from the three figures; they fill the picture plane almost completely. Everything appears clear, simple, and direct, except for the curtain about to be silently pulled aside, but which will keep its shadowy figure hidden forever.

The use of drapery elements to preserve mysteries and to entrap and transmit light is a very important device for Tooker, and one which he uses frequently. Often, the drapery almost conceals an object or person behind it, but on several occasions he has painted just the drapery itself, for his rendering of the folds, billows, and swags of drapery with conviction is a technical tour de force. Early on, he painted several smaller works, shelves containing still-life objects, or just the curtains covering the shelves, as potboilers, quickly created and priced to sell even when his more important work found no market. *White Curtain* (1951) is one such painting. It is rendered to maximize its *trompe l'oeil* effect with the fabric touching the bottom of the "frame" of the opening and falling forward out of the picture plane. Tooker has always placed these works in a lower category of achievement and signed them only with his initials – a way of distancing himself a bit from the necessary if slightly distasteful task of making popular images

**GYPSY** 1951.
Egg tempera on gesso panel,
23 x 17½ in.

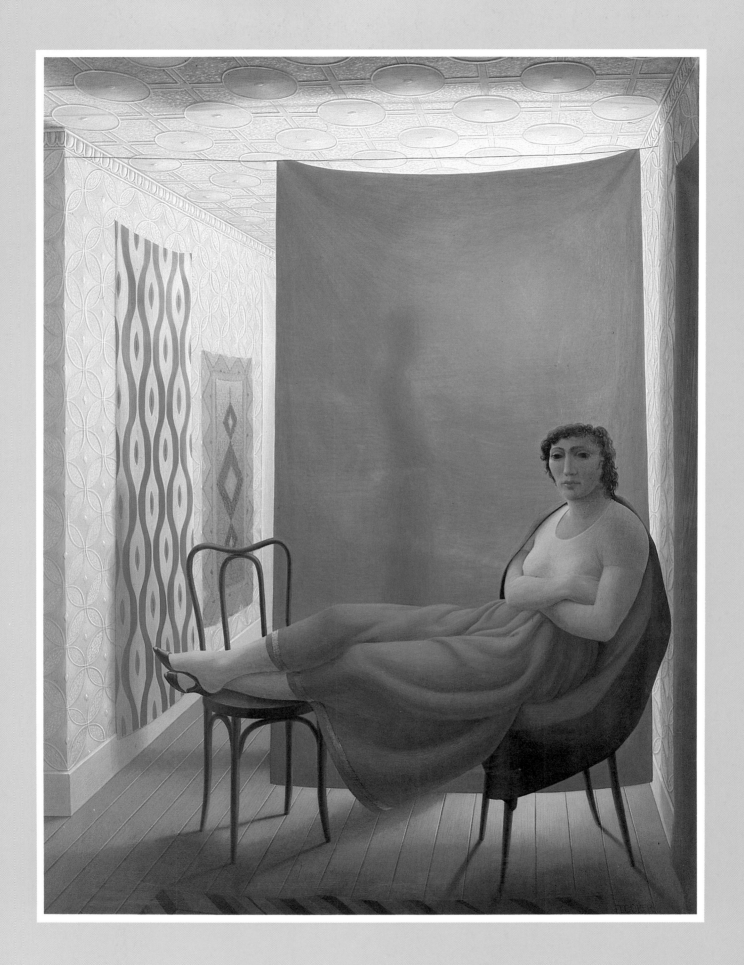

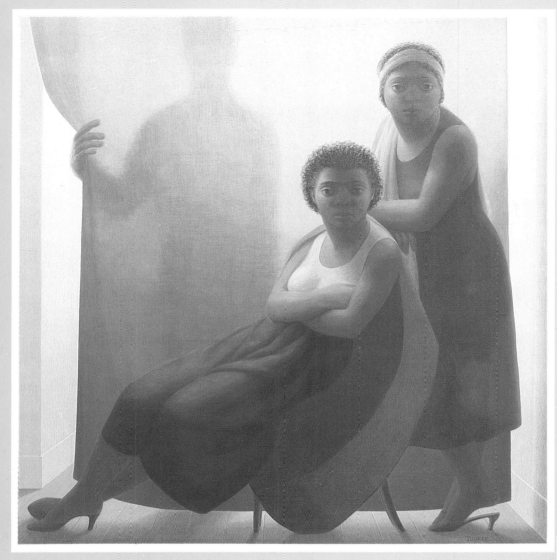

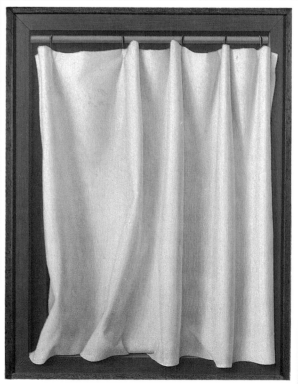

**GYPSIES** 1968.
Egg tempera on gesso panel,
23 x 23 in.

**WHITE CURTAIN** 1951.
Egg tempera on gesso panel,
17½ x 13½ in.

designed for quick sale.

Another picture of this time, *Builders* (1952), harks back to Tooker's very earliest mature paintings in its emphasis on a dynamic enclosing structure. The artist has taken liberties with the architecture, placing the joists of the ceiling at right angles to the roof framing, using these incorrectly placed structural members to create a deep and enclosed space. The picture was an homage to Paolo Uccello and Piero della Francesca in the manner in which these quattrocento Italians created spatial perspective. Of greater importance, however, is the fact that *Builders* marks the first appearance of the Tooker "seer," an oracular figure, always a woman, marked by huge eyes and quiescence of stance that suggests an altered state of consciousness. The workers accord her rapt attention. She is not doing the building, but they are following her seemingly telepathic instructions.

*Jukebox* (1953) was completed in the early part of the year and is one of Tooker's most successful pictures. The structured architecture, with a certain amount of all-over surface patterning, was further elaborated with swags and garlands of crepe paper. The two young women who lean languorously against the jukebox are wonderfully illuminated from below by the light projected through the multicolored case of the jukebox. The depiction of the two heads above the jukebox is particularly successful. The unusual angle of the light coming from the jukebox gave Tooker an ideal opportunity to model facial structure, particularly the curve of eyesocket as it turns down into the bridge of the nose. One curious feature of the composition is the almost mannerist compression with which these two figures have been fitted into the pictorial space. It is a device Tooker used often, citing as one of his reasons his fascination with Italian early-Renaissance relief sculpture that contained so much illusionistic detail within a very shallow relief.

In 1953, Tooker and William Christopher bought an old brownstone on State Street in Brooklyn Heights. The move was traumatic but positive, and painting slowed while the house was being reconstructed, preceded, of course, by the battles at Borough Hall that led to *Government Bureau*. The Brooklyn Heights neighborhood was then as unfashionable as Eighteenth Street, but was entirely residential, a dense mixture of small apartment buildings and rooming houses. This rich mix of faces and figures served Tooker well over the almost ten-year period he lived there. *Red Carpet* (1953) is a picture based on a glimpse into a basement room in a Puerto Rican apartment house in the neighborhood. From that glimpse, Tooker reinvented the scene, investing in the simple room and its occupants a complex visual iconography influenced, in turn, by his reading of Robert Graves's interpretation of the theme of the White Goddess. This creature, a synthesis from a number of mythological and religious sources, is an extension and embodiment of the three Fates of Greek and Roman mythology, those three figures of destiny that rule birth, life, and death. The figures in this painting are not dancers, as some commentators have assumed. Three women are seated on the floor, smoking cigarettes. Their

faces, devoid of all expression, are unusual even considering the geometric liberties to which Tooker often subjected the human face. They appear to wear finely formed masks that strip away any emotion from their faces. The composition supports the curious stares of these three figures. Two of them gaze across the almost empty expanse of room, and their placement at the lower left corner gives emphasis to the closed geometry of the space, pressed forward by the remarkable red rug – a Tooker invention. The color is that of passion, this time a passion of the imagination, of the transformation Tooker has wrought upon these figures and the new meaning he has cast upon them. It is perhaps the figure at the left, the one who stares out beyond the picture plane, that most captures our attention. The eyes appear to see the viewer, yet without making eye contact. She appears to be transfixed, utterly lost in thought. She is the seer who has been found in a Brooklyn basement.

This is another appearance of the Tooker seer, a figure in an altered state, a trance which is neither sleep, nor death, nor consciousness. It is a riveting image, one which will appear in many forms in many pictures and one which always raises the question, what is their state and what do they see?

Just before the move to Brooklyn Heights, Tooker painted *Doors* (1953), a free interpretation of a crowded hallway in the Eighteenth Street loft. It is a painting that Tooker enjoyed for its strongly architectural yet abstract qualities, with the two human figures severely cropped – and dominated – by the architectural elements in the composition. The semi-nude woman entering from the right gives the work a sense of portent which extends beyond form, even though the sunlight shapes and models these crisp wooden doors so luminously. The doors push the image closer to the picture plane, abruptly terminating the view into the picture. Despite all the attention focused on the three doors and the shallowness of space, the true subject of the painting is the event that seems about to happen. For, through the central door, another fragment of a figure (unidentifiable as necessarily male or female), apparently also nude, can be seen sitting on a bed. The situation can only come to a conclusion in the imagination of the viewer; in the painting, the moment is suspended, forever unresolved.

In late 1954 or early 1955, Tooker began the series of *Window* paintings, his longest cycle on a single theme to date. It consists of nine numbered works (I through IV, and VI through X; the number V was inadvertently skipped, Tooker apparently losing track of the sequence in the two years between *Window IV*, 1960, and *Window VI*, 1962), and a number of other paintings with various titles that refer to the theme of figures in a window.

The great number of window paintings in Tooker's *oeuvre* attests to his attraction to this thematic concept as a "natural" framing device, which provides containment and compositional order at the edges of the painting while it emphasizes the dense and dramatic arrangement of figures within the frame. The window concept even allows an occasional witty play of illusionist ambiguity

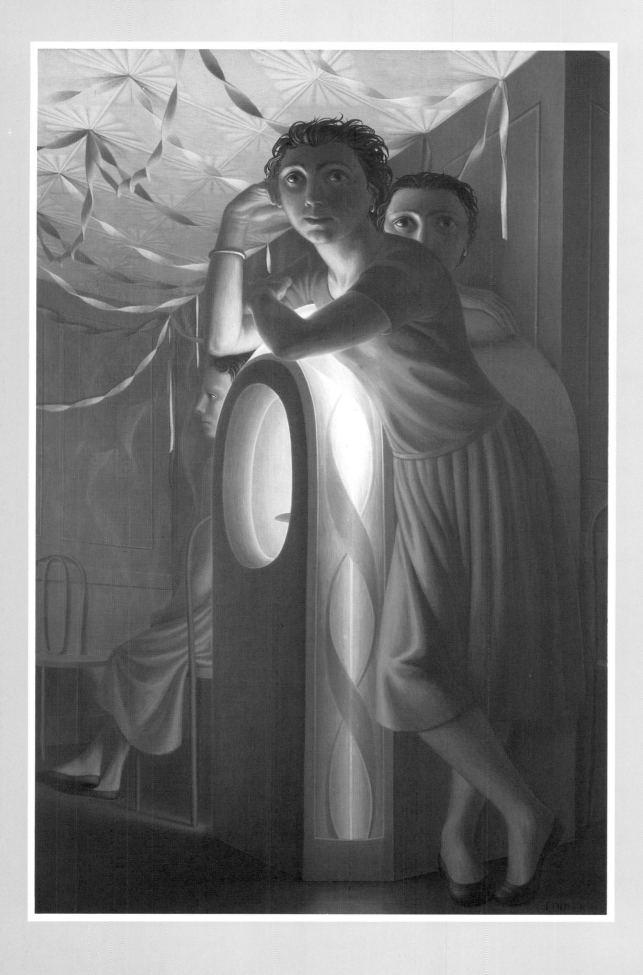

**RED CARPET** 1953.
Egg tempera on gesso panel,
16 x 20¼ in.

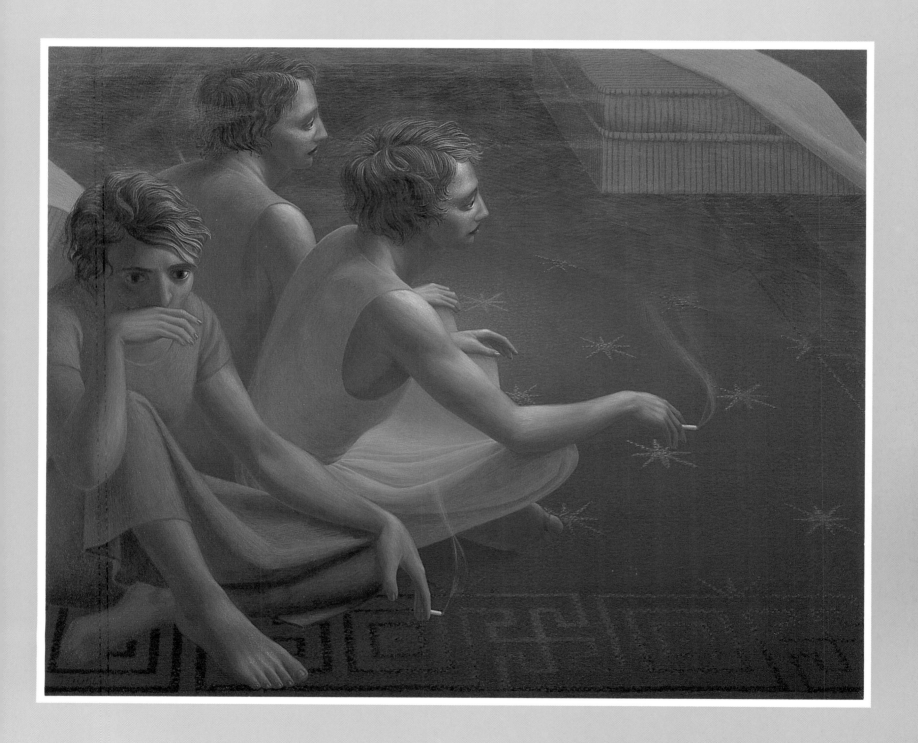

**DOORS** 1953.
Egg tempera on gesso panel,
12½ x 17½ in.

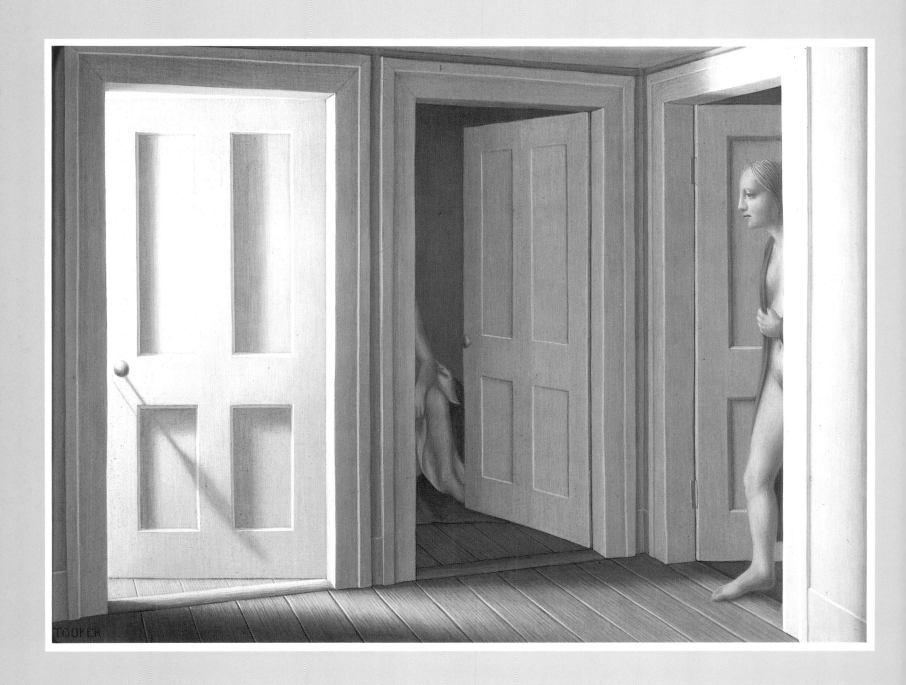

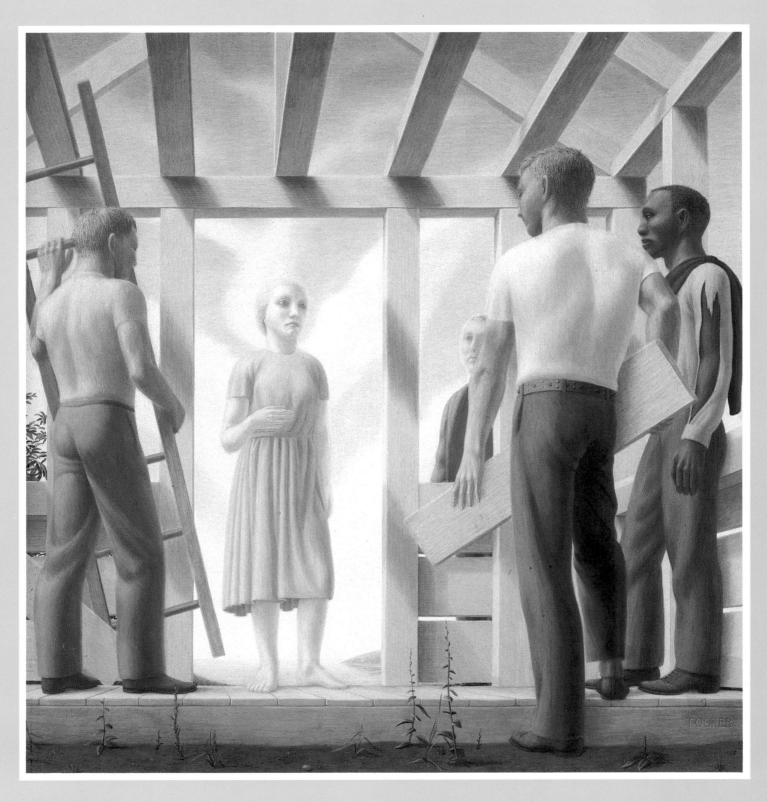

**BUILDERS** 1952.
Egg tempera on gesso panel,
16 x 16 in.

within the picture plane.

While the windows of Bleecker Street and Manhattan's Chelsea district where Tooker had lived previously were often filled with figures on warm summer nights, it was not until he moved to Brooklyn Heights that he really experienced "window life." This area of Brooklyn, originally developed as a proper, middle-class residential area in the mid-nineteenth century, featured narrow streets lined with three-to-five-story brick and brownstone buildings. The windows were open and crowded with people all summer long. *Window I* (1954-55) is, like *Red Carpet*, based on a quickly glimpsed scene that Tooker witnessed in the rooming house across from his own building on State Street, but the composition recalls the earlier *Gypsy*. A black woman sits looking out of a window, a translucent yellow window shade drawn down behind her, while a man looming behind her thrusts his arm forward in the act of lifting the shade. Except for the muscular arm, he remains an ominous shadow against the gauzy fabric. The partially lifted shade creates a backlit aura behind the woman, highlighting her arms, hands, and part of her face, and reveals a black man at the back of the room, stripped to the waist and idly toying with his fly. There is no physical contact; the figures do not even look at one another, but the implications are clear. It is a sexually charged yet chilling image, which Tooker emphasizes by the acidulous yellow color of the window shade and the woman's long fingers, twisting in her dark hair.

During the next five years, Tooker painted four variations on this theme. In *Window II* (1956), an entirely invented image, the sun washes across a window opening (the sash and glass have been left out in a perfectly acceptable use of artistic license), illuminating the figure of a well-muscled Hispanic man in an undershirt who lifts the battered cloth of an old green window shade to gaze into the street below. A second face, that of a woman, is just discernible in the shadowed interior below the shade in lower left, staring straight out at the viewer. The man holds an orange against the window ledge but seems to lack the interest or energy to eat it. Perhaps it is morning, perhaps a drowsy time following an afternoon of love, but the face beneath the shade suggests something else, both mysterious and ominous. She is a riveting emotional foil to this otherwise languorous picture.

Tooker was building upon his interest in using simple, bold forms, pressing them forward to the picture plane and combining them with large areas of strong color. The white of the man's undershirt contrasts strongly with his darker flesh, the curtain, and the shadows of the room. The paper flowers that rest on the window ledge are there not only for a bit of color but for a play on space as well, for the petals of the light-colored blossom that extend over the edge of the window sill (into which Tooker has "carved" his name at the far left) imply that the image extends beyond the edge of the picture plane and into our own space.

Tooker recalls that at this point in the series, the formal aspects of the work began to show the influence of his interest in Italian fifteenth-century relief sculpture, particularly the work of Agostino di Duccio he had seen in the Tempio Malatestiano in Remini. The shallow relief in those sculptures was composed into a series of discrete panels, each framed with architectural elements. Those panels suggested windows, and he developed his ideas in that form. He thinks of paintings "in terms of carving, of bas-relief, a solid form supported from behind. Some artists paint atmosphere, but I work to cut it out, to compress space, to push it to the front of the painting as much as possible."

This spatial carving and compression resulted in substantial changes in the composition of the window paintings. In *Window III* (1958) two amply proportioned, somnolent-looking figures lean out of a window, with a curtain and venetian blinds pressed up close behind them. Lighted from below, they themselves are pressed forward in the picture plane in a mannerist way, and take up almost the entire space of the window without somehow disturbing the venetian blinds. In fact, those venetian blinds hang improbably on the room side of the rich red drapery which has been pushed aside by the man's naked arm and shoulder. The window frame itself is only suggested by the horizontal color bands at the top and bottom of the painting, which serve primarily as support for the hands and arms of the figures.

*Guitar* (1957) followed the arduous creation of *The Waiting Room* and is as intimate and pleasurable in its vision as *The Waiting Room* is disquieting. The window is suggested only by the sill running across the bottom and the red draperies at either side. The light enters from an angle as if through a window, illuminating the hands and face of the black guitar player as he caresses his instrument with a gesture more sensual than musical. His companion, a nude blonde woman, reclines upon the rumpled bed, her ripe features reflecting the light that filters into the dim interior. The title of the work has a double meaning. It refers not only to the musical instrument but to the shape of the classic female torso. Despite its air of casual voluptuousness, the painting was intended to shock and, indeed, it did when it was first shown. The black man's long fingers delicately caress the finely grained wood of his instrument, which is clearly a metaphor for the exquisite flesh of the woman. Tooker, however, does not let the heat of the moment overcome his sense of order, and the picture is as highly organized as a Raphael. The two "guitars" oppose each other in an inverted V, with the figure of the man and the opposing drape forming a secondary framing gesture. In the final drawing for the picture, a glass of water refracting the light stood on the window ledge to the right of the guitar. Tooker wisely left it out. The ledge and curious little ribbons from the guitar strap were enough to establish the space of the picture without visual theatrics.

*Window VI* (1962) is a variant of *Window III*, with two black figures, a partially nude man and a nude woman, standing at the window. They are pressed right to the limits of the window ledge, again nearly filling the picture plane. It is a composition of interesting geometric order in which the arms and torsos of the two

**WINDOW I** 1955.
Egg tempera on gesso panel,
23¾ x 16½ in.

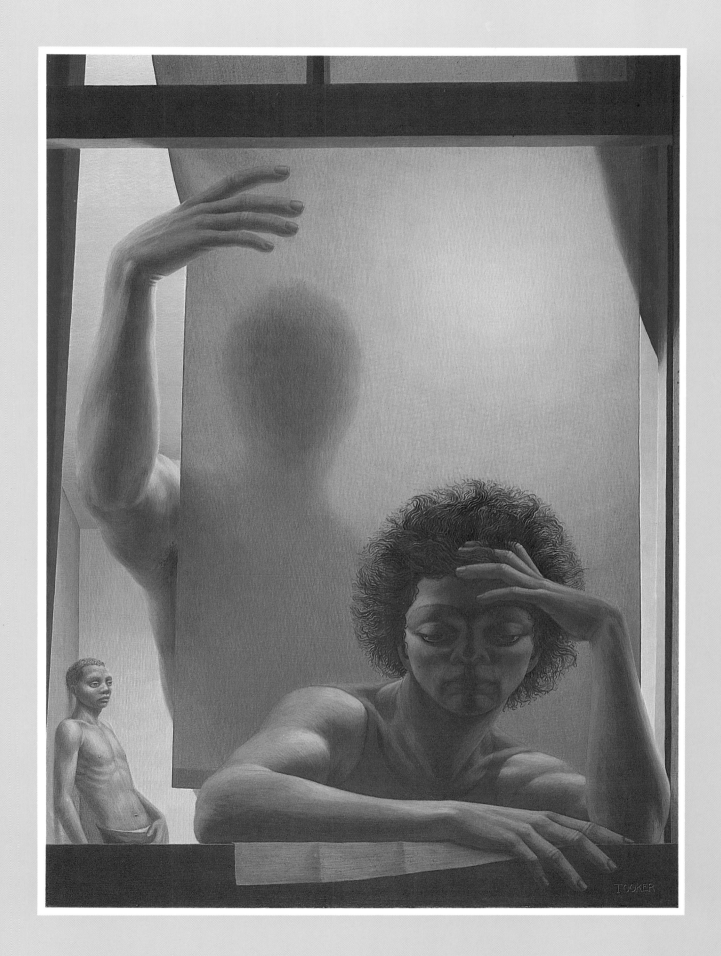

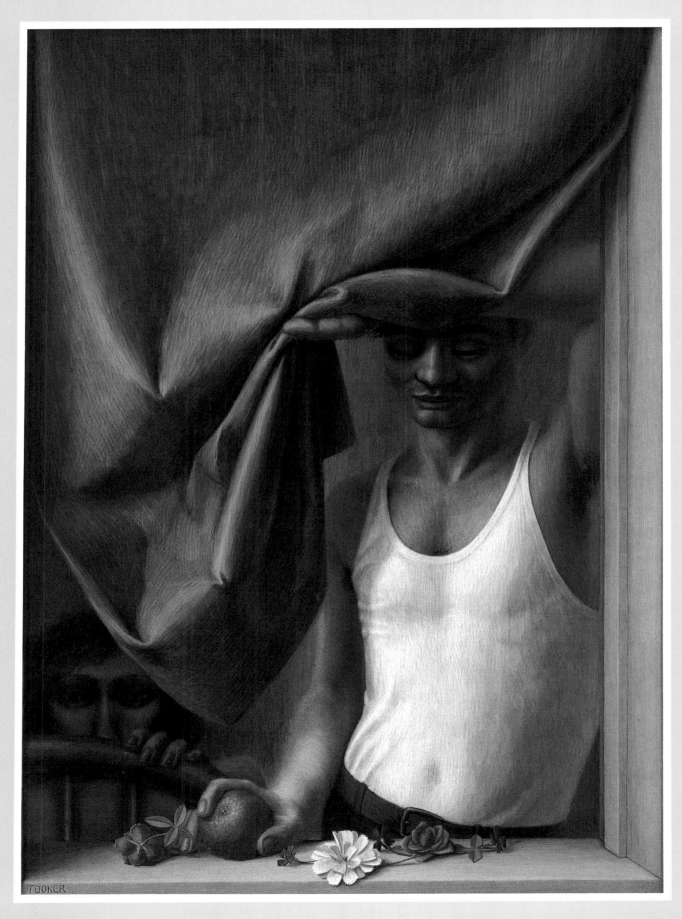

**WINDOW II** 1956.
Egg tempera on gesso panel,
24 x 18 in.

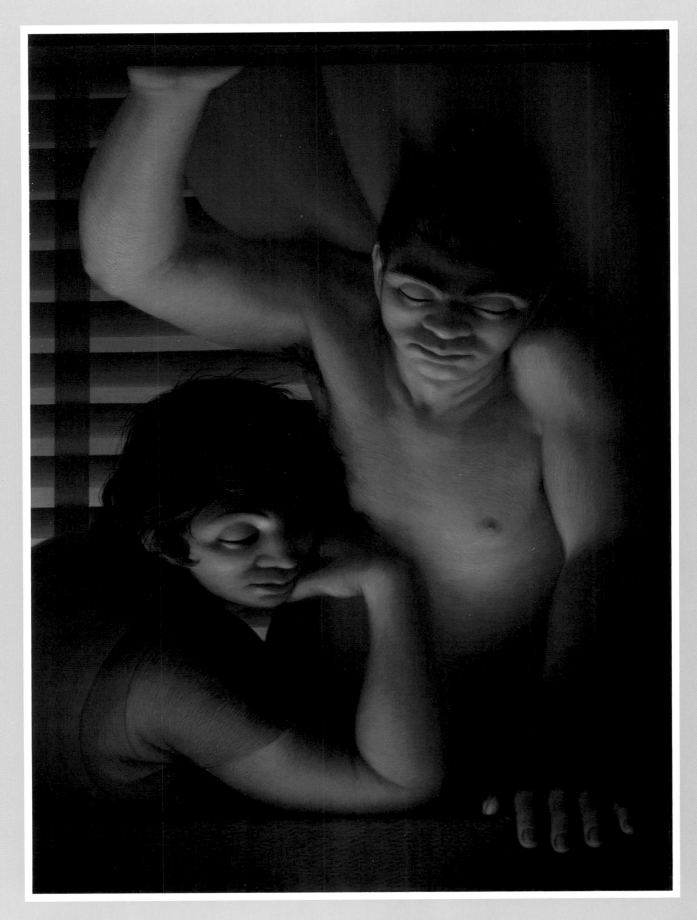

**WINDOW III** 1958.
Egg tempera on gesso panel,
24 x 18 in.

figures form a curious rectilinear shape, a grouping that could be rather graceless if the figures were not so elegant and sensuous. The attraction of these figures for one another is subtly shown, particularly in the gesture of the head and right hand of the woman. She appears to be caressing and nibbling the upper arm of her lover, a gesture which is at once demure, coquettish, intimate, and passionate.

In contrast to the dominance of the male figure in *Window VI*, a full-figured nude young woman dominates – indeed, occupies most of the picture plane – in *Window VII* (1963). She is shown lifting aside a gold curtain bathed in light and peering out obliquely. At the extreme upper left of the painting, behind her right shoulder, is the head of a handsome black man whose look confronts us directly. The drapery shields much of the woman's body from the direct rays of the sun, which fall strongly upon her "divine belly," while the rest of her body is softly illuminated from the diffuse reflections of the light-drenched curtain. Once again, the window is indicated just by a curtain and a frame running along an edge of the picture (here, the top) suggesting a proscenium for a stage populated with gargantuan figures. Only a fragment of the room may be seen. The wall is a passionate red, with a patch of rumpled drapery below it – the bed, perhaps? The nude here is unusual in Tooker's work for the pronounced Teutonic character of her face and head, with a small nose, pointed chin, and blonde hair. In fact, this painting is atypical in the way Tooker has strongly emphasized the differences of the races. The scene conveys a strong sexual tension; the couple appear

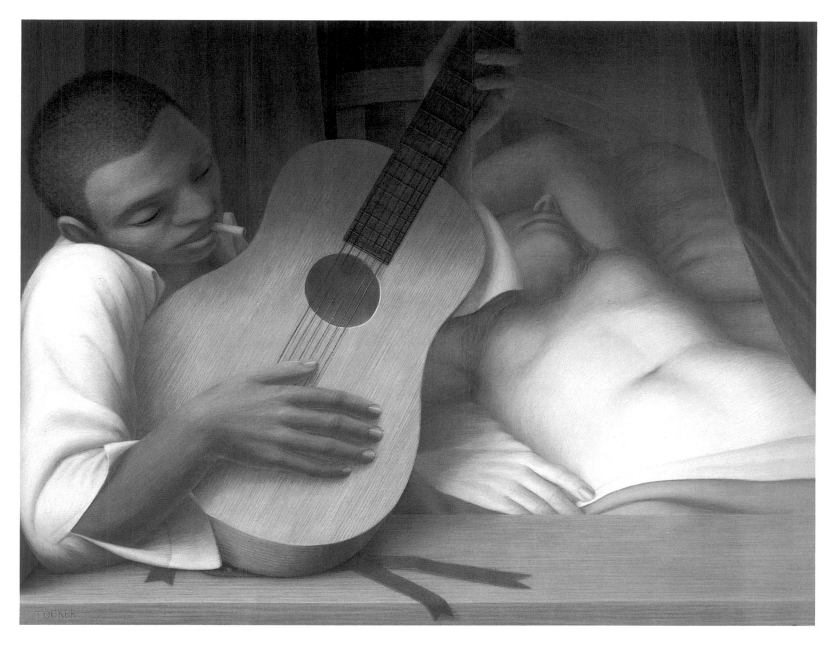

**WINDOW VI** 1962.
Egg tempera on gesso panel,
24 x 18 in.

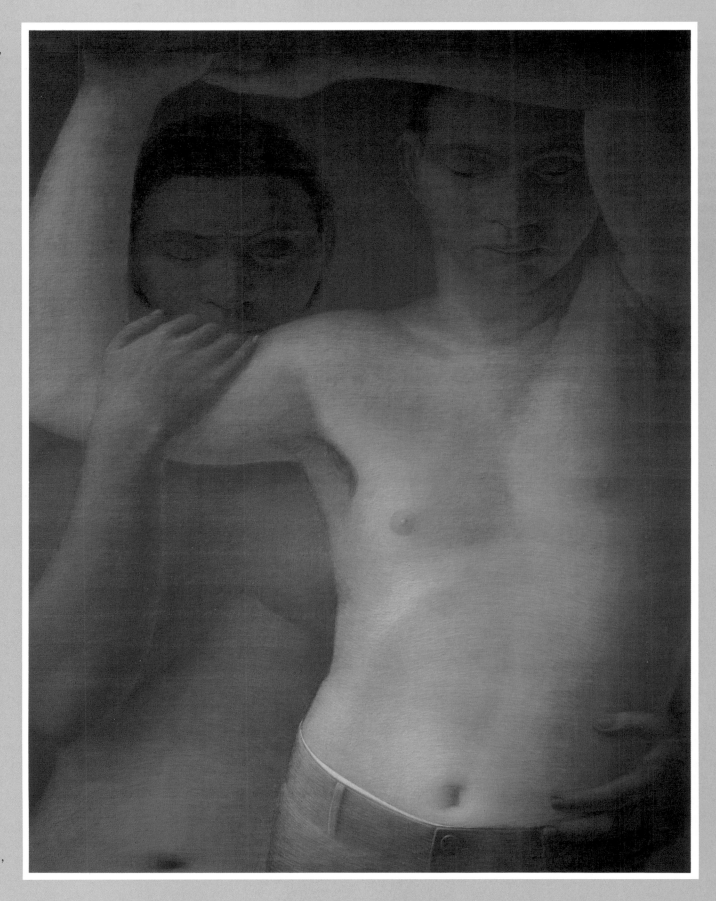

**GUITAR** 1957.
Egg tempera on gesso panel,
18 x 24 in.

(Opposite)

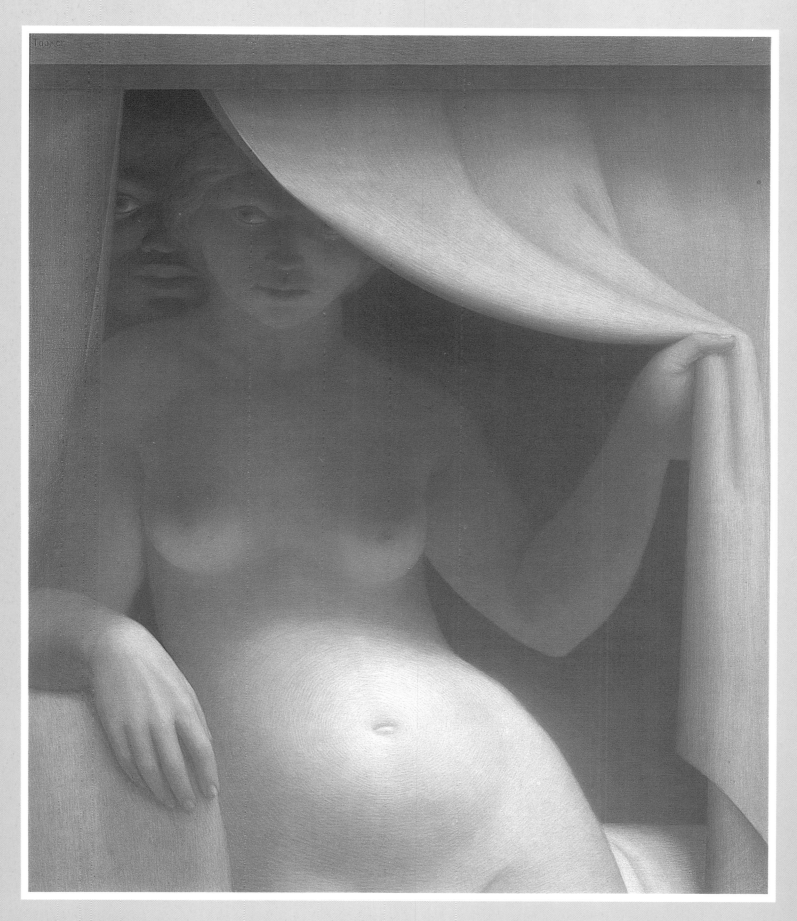

**WINDOW VII** (DESDEMONA) 1963.
Egg tempera on gesso panel,
24 x 21 in.

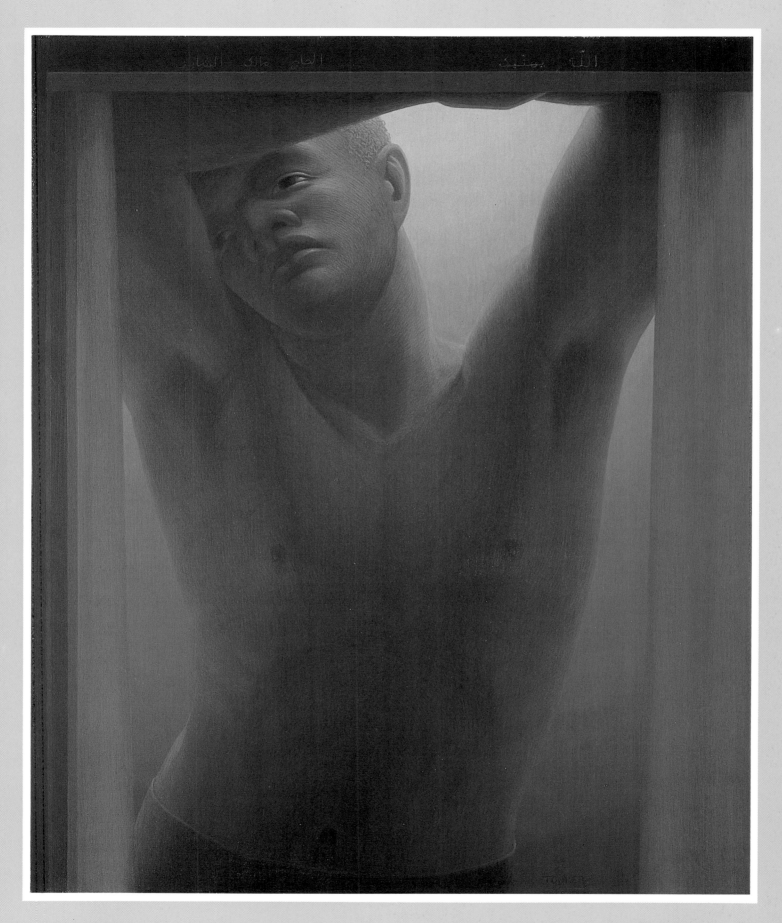

**WINDOW VIII** 1966.
Egg tempera on gesso panel,
24 x 20 in.

to be gazing from the window before letting the curtain fall on the world outside, at least for the remainder of the afternoon.

*Window VIII* (1965–66) shows a lone black man, nude to the waist, who stands in a window at night, his arms upraised and crossed, resting against the open sash and revealing his full upper body to us. Although the pose is reminiscent of the male figure in *Window II* and *Window VI*, the figure here is stronger and more visceral. And unlike many of the previous window paintings, this figure neither looks directly at the viewer nor does he look down into the street. His gaze is abstracted, and his eyes, half hidden by the crook of his right arm, look into a middle plane. The picture is, in fact, a memorial to Malcolm X, whose name in Arabic is carved into the window sash framing the upper part of the picture. The artist had been much impressed with the change in Malcolm X after he returned from his pilgrimage to Mecca, after which his narrow racism was replaced by a new sense of universal brotherhood. The

pose, while set within the familiar window structure, is very consciously derived from the prototype of Michelangelo's *Dying Slave*, created for the unfinished tomb of Julius II.

This figure standing thus, hands over the head, is a universal symbol of vulnerability, a vulnerability that is intensified by the very gloom of the work. The only source of illumination is the light behind the figure, from within the room; there is no moonlight or streetlight. It is a painting of melancholy, but one also in which the strong physical bulk of this powerful man makes an indelible impression. He seems strong enough to take the risk of placing himself in the window, perfectly silhouetted, the dreamer framed as a perfect target. It is, too, a technically bold work, portraying a black man in silhouette on a dark night, yet retaining its detail within the shadows which are suffused with the smokey red-orange of the curtains.

*Window IX* (ca. 1968) swings the window viewpoint dramatically,

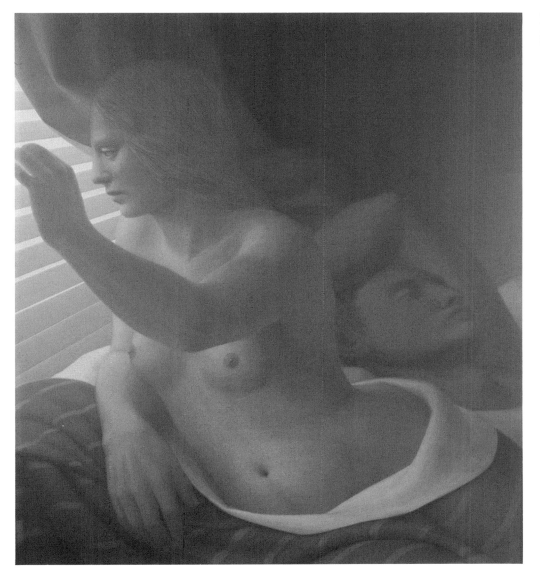

**WINDOW IX** 1968.
Egg tempera on gesso panel,
24 x 22 in.

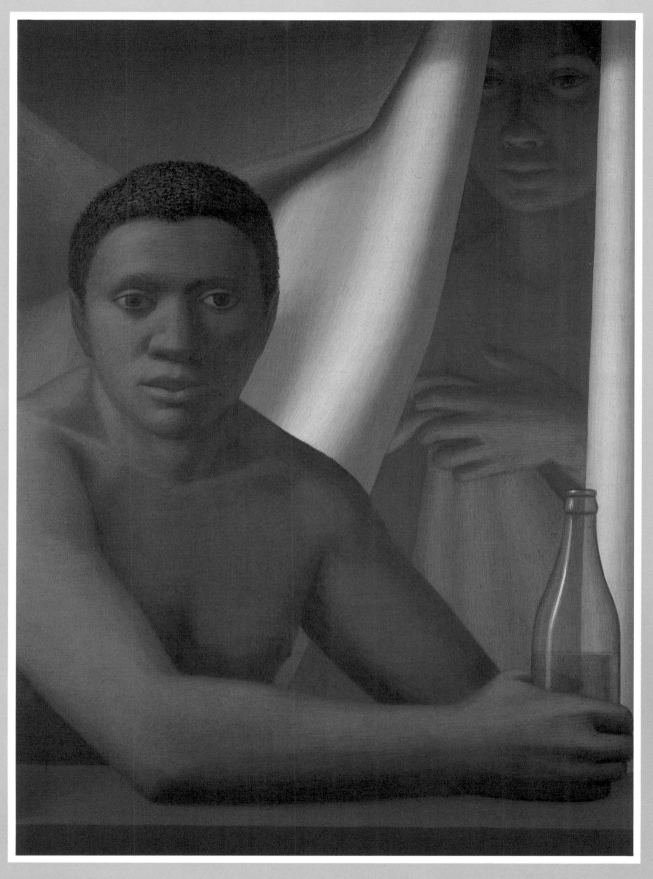

**WINDOW X** 1987.
Egg tempera on gesso panel,
23½ x 17¼ in.

**UNTITLED** 1991.
Egg tempera on gesso panel,
19 x 23½ in.

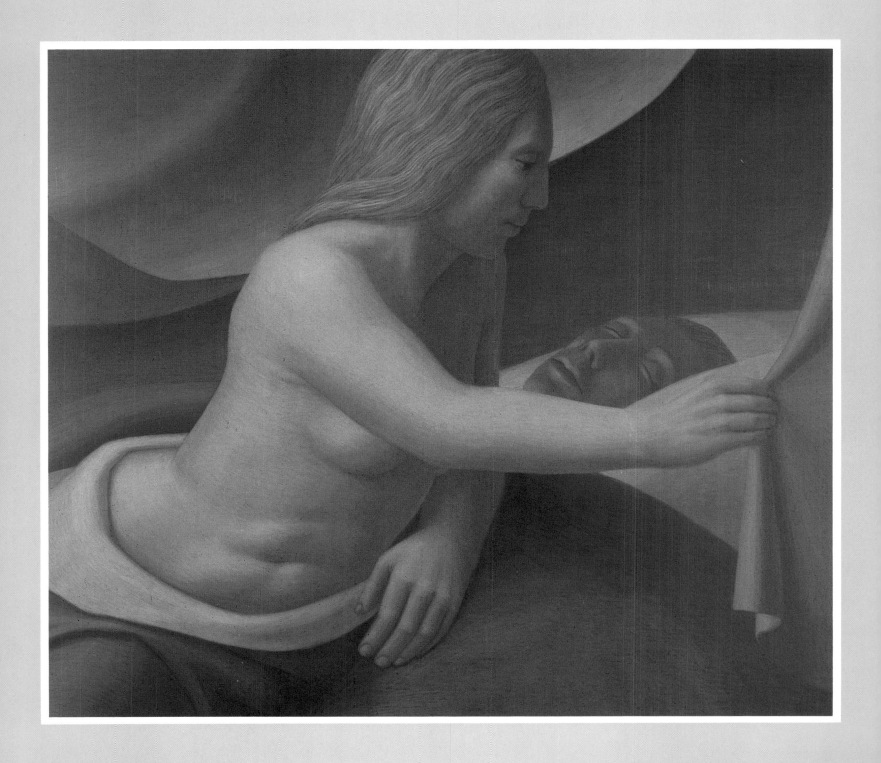

turning from outside to inside the room. A man and woman lie upon a bed, and the woman is the prominent figure here. She is nude and has turned away from her sleeping lover to peer through the slats of a venetian blind through which soft, volume-shaping light washes her form. Her figure is that of the classic *odalisque* and another, almost sculptural, variation of the female torso as guitar. In 1991 Tooker painted an untitled reprise of this work (and Tooker's only untitled painting). In this latter work the window is entirely eliminated and the well-fleshed figure of the woman has turned back to face her still sleeping lover. This time, however, she makes a modest but loving gesture to him by pulling the curtains more closely around them. Of course it is another opportunity to render the "guitar," and this work does it in a most tender way.

Window X (1987) is a variant on *Window VII* but reverses the earlier composition. *Window X* places the figure of a black man in the foreground while his white companion appears in the right background, lighted in the reflection from the curtains.

The window idea, if not the specific window structure appears many other times in Tooker's work. *Toilette*, although not explicitly a window painting, is related to the theme in its depiction of a nude woman framed by drapery and four figures crowded behind her in a compressed space. Between 1962 and 1979, Tooker explored an interesting variation of the window theme in a series of four *Mirror* paintings. And in Spain in the mid-1970s he created several classic window paintings, especially *Pot of Aloes* and *Woman with Oranges* (discussed later in "The Spanish Pictures"). What they all have in common is a clear sense of drama within a closely delimited space, and figures whose corporeality and density are felt as palpably as if they were carved from stone. The intensity of the images emerges as much from the visual drama of the space as from the dramatic tension of the scene.

In *Toilette* (1962) and the four *Mirror* paintings, Tooker focuses on the female face and body, in meditations on youth and age, beauty and ugliness, themes that Tooker touched upon as early as 1947 in *The Chess Game*. All of these paintings are variations on the traditional vanitas portrait, in which youth and beauty are shown to be transitory, and age and death inevitable.

*Toilette* contrasts the beauty of the young woman with the four older, bloated figures behind her who are in the process of adorning her with beautiful clothes and jewels. Although she accepts their ministrations, she appears to be ill-at-ease. They, on the other hand, are absolutely self-assured as they dress her. The doubts and beauty of youth are replaced by the complacency of age. The healthy, rosy color of this young woman's flesh will be transmuted by age into the sickly pallor of the figures who surround her. *Toilette* is intriguing in its use of mannerist spatial abstraction. The relief is now so compressed that it is difficult to imagine how the hands that drape the fabric on the young woman's body or hold the jewels for examination are able to penetrate that solid wall of figures that press up against her so tightly. In the draping of the body Tooker uses another convention, later to become more

pronounced, the curving of background into foreground, which confounds traditional ideas about pictorial space. The man directly behind the young woman wraps her figure with a swag of rich red fabric. He is pulling the cloth from the panel hanging at the back of the painting and curving it around her torso in the foreground, thus connecting the two.

The four *Mirror* paintings extend the vanitas theme in compositions that display Tooker's highly refined sense of geometry at its best. The placement of a table or other object in front of a portrait figure to develop pictorial space, a traditional seventeenth-century device, is used here in the way Tooker uses the sill in the window paintings. In *Mirror I*, *Mirror II*, and *Mirror IV*, the table in front of the figure and the architectural details behind the figure define and limit the space. The mirror held by each woman appears as an opaque silhouette against the soft light of the room at the same time that it reflects the light to illuminate the faces from that low angle which Tooker so favors. The mirror is much larger in *Mirror III*, occupying the entire picture plane, and the frame of the mirror defines and limits the space by its literal congruence with the edges of the picture.

In *Mirror I* (1962) the hauteur of the young woman, her vanity, her desire for beautiful adornment, is directly contrasted with the death's head behind her left shoulder, of which she seems happily unaware. In *Mirror II* (1963), where the figures of youth and age together stare fixedly into the mirror, youthful self-adoration is replaced by awareness of the inevitable changes time will bring.

Of these two paintings, the artist himself much prefers *Mirror I*, citing the strong composition – the variation on the circle offered by the ovoid disk of the mirror and the more solid spherical shapes of head and skull – and naming Georges de la Tour as the master from whom he derived the form and light of this painting.

*Mirror III* (1970–71), (illustration on page 146), which shows not only the face but the partially nude figure of a young woman, is more explicitly sensual than the first two paintings. Standing in front of a three-quarter-length mirror, the young woman has begun to remove her loose-fitting robe, while an old crone peers over her left shoulder. Their faces are seen only in reflection and are slightly distorted by the beveled edge of the glass. As in *Mirror II*, the older face is a vision of the future.

*Mirror IV* (1976–79) portrays the same young woman as *Mirror I*, but the skull is replaced by a rose as the traditional symbol of mortality and the ephemeral nature of beauty. It is a more subtle and brilliant variation of the earlier work, confirming Tooker's strength as a master of light and structure. Five planes define the composition, from front to back: the horizontal table edge, the vase and flower, the mirror, the young woman's head, and the wall with its vertical molding. But only the head – lighted from above and from the light reflected in the mirror – is developed volumetrically.

The spectator looking at these four paintings, amid all this adoration of flesh and beauty, is somehow denied a sense of participation with these figures. Perhaps the presence of the mirror,

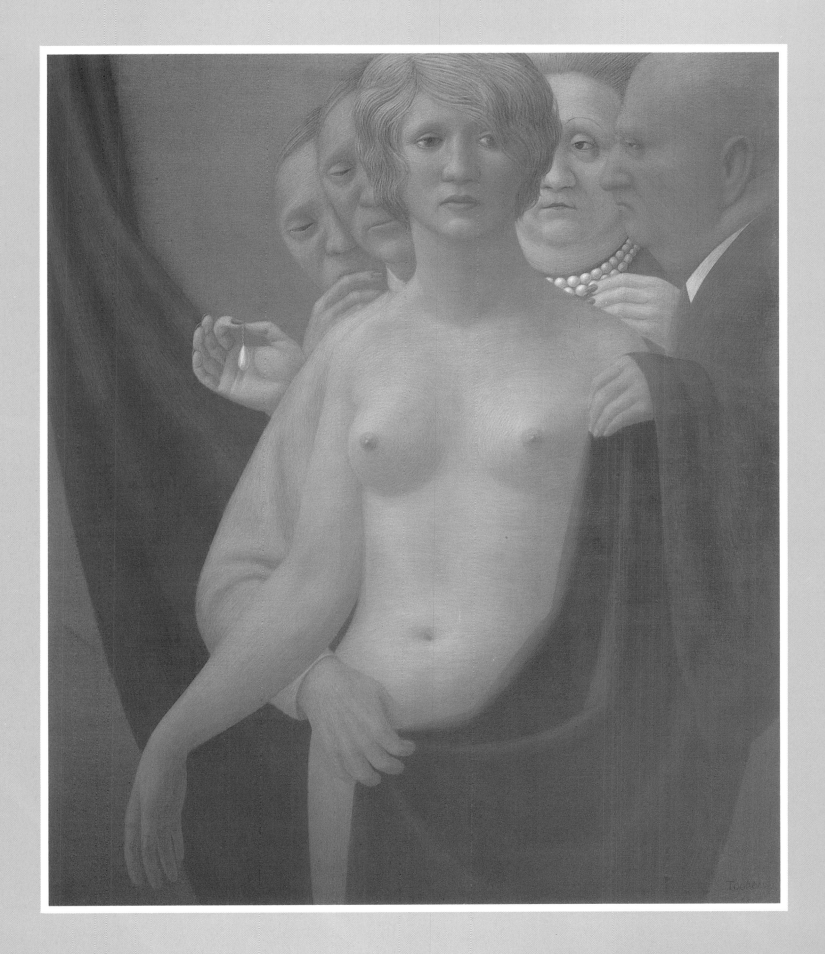

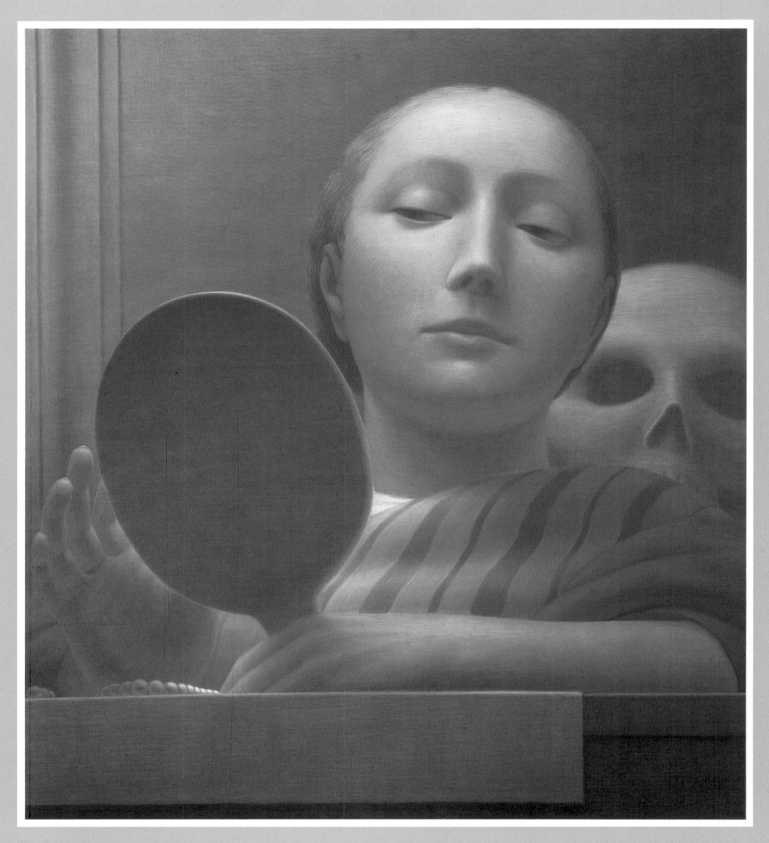

**TOILETTE** 1962.
Egg tempera on gesso panel,
20½ x 17½ in.

(Opposite)

**MIRROR I** 1962.
Egg tempera on gesso panel,
20 x 18 in.

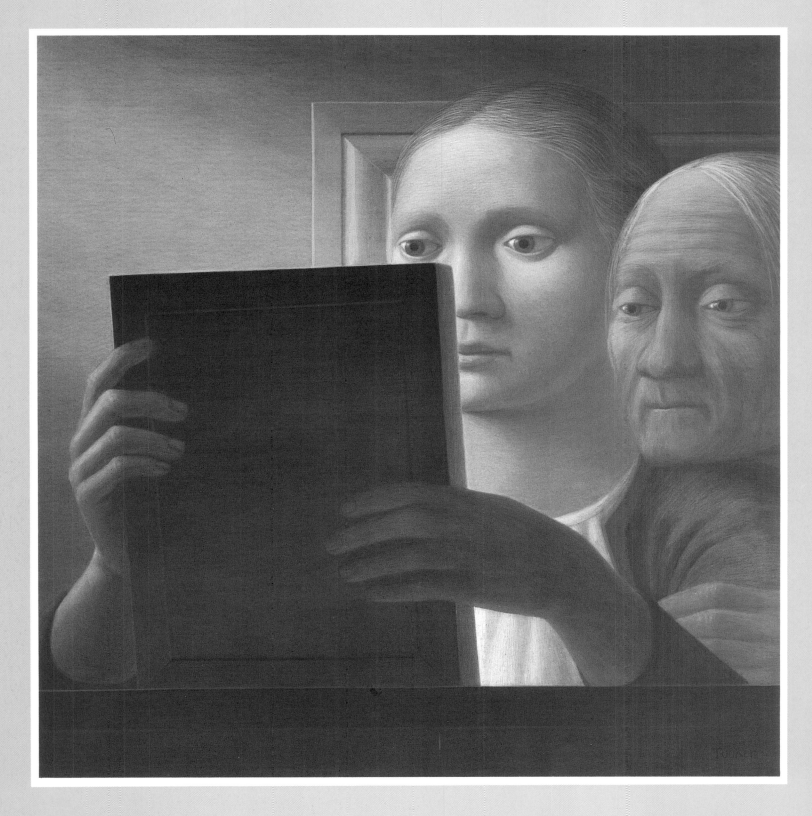

**MIRROR II** 1963.
Egg tempera on gesso panel,
20 x 20 in.

**MIRROR IV** 1976-79.
Egg tempera on gesso panel,
24 x 20 in.

(Opposite)

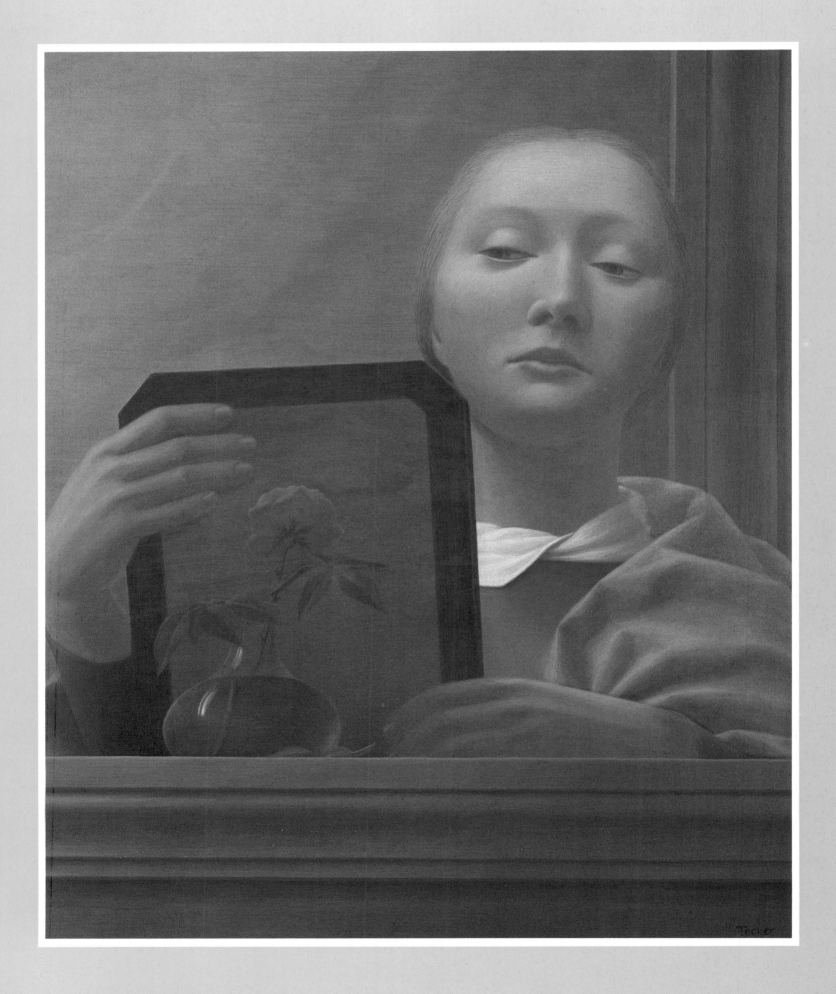

a strong physical barrier, creates an unbridgeable distance. Perhaps it is the young women's complete self-involvement with their own images that shuts us out. Even though the color and light of the paintings are ingratiating, the steely impression of time stopped tends to frame and isolate these subjects from us just as within the works they are so often isolated from one another.

This chapter concludes with two recent variations on the window theme. In *Girl with Basket* (1987-1988) the window elements are used almost as framed pictures to articulate the background. It is a rare picture for George Tooker because it has no program—other than the desire to render a figure in the pale blonde light that tempera handles so well. The young woman is seated between two windows, her head strongly modeled by the light entering from either side of the panel. She holds a basket of fruit in her arms, and one might say that this painting reflects the work of Vermeer, if he had painted in fifteenth-century Italy. This picture is not a variation of an earlier work (save that Tooker uses the motif of the sweater draped over the shoulders and tied under the neck) but rather is about beauty, both in the form rendered and in the manner of its rendering. It is one of his most ingratiating works.

*Woman with a Sprig of Laurel* (1992) is a reprise of a number of other "window" variants, of which this is one of the most gentle. The brilliance of the window ledge (or table) only draws one's eyes into the shadows, and inevitably to the eyes of the figure. Perhaps it is another variant of the Tooker "seer," but now the look is less piercing; it is just as wise, but much more kindly.

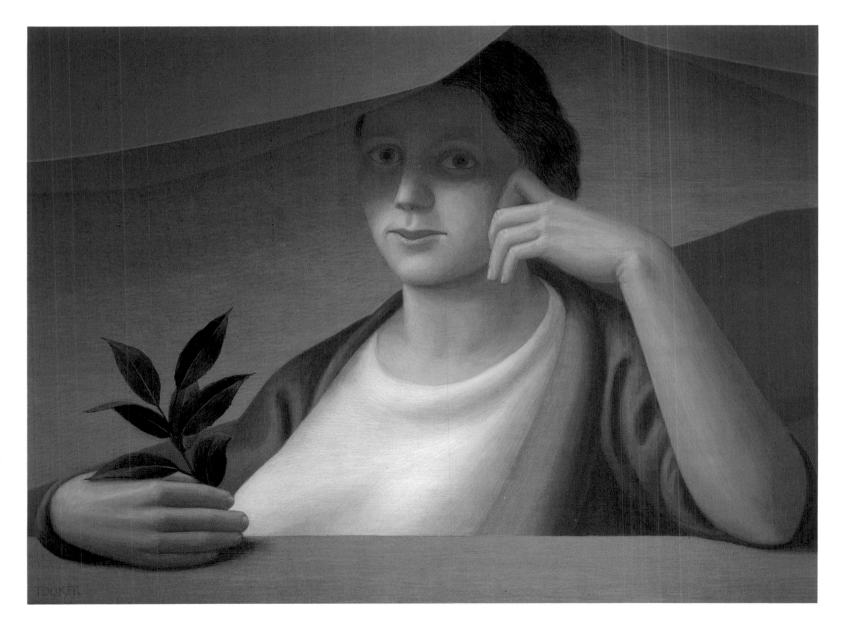

**WOMAN WITH A SPRIG OF LAUREL** 1992.
Egg tempera on gesso panel,
18 x 24 in.

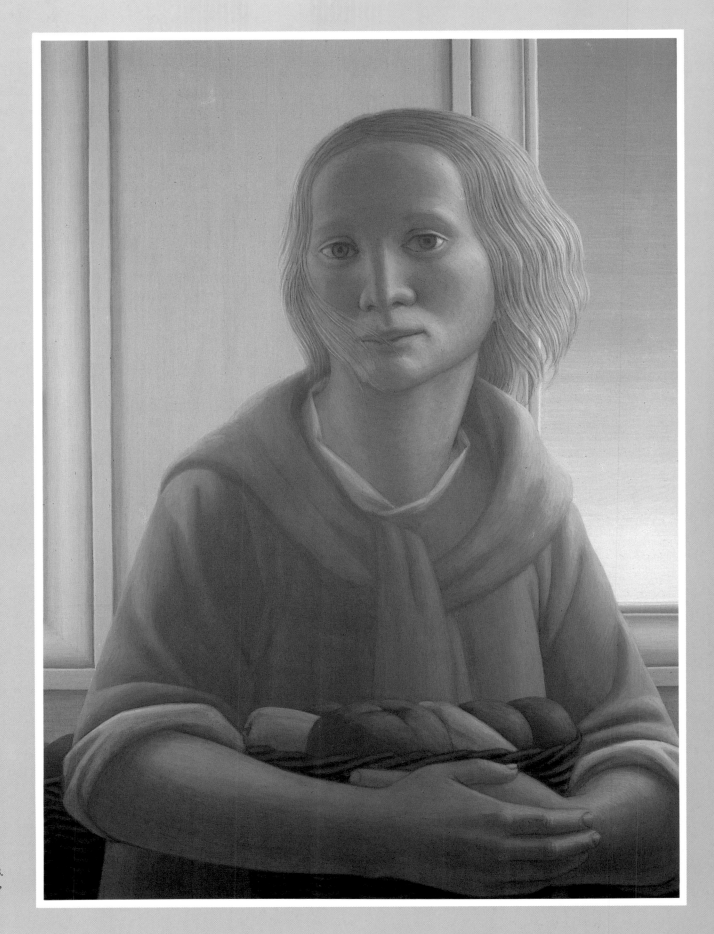

**GIRL WITH BASKET** 1987-88.
Egg tempera on gesso panel,
24 x 18 in.

## INNOCENT DIVERSIONS

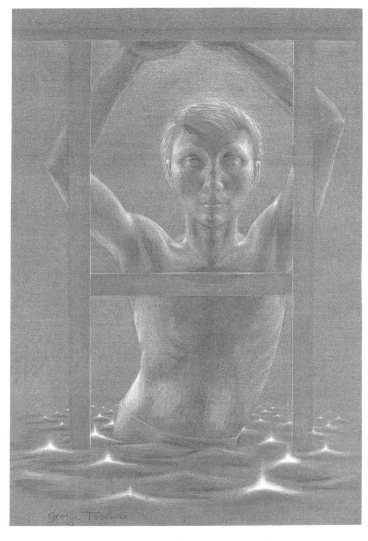

SELF-PORTRAIT OF THE ARTIST (Study for DIVERS), 1952
Silverpoint and egg tempera on hand-toned paper, 12 x 19¾ in.

**A** small number of paintings seem to defy classification within this loosely structured system of Tooker's work. The subjects are pleasures of the past – of childhood – recalled by Tooker in his paintings as one might recall the memory of a special celebration, special because of its distinctness from everyday life.

*Bathers* (1950) stems directly from Tooker's childhood memories of swimming at the Old Inlet Bathing Beach on the south shore of Long Island near Bellport. One of Tooker's brightest, most luminescent works, it glows with the intense, reflected beach light of a sunny afternoon. In order to verify the perspective and to "balance" his composition, Tooker made a remarkably complex drawing for the work, reminiscent of the perspective studies that Thomas Eakins regularly prepared for his paintings of rowers on the Schuylkill River. The construction of Tooker's picture, with its elaborate patterns of wooden siding and boardwalk, hearkens back to his recently completed *The Subway*. The wooden wall is perforated by a series of narrow openings, each one showing a fragment of ocean or dressing rooms beyond. The figures of the three young girls, originally given short skirts in the drawing, have been reduced to smooth, nearly abstract forms, suggesting Italian fifteenth-century portrait sculpture. The moment seen here is a reflective one. It marks the end of the visit to the beach, perhaps, when hours of sun, play, and swimming have taken their toll, and pleasurable fatigue wins the day.

*Divers* is another "summer picture," painted in New York either in 1951 or 1952. Its structure bears a strong resemblance to *Bathers* and to *Coney Island* in its use of wooden planking as a major compositional and framing element. For Tooker, it is a happy picture, and the thin figure on the ladder is an acknowledged self-portrait. It is one of Tooker's most schematized paintings. The back-lit wavelets are as geometrically constructed as the sawn timbers of the dock, and unquestionably influenced by Italian quattrocento painting. The great pleasure of this picture is the light which wraps the attenuated, almost nude figures in a cool glow – the light of a Northern summer. Tooker has even lighted his signature, painted on one of the dock's stringers, to resemble one that had been carved into it. It is the last of the beach paintings, which moved steadily away from their Reginald Marsh prototypes before vanishing from Tooker's *oeuvre* altogether. It is also the most stylized of the beach paintings. The highlights of sun on the water are schematic rather than illusionistic renderings, stressing form and pattern. The figures plunging from the dock into the water – more flopping than diving – are devoid of fluid motion, yet they epitomize the repetitive study of the single semi-nude figure from different angles that so fascinated Tooker at this time. Notice too the construction of the dock, particularly the right side, in which space is funneled away from the picture plane, a device rarely used by Tooker.

Four other paintings, all featuring Japanese lanterns, complete this brief chapter. The earliest, *Garden Party* (1952), is based on memories of the artist's childhood. In the late 1920s and '30s, his parents used the July Fourth holiday as an occasion to have a

**BATHERS** (BATH HOUSES) 1950.
Egg tempera on gesso panel,
20¼ x 15¼ in.

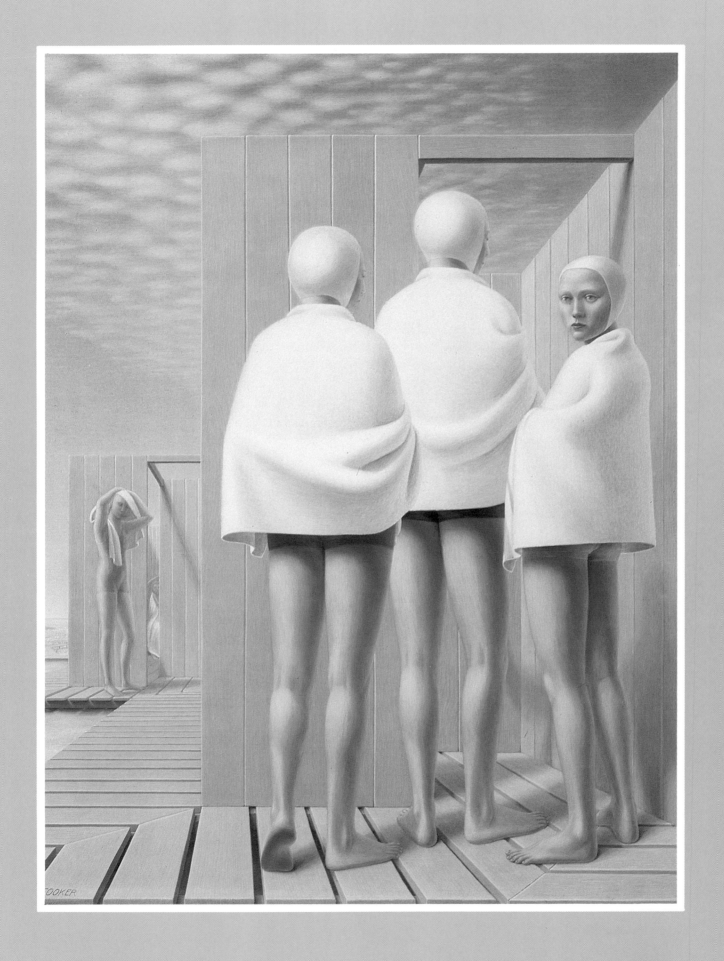

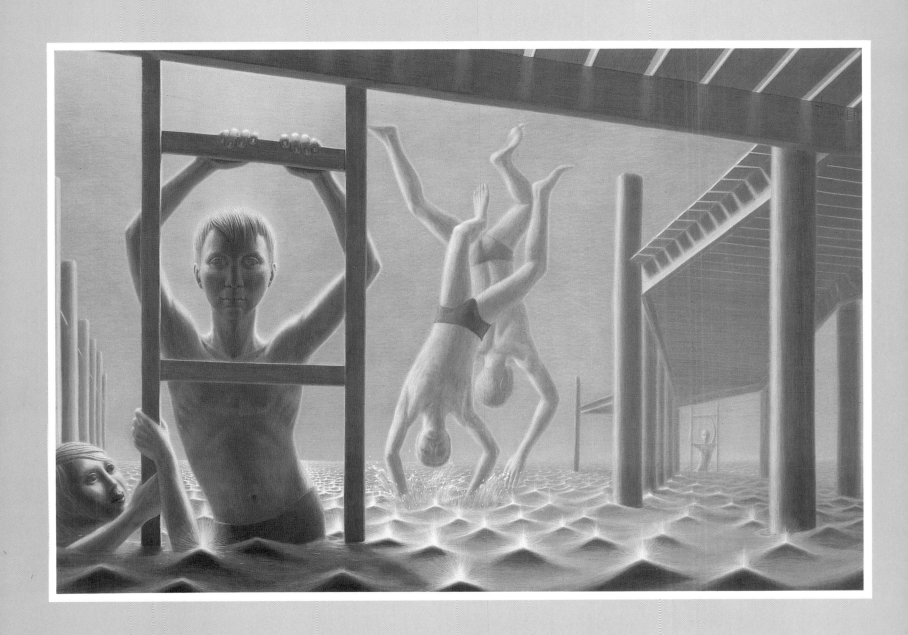

**DIVERS** 1952.
Egg tempera on gesso panel,
12 x 18 in.

midsummer garden party for their extended family. Cousins, uncles, and aunts would come to visit at the Bellport house. The family did not shoot off fireworks, but later in the evening, as it grew dark, the children would each be given a lighted Japanese lantern to hang somewhere in the garden. Tooker recalls the image of the young children moving through the twilight with their lanterns as "very magical." He included himself in the painting as the boy at the extreme right lighting the lanterns and passing them along to the others. The composition of *Garden Party* utilizes the device prevalent in the early paintings of deep space to the left, shallow space to the right; this is also true of *Bathers*.

The use of Japanese lanterns is repeated again in the painting *In the Summer House* (1958). The vista of the pergola of *Garden Party* of a few years earlier has been compressed into an interior of a summer house which frames the figures of two young girls as they prepare their lanterns for hanging. The wooden trellis, here given a latticework diamond pattern, serves the same compositional function as the pressed-tin walls and ceiling patterns found in earlier paintings. Its crisp, rectilinear lines nicely offset the softer shapes of young bodies and lighted lanterns. There is a curious languidity to the figures, as though bone had turned to putty, perhaps due in part to the creamy glow of the light that infuses the picture.

*Lantern* (1977) was painted in Baltimore. Tooker had gone there to stay with a friend who had suffered a personal tragedy. Recognizing that he might be in Baltimore for some time, Tooker brought along a gessoed panel already framed on which he could work during his stay. (He often prepares a number of panels and orders frames to fit well in advance of using them. This allows him to make decisions about the dimension of a painting by selecting from the several size panels available, and the frame protects the painting when it is moved.) The panel, frame, porcelain watercolor palette, several brushes, and small containers of dry pigment are all that are necessary to move Tooker's "studio." All the tools for his painting can be contained in a small suitcase.

*Lantern* is a triumph of the painting of an internal light source, similar in intensity and angle to the reflected light in the mirror paintings. Tooker's often-used device of extending an object (the figure's left hand in this case) beyond the table edge only emphasizes the shallow space of the work and the ambiguity of the placement of the figure, which appears to float somewhere in front of the picture plane, even if still within the frame. The single androgynous figure (Tooker considers it to be a woman) confronts the viewer with an expression that is hard to fathom. It is not unemotional, nor is it quizzical. It is another manifestation of the Tooker "seer," a figure that seems to look out beyond the frame directly at us. Those eyes have an intelligence and a curiosity that seem to encourage the sharing of confidences. Indeed, this painting may not really be an image of an innocent diversion, for the figure seems possessed of a knowledge that verges on the oracular.

*Lanterns* (1986) is the most recent variant on this theme. Here

(and in the other paintings of the "Lantern" series as well), what might have been a painting of cloying sweetness is given presence and monumentality by Tooker's reductive, idealizing geometry. By means of this rigorous visual order he isolates the critical elements from the deluge of extraneous detail. Within the almost square panel are variations on a single head, the "Tooker person," seen

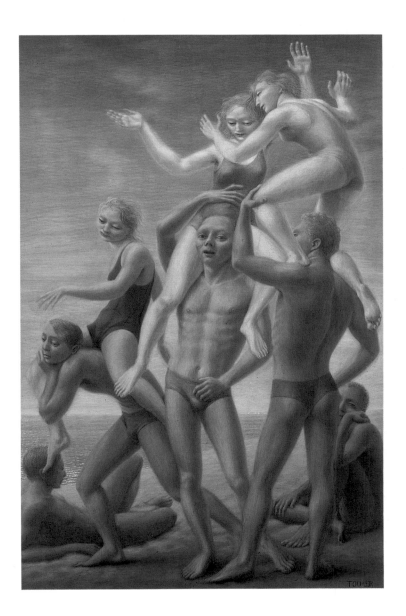

**ACROBATS** 1950-52.
Egg tempera on gesso panel,
24 x 16 in.

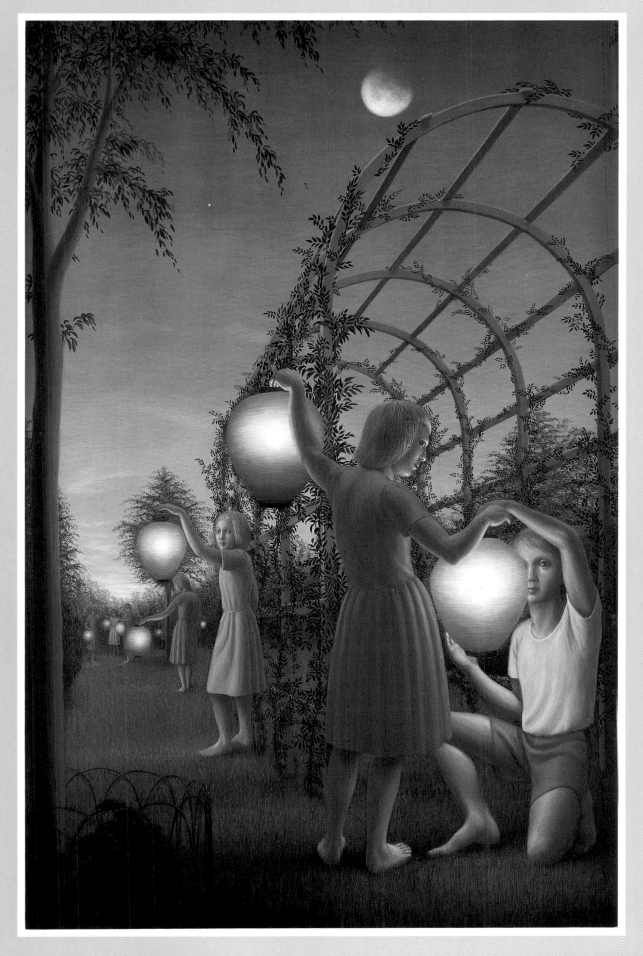

**GARDEN PARTY** 1952.
Egg tempera on gesso panel,
18 x 11¾ in.

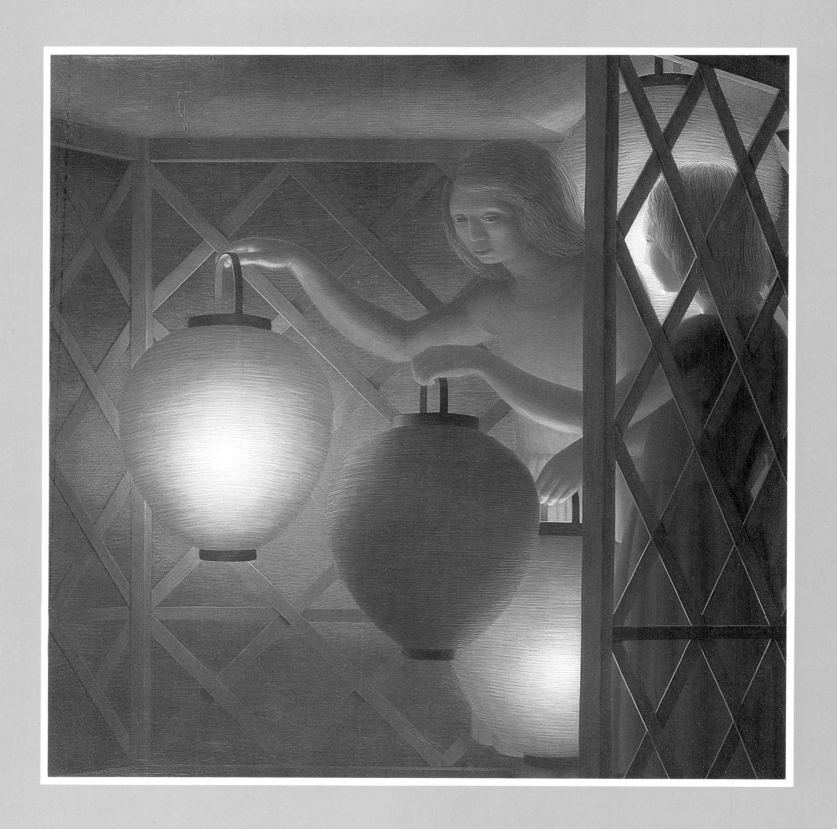

**IN THE SUMMER HOUSE** 1958.
Egg tempera on gesso panel,
24 x 24 in.

**LANTERN** 1977.
Egg tempera on gesso panel,
18 x 16 in.

**LANTERNS** 1986.
Egg tempera on gesso panel,
22 x 26 in.

(Opposite)

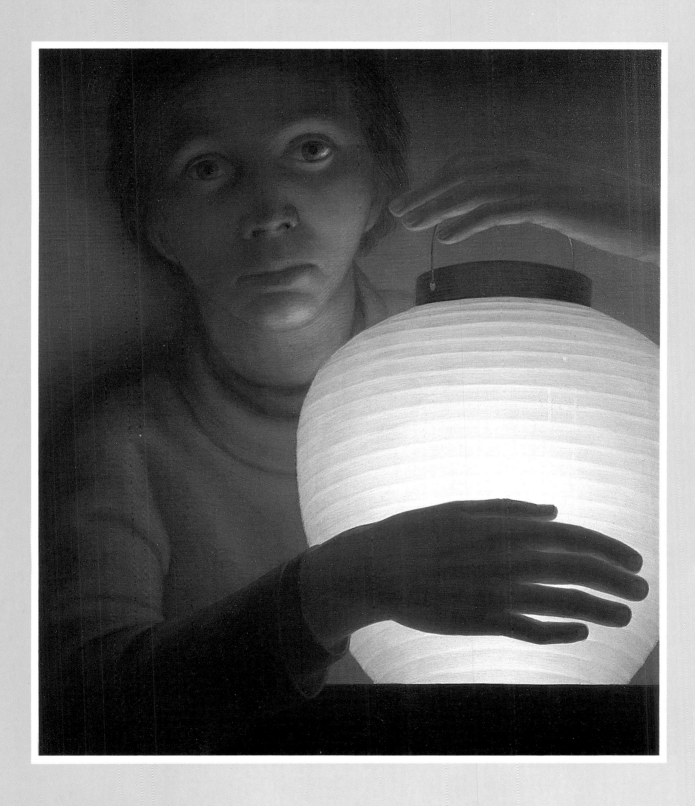

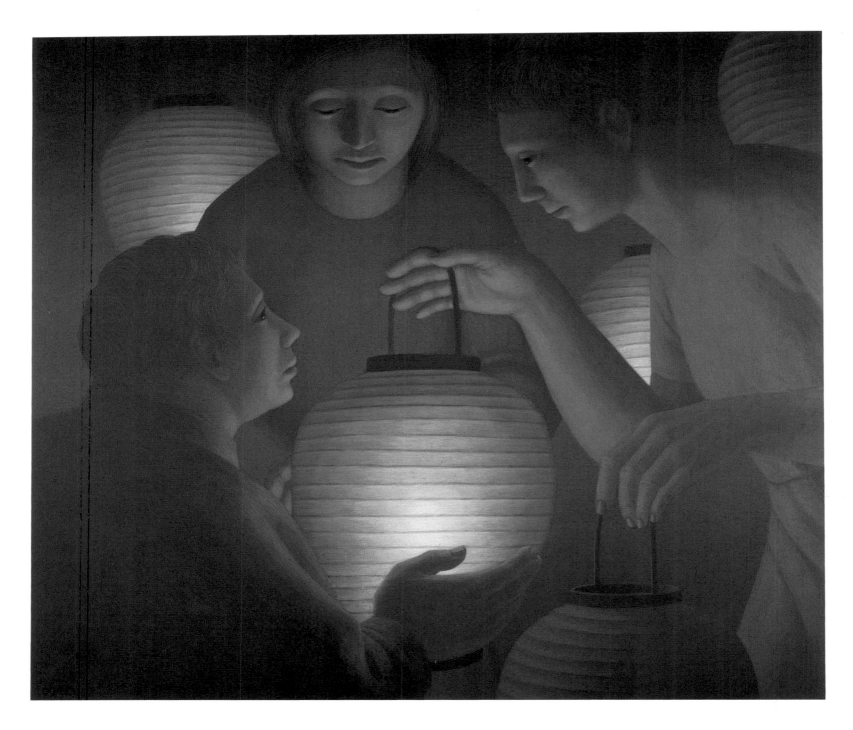

profile and full-face. Individual diversity gives way to common-alities. Again the gender of these figures is ambiguous (or not important). All evidence of the specific moment or precise location is stripped away. Monumental in scale, the powerful forms confined within the small panel establish a counterpoint between the glowing lanterns and the pensive young faces illuminated by them.

*Lanterns* is not specifically a religious picture, although the glow of the candles, like those of votive lights in a darkened church, evokes the spiritual through the evanescent and luminescent flame.

*Lanterns* depicts the penultimate moment, the instant before the resolution and completion of an event, a time to gather strength inwardly through contemplation and introspection.

The four "Lantern" paintings possess such stillness, contempla-tion and reflection that a deep spiritual intensity seems to permeate this modest activity. The act of lighting a candle in a paper lantern has become a testament, an offering of light to the darkness of the world.

## DOORS AND WALLS

In the decade from 1962 to 1972, Tooker created a group of pictures that documented his deep concern about the apparent failure of communication in American society. He attributed the problem, in part, to self-imposed barriers of which to some extent we are all guilty. Enough has already been said about the 1960s as a time when our most closely held social beliefs underwent their most rigorous challenges. Obviously, the spirit of the time affected Tooker strongly.

*Voice I* (1963) was the earliest of these paintings. Tooker has commented that "the figures on either side of the wall are identical. The painting is about non-communication." Shown here are the futile efforts of "two human beings, just plain people" to communicate, separated by a barrier as thin as a door yet as impermeable as a yard of steel. We have no idea what they are trying to communicate, only that it is very important, and that the voice of one or the hearing of the other is too weak to make the message clear. The speaker is trapped in darkness, and his face expresses the urgency of the message; his hand is partly raised, as if to knock on the wall to emphasize his point and to aid in being heard. The listener, intent yet uncomprehending, has pressed an ear close to the wall, and placed his hand against it, too, almost as though its slightly cupped form might help him to hear better. It is a poignant picture, all the more so because we cannot imagine what is preventing them from simply walking around the partition.

*White Wall* (1964-65) is an odd composition for Tooker, with more than half the painting given over to a flat, white surface, completely uninflected. The title of the work is symbolic. Tooker had invited an old college classmate, a friend fondly remembered, for a visit to Vermont. When he arrived, Tooker discovered that the fellow had become rabidly anti-black. "He was so afraid of blacks and so upset by them that he was hiding behind a white wall . . . he was so terribly crippled." *White Wall* is an emotional portrait of his former friend, and Tooker has compressed and buried this man into a niche in his wall of whiteness, a niche which offers little shelter. He stands with arms crossed, the classic stance of emotional self-defense, while the relentless glare of the light, implacable in its whiteness, has bleached him to a pale shadow of his former self.

*Two Heads* (1966), a rapidly executed work, followed the laborious process of painting *Landscape with Figures*. It is in some ways a reprise of *Voice I*, but in this picture the two figures of young black women are less intent upon communication with each other than with an outside world.

*Door* (1969-70) is a variant of the "know nothing" theme. The figure now takes an active stance. No longer content just to hide from life around him, he energetically throws his weight against the door, as though by his own stubborness of will and physical power he will be able to keep out the weight of history.

*Farewell* (1966) is an anomalous picture in Tooker's *oeuvre* in that it is by far his most abstract. He based it on a memory of the hospital corridor where his mother died, although another painting,

**VOICE I** 1963.
Egg tempera on gesso panel,
19½ x 17½ in.

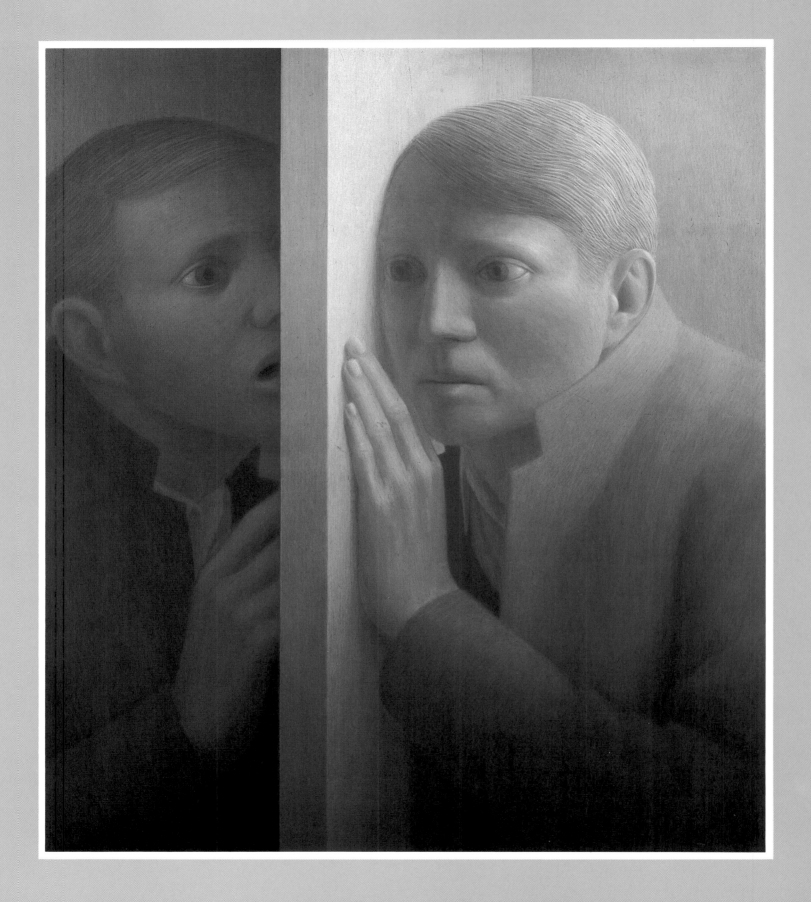

**TWO HEADS** 1966.
Egg tempera on gesso panel,
12 x 16 in.

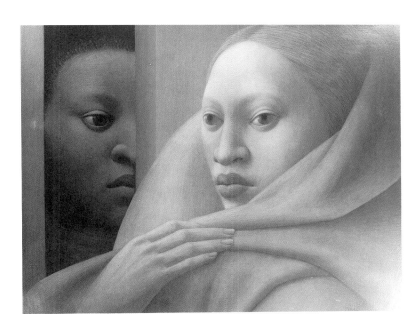

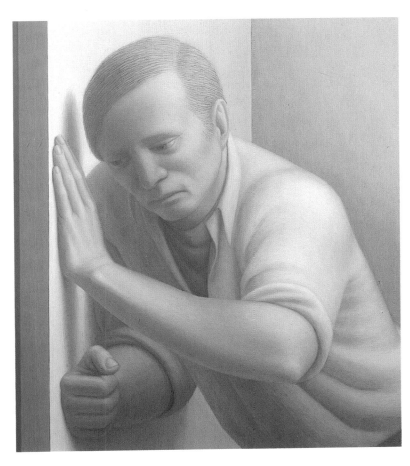

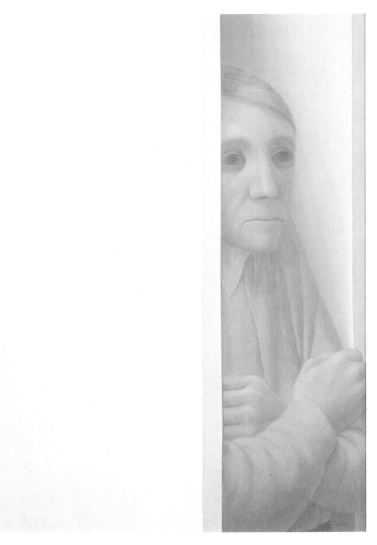

**DOOR** 1969-70.
Egg tempera on gesso panel,
20 x 18 in.

**WHITE WALL** 1964-65.
Egg tempera on gesso panel,
24 x 18 in.

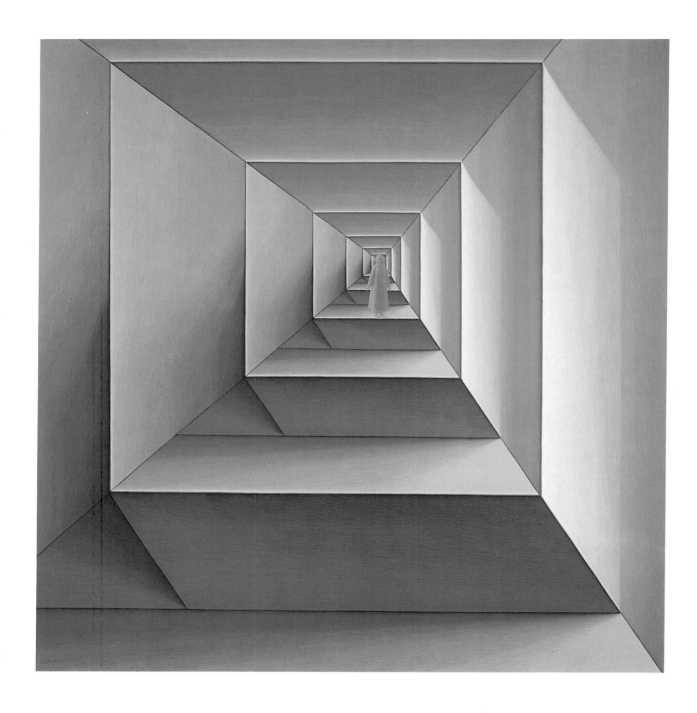

**FAREWELL** 1966.
Egg tempera on gesso panel,
24 x 24 in.

*Meadow I* (1960–61), is the work he created as a memorial to her. The structure of the corridor, with its alternating spots of light marking the open doors to the hospital rooms and darker areas between, has been transformed into a series of diminishing squares. The image is predominantly gray with just a line of dull red used to form the squares. The figure of a woman in a dressing gown – just a pale shadow – appears in the distance, standing within one of the squares, her head placed at the confluence of the vanishing point of the composition. The painting remains an emotional one for Tooker, but he feels it is not successful compositionally. Others have disagreed with him, but in this painting an obvious geometry has replaced Tooker's more subtle use of a geometry imbedded in a figurative style, and the melancholy of the subject may well be inhibited by the formal construction of the work.

*Man in the Box* (1967) is a variation on a
theme originally developed in a different way.
In the final drawing, the features were more
Caucasian, but by the time Tooker traced the
drawing onto the panel his thoughts about the
picture had become much more focused. It is an
allegorical work, a direct comment on the status
of black mankind in a white society. The picture
was upsetting to a number of people who saw it
early on, as the box appeared to be some sort of
torture device. Tooker had not intended the box
to be seen that way, but in fact it is a symbol of
emotional torment. The figure seems to accept
his fate as passively as do those young faces in
*Landscape with Figures*, which is one of this
work's most disquieting aspects. The box itself is
curiously rendered. The bottom and sides are of
equal, rather shallow, depth, but the top is much
deeper. *Man in the Box* is one of those works
that demonstrates Tooker's deep involvement
with issues of modern life. The painting itself is
warm in its depiction of the human figure, but the
message is chilling.

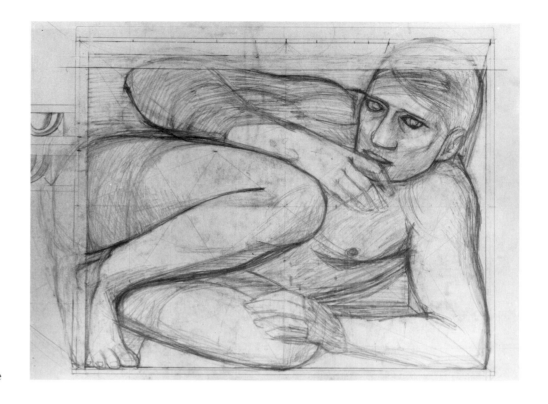

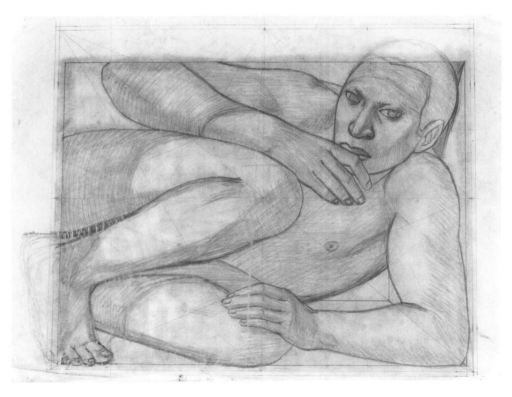

Study for MAN IN THE BOX, 1967.
Pencil, 19½ x 24 in.

(above)

Study for MAN IN THE BOX, 1967.
Pencil and wash, 20 x 24 in.

(below)

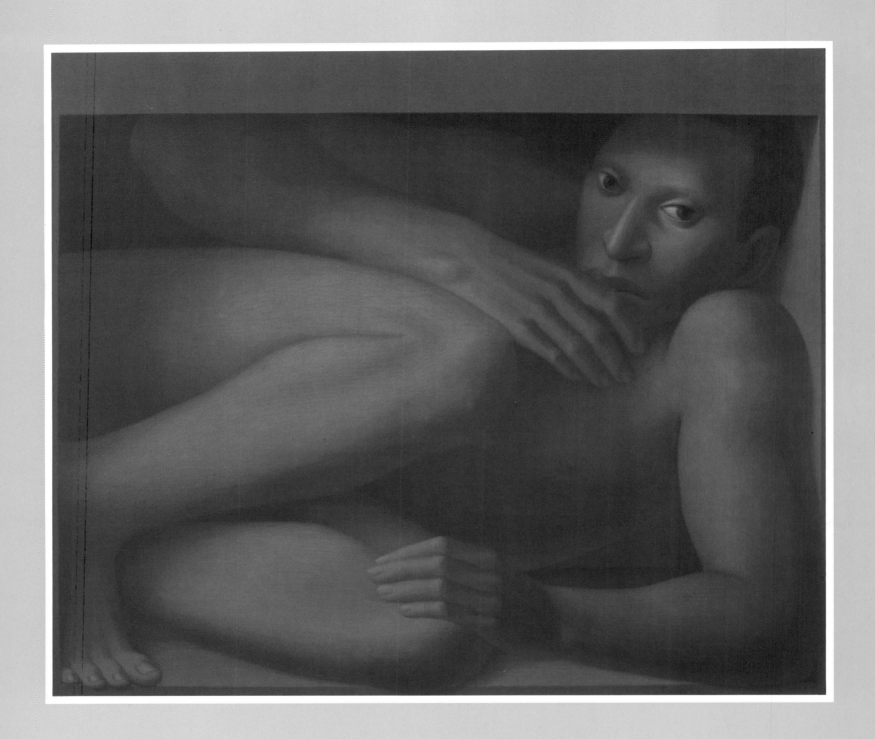

**MAN IN THE BOX** 1967.
Egg tempera on gesso panel,
20 x 24 in.

## THE SLEEP OF MORTALS,
## THE WATCH OF ANGELS

In his introduction to the 1950 London exhibition, "Symbolic Realism in American Painting, 1949–50," Kirstein first points out that the artists seen there, of whom Tooker was one, were attempting, "to find a coherent set of symbols, objective yet humane."[8] Kirstein found in American painting a certain lack of elegance, but that was replaced by "a firm sense of candour, personal and topographical, . . . concern for the Social Order not rendered visually in European prototypes but in the Transcendentalism of Emerson, Poe, Hawthorne, and Whitman in which the reality of the objects is less substantial than the 'unseen soul' embodied within them."[9]

> *Prophetic painters throughout our Nineteenth century attempted to find, with slight reference to classic or Christian iconography, symbols for a superior order. Since they were artists in a province arid of much activity save the muscular, they found them in an expression of chronic loneliness or personal despair which has provided, in terms of isolation, violence and conflict, tragic constants. Symbols were sought for the Transcendental and the nature of evil; they were found in personal allegory or individual lyricism. . . .*

> *The prophetic painter or painting, consciously or unconsciously, attempts to inscribe a synthesis of superior or unifying order, as unattached to dogma as to practical politics. The attitude is neither tragic nor ironic, but lyric."[10]*

Kirstein's observations, written before almost all of the paintings seen here had been executed, serve to introduce a group of paintings that appears to be Tooker's least understood work. These are the paintings of oracular prophecy in which the symbol – the signifier – replaces the individual, be it an object, a personality, an incident, or a gesture. Tooker has sought to represent in these paintings a deeply meditative state rendered in a traditional manner. In many of his most strongly prophetic paintings the figures are in a state of suspended animation, of disengagement from life, all too often misinterpreted as the artist's representation of death. They are surely not dead, but are in a different state of consciousness, and in this transcendent state they have lost neither their consciousness nor their soul. In these works Tooker has attempted to find his own symbols for that "superior order" which might be possible in this world.

An early example of this urge to seek that "coherent set of symbols, objective yet humane," of which Kirstein speaks may be seen in *Fountain* (1950). A fountain (based on the one located in New York City's Washington Square Park) is circled by eleven male figures, barefoot and stripped to the waist, some standing, some sitting on the stone coping. The young men, all nearly identical, are an early version of the Tooker person, and appear almost architectural in their placement and their solid, rounded forms, like columns circling an ancient temple. The iridescent "water" that jets up and cascades down seems to lack most of the normal properties of

water, such as wetness. The envelope of air that surrounds the water is suffused with a special kind of energy through parallel striations in the brush strokes, creating radiant lines of water and light. This is not an ordinary fountain but the fountain of life, and these monumental figures seem to derive their energy from it, to bask in its mythic energy.

Only a year or so before *Fountain* was painted, Paul Cadmus had painted *Playground*, and a brief comparison is instructive. *Playground* is an intensely physical and sexual painting. The location is a crowded and scuffy urban playground. High wire fences enclose the space and papers blow around on the concrete. The light filters in from the front of the picture leaving the background of buildings in shadow. It is a painting filled with activity, a cumulative portrait of gestures and vignettes including a ball game in progress and a young man's foolish clowning as he hangs dangerously from the high fence. To the left another young man seated on a bench has spread his legs and his girl friend stands between them as each touches the other. It is the boy in the foreground that rivets one's attention, however. A well-muscled blond, he has unbuttoned his pants and seems to be pushing them down over his hips. It may be an act of playground exhibitionism, but he looks directly out of the picture, a challenge more to the viewer's perceptions of correct behavior (an issue more sharply drawn in 1948 than today) than a dare to his pictorial companions. The street noise – the calls, whistles, and shouts – can almost be heard in this painting. In contrast, *Fountain* is a silent work. Gone are the individual gestures, the evidence of particular human passions. Things of the moment have been transcended; here, the universal spirit reigns.

Within this world of the spirit, certain images appear again and again in Tooker's work, continually modified and reshaped. Most numerous are the elegiac paintings of "sleepers," figures who are neither sleeping nor awake, but rather in some profound and unnameable trance.

In *Sleepers I* (1951) three young men are asleep on a beach, nestled in the furrows of sand that curve along a gradually sloping shore. Two of the figures, nude and only partially covered by thin blankets, are prone and appear to be fast asleep. The figure nearest to us, however, clothed in tee-shirt and pants, is on his back, propped up on one elbow, his eyes open (though "eyeless") and staring into the heavens, in that meditative state of consciousness that expresses the unseen soul's communion with the universal spirit. The light, though bland and almost without contrast, delineates figures and landscape in solid volumetric relief. The influence of the Italian quattrocento – especially Mantegna – is noticeable in the modeling and features of the foreground figure; Tooker has also indicated Etruscan terra-cotta funerary sculpture as a source. These influences were tempered by the art of his own generation, most strongly in this case by Jared French, who had done paintings and photographs of semi-nude men on the beach several years before *Sleepers I*. As an early work, it may lack some of the refinements of composition in its ordering of space and

**FOUNTAIN** 1950.
Egg tempera on gesso panel,
24 x 24 in.

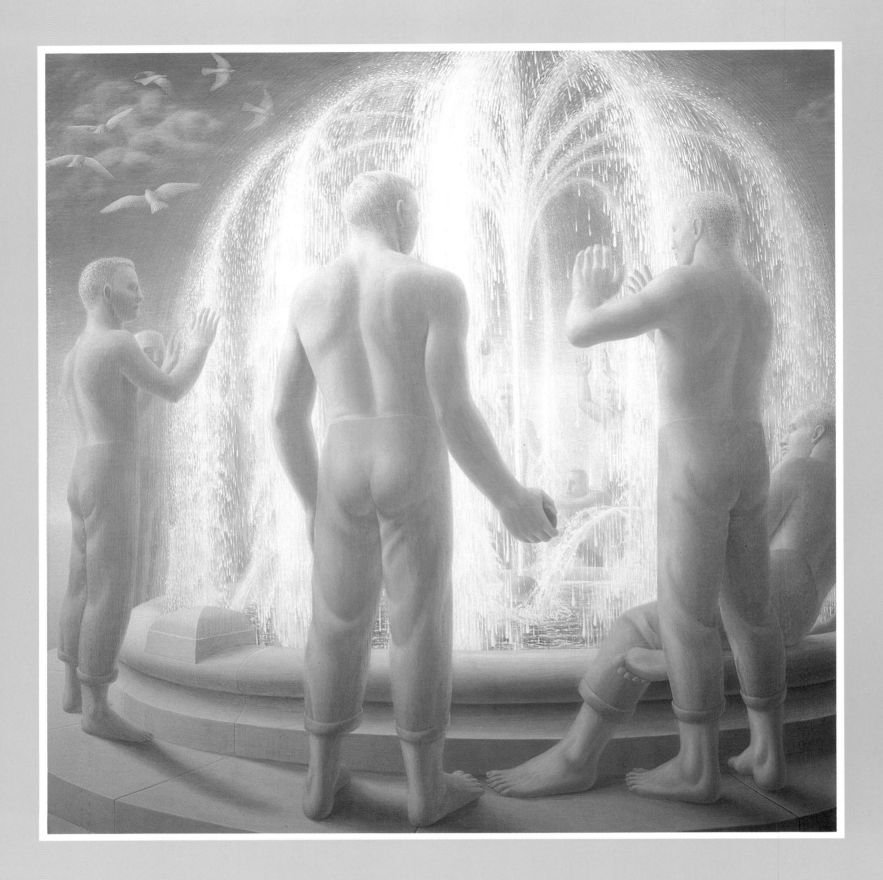

**SLEEPERS I** 1951.
Egg tempera on gesso panel,
18 x 30 in.

dramatic tension that mark Tooker's later work, yet, in its sources and execution, it is one of his most intensely felt paintings. It was in fact a memorial to his father, who had died suddenly the year before, and was inspired by Matthew Arnold's poem *Dover Beach*.[11]

Tooker's exploration of this transcendental state of consciousness resumed with *Sleepers II* (1959) and continued in several works of the 1960s – including *Night I* (1963) and *Sleep* (1964) – and in the 1970s with *Night II* (1972), *Dreamers* (1975) and *Sleepers III* (1975-76). In *Sleepers II* seven figures of indeterminate sex appear to be resting beneath an endless eiderdown quilt, with only their heads visible, like monoliths upon the billowing sands of a never-ending desert landscape. They seem to be in suspended animation rather than asleep, for their eyes are open and they stare fixedly at the heavens. They might almost be taken for corpses wrapped in an endless shroud, and many commentators have interpreted the painting as a portrayal of death. It is not, but rather Tooker's most graphic representation of the profound trance state that is neither waking nor sleeping. Here the spiritual communion is mixed with a certain apprehensiveness. By the time of *Sleepers II*, Tooker had painted *Government Bureau* and *The Waiting Room*, and his vision

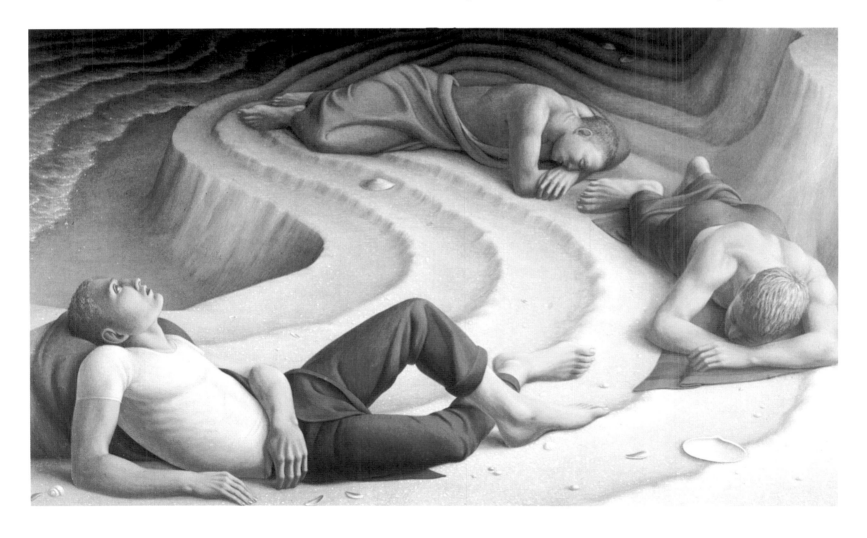

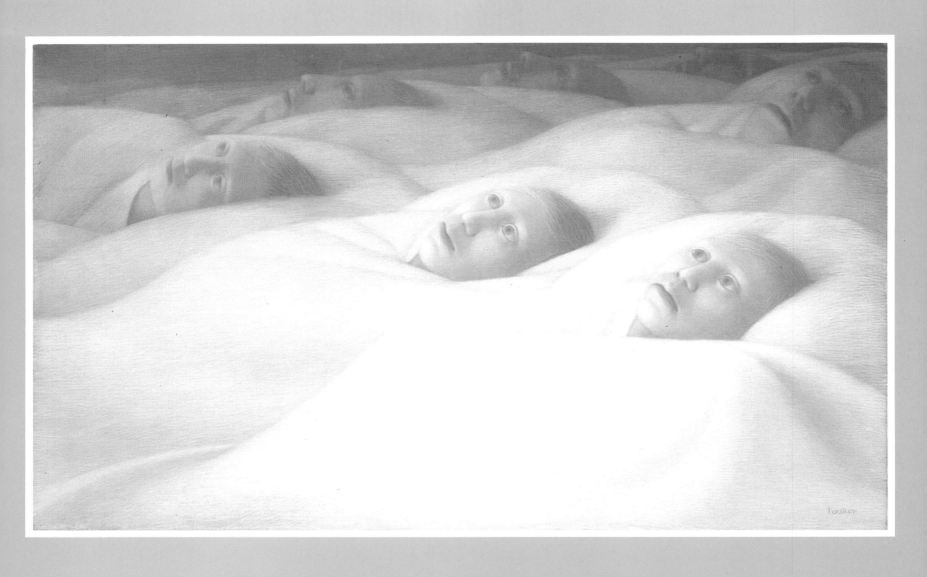

**SLEEPERS II** 1959.
Egg tempera on gesso panel,
16⅛ x 28 in.

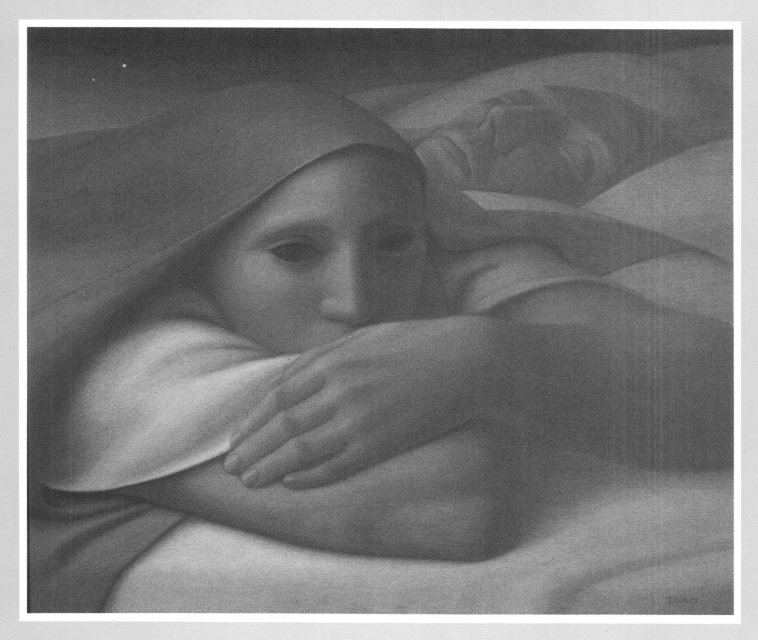

**NIGHT I** 1963.
Egg tempera on gesso panel,
14½ x 17½ in.

**SLEEP** 1964.
Egg tempera on gesso panel,
18 x 24 in.

of the "unseen soul" had undergone much change.

In *Night I* (1963) there are only two figures. One, a woman, is clearly awake and is the watcher while the other, whose gender is indeterminate, is in a deep and profound slumber, perhaps even the sleep of the dead. The theme and imagery of the preceding paintings have been combined: the figure who is awake in *Sleepers I* has been introduced into the billowing landscape of *Sleepers II*. But here, it is a watchful woman who rests her head on folded arms, the thoughtful concentration of her face a contrast with the unconscious mask behind her. What is the significance of this figure? The "watcher," one who is awake and alert while others sleep, may be a visual surrogate for the artist himself.

Tooker's fascination with classical Greek mythology reinterpreted in contemporary terms led to several paintings in the mid-1950s that have no precise parallel in contemporary urban life. One of these is *The Artist's Daughter* (1955). The source of the title is ambiguous; Tooker thinks it may have been suggested by Jared French, even though Tooker had no daughter. The young girl has been conceived of as the youthful embodiment of the White Goddess. Tooker has mentioned that he perceived the large-eyed child both in the form of an archaic Greek *kore* figure and as an owl, very wise but elusive. She seems to know everything, even those things we do not wish her to know. It is a "mysterious appearance of a supernatural creature," an apparition whose physical substance is lost in the dappled light of the wall behind her and half-hidden by a screen of diaphanous foliage. It is a successful transliteration from myth to reality of a creature from both worlds who possesses attributes of both.

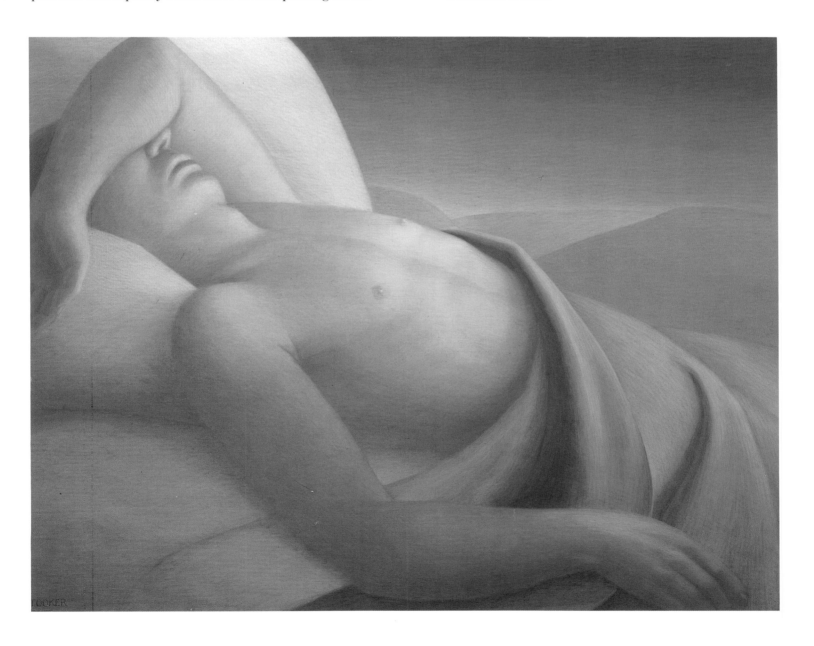

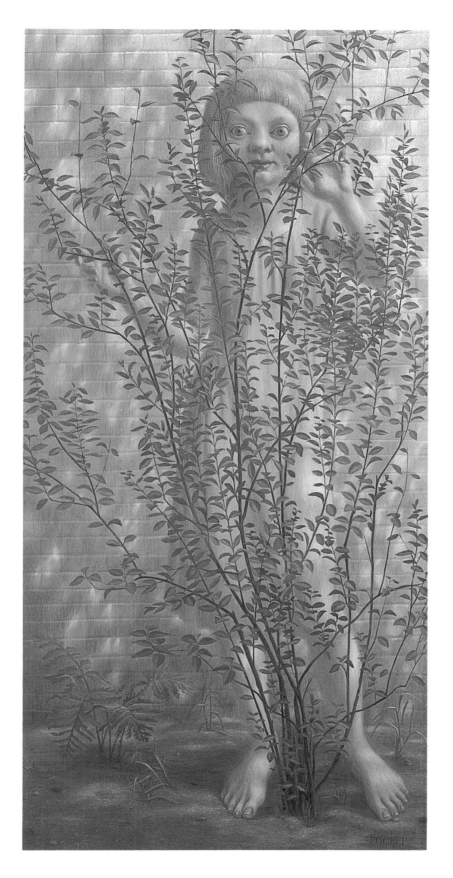

Another painting of 1955, *Fig Tree*, continues the theme. The center of the composition, set in a Brooklyn back yard, is a fiddle leaf fig, uncommon and hard to grow in that climate—but easy enough in Greece. Two young boys are in the tree, floating more than climbing, while several women, young, old and middle aged, look on indifferently. In the background a young nude woman stands in a pale bower, again unnoticed by the temporal witnesses. She is another manifestation of the White Goddess and the two boys are Castor and Pollux, the twin sons born to Leda following her liaison with Zeus, who came to her disguised as a swan. Greek mythology held Castor and Pollux in high regard for their brotherly affection, and Tooker enjoyed the artistic idea of bringing figures from another time and place into his own backyard—and having the neighbors totally oblivious of the fact. It is worth remembering that when Tooker paints the commonplace he may make it look not quite of this world, but when he brings in figments from other times or places he may set them into situations of utmost banality as here, a brick-lined tenement backyard.

As Tooker's own experience widened, the need for specific mythological references in his work diminished, although the oracular sensibility remained and, if anything, became more intense, as in *Entertainers* (1959-60). Here, three young women, a singer flanked by two tambourine players, are seen close up, dramatically lit from below. They occupy almost the entire picture plane, with an overscaled egg-and-dart molding barely visible behind them, as if they were massive sculptures in a temple. Their features and costume are identical, and their eyes are blank. The ghostly light keeps everything in shadow except their necks and the lower part of their faces, which are brightly illuminated. Only the central figure speaks, her mouth a dark cavity against the glow of flesh surrounding it. She might indeed be an oracle—a priestess of ancient Greece through whose lips the voice of a deity was believed to have spoken. *Entertainers* shows Tooker's skillful manipulation of light and masterful handling of sculptural forms (here, once again, variations on the circle and the sphere).

*Three Heads* (1967) was painted in the remarkably short time of three weeks as a last-minute addition to Tooker's 1967 exhibition. The entire picture plane is taken up by three female heads, all shown frontally; there is no ornamentation whatsoever in the depiction of the figures or in the background. Their dress is simple to the point of severity, almost the same shade of blue as the sky beyond. The three heads seem to float in this shadowless space, disembodied, like three copies of a portrait bust. Although not a reprise of any of the earlier works, *Three Heads* has certain features in common with some of them. As in *Entertainers*, the faces and costumes of the three figures are identical and their eyes are blank. With their straight blonde hair pulled tightly back, they resemble more closely the female figure in *Watchers*; the slightly fuller lips and broader noses, however, are more typical of Tooker's depiction of blacks. Again as in *Entertainers*, all three

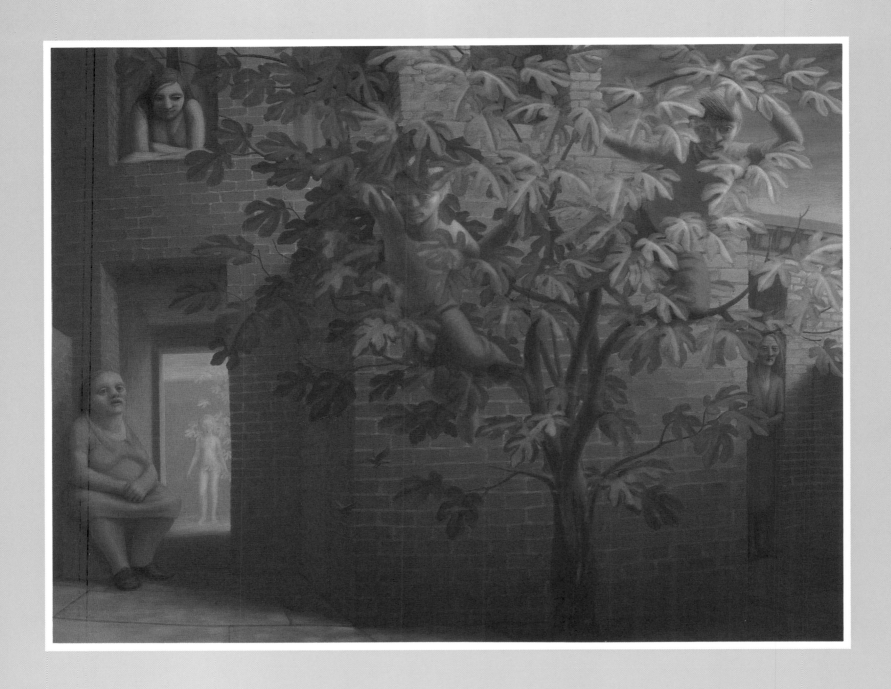

**THE ARTIST'S DAUGHTER** 1955.
Egg tempera on gesso panel,
24 x 12½ in.

(Opposite)

**FIG TREE** 1955.
Egg tempera on gesso panel,
18 x 24 in.

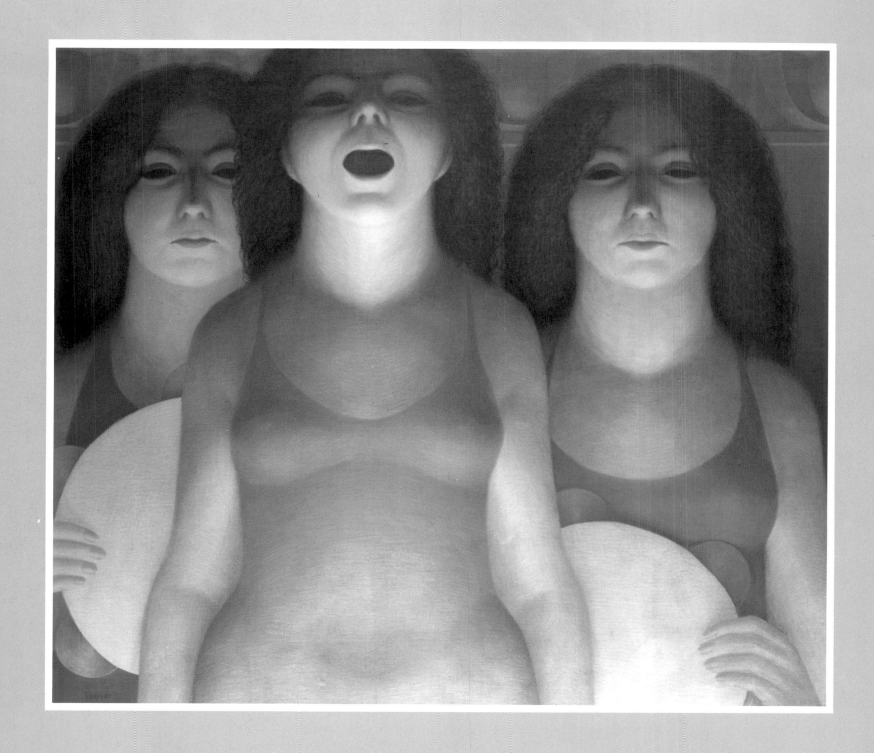

**ENTERTAINERS** 1959-60.
Egg tempera on gesso panel,
20 x 24 in.

women stare directly out at us with a penetrating gaze, and the arrangement of the figures is the same. The lighting, though, is exactly the reverse: the upper face and forehead are brightly illuminated while their necks and the lower part of their faces are in shadow emphasizing the impassive nature of these silent souls.

The figures in *Three Women* (1959-60) are observers of a more physical sort. Only their cats' eyes indicate that these figures are other than a group of well-fleshed Hispanic women. Tooker now regards these eyes as "most probably a mistake," although they add an edge of ambiguity to what is otherwise a painting that is primarily formal. The fleshly forms are shaped and rounded into volumetric variants on circles and cylinders, and, as in *Toilette*, Tooker extends the background into the foreground by draping the gray diamond-pattern fabric of the background over the arm of the central figure. However, in the deep left background, he adds a red and gold variation of this same fabric, upsetting the neat seamlessness of the foreground/background relationship, but creating, in the process, a strong element of shadow and depth in the otherwise shallow space of the painting.

*Watchers* (1962-63) is a picture of four figures against a featureless background. The principal figure, a man, is flanked by a man and a woman; all are heavily dressed. Only a part of the fourth figure's face is visible over the woman's shoulder. In fact, our attention is focused in this painting on faces and hands. The central figure's right hand is placed across his abdomen just below his heart – it is a gesture seen in the central figure of *Subway*, an involuntary movement of self-protection – while the woman behind him is anxiously clutching at his left arm. Their faces are all vulnerable, exposed; and their large eyes are fixed not directly on us, but on something off to one side. Tooker has commented that the painting "is about people watching things happen to them and being unable to do anything but watch. They are not oracles, but maybe they are listening to one." The figures possess an intense anxiety that is present in few other of Tooker's paintings. These people are ourselves, spectators to a drama we cannot control. He has acknowledged that the subject of this painting was related to the growing threat of atomic war and our inability to prevent it.

Tooker painted *Meadow I* (1960-61) as a memorial picture for his mother, who had died in 1959. This work is a strongly elegiac painting, much more so than *Sleepers I*, painted ten years before as a memorial to his father. In *Meadow I*, a man kneels stoically beside the madonna-like figure of a dead woman laid out beside him in a field. It is the field outside the window of Tooker's studio in Vermont, a field kept cropped by the cows from a farm nearby (although the trees are invented). Neither figure is a likeness of the artist or his mother, but there is great poignancy in the differences between the faces. The woman's is severely sculptural, but the

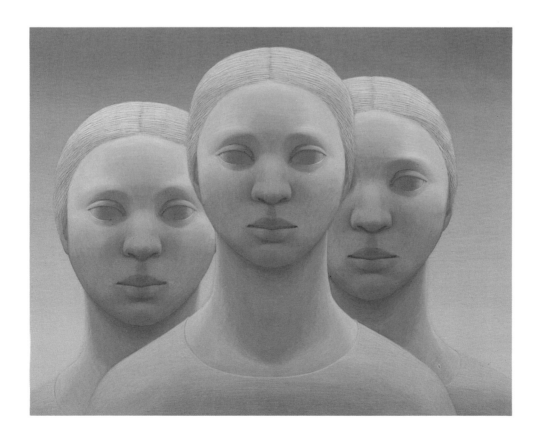

**THREE HEADS** 1967.
Egg tempera on gesso panel,
size unknown

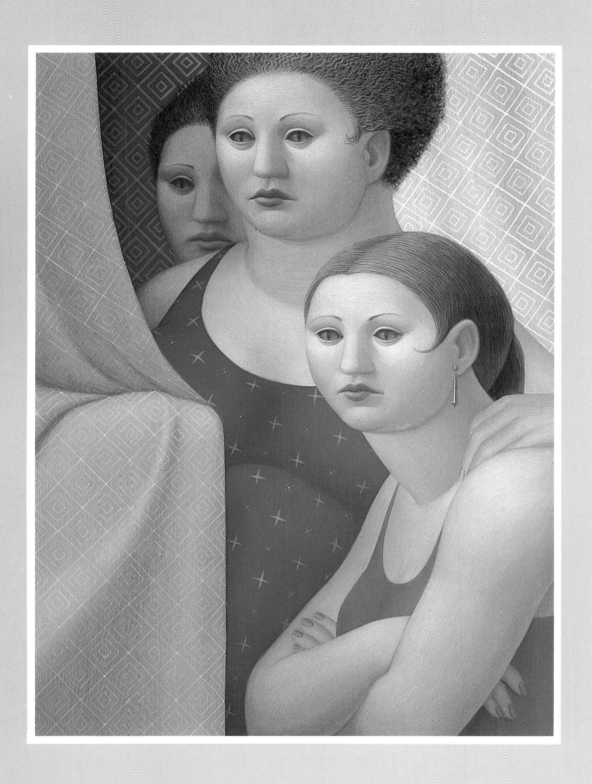

**THREE WOMEN** 1959-60.
Egg tempera on gesso panel,
23½ x 17½ in.

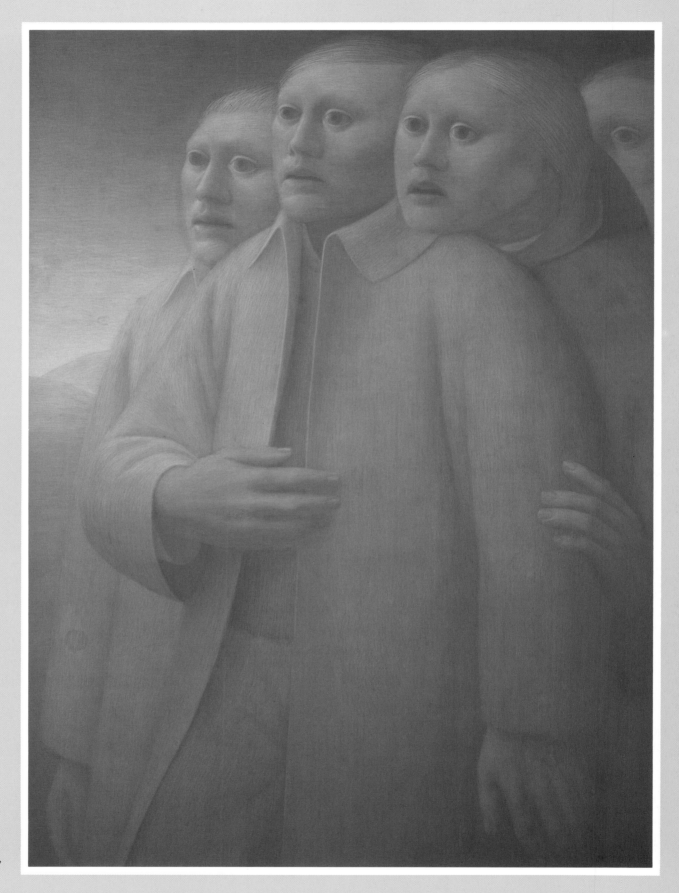

**WATCHERS** 1962-63.
Egg tempera on gesso panel,
26 x 20 in.

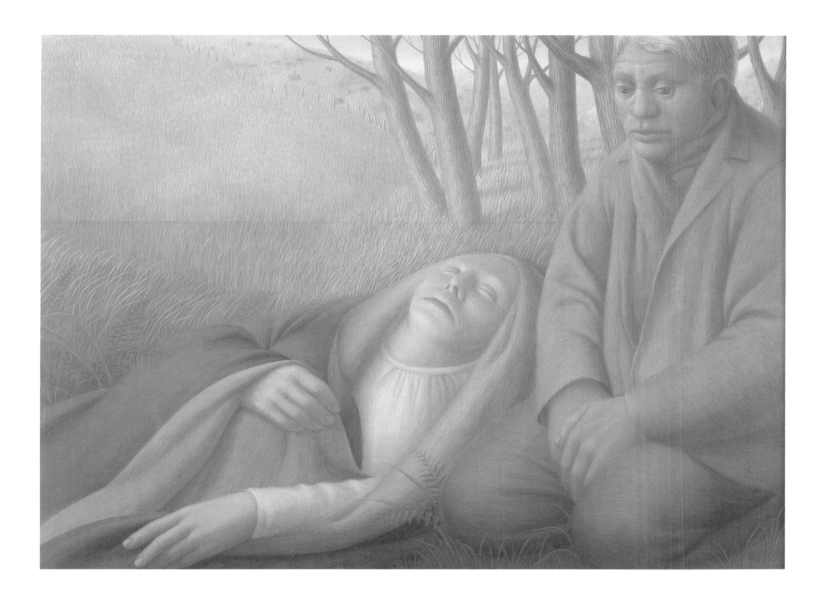

animating forces have left it, while the man's face, deeply saddened, remains vital and, even in sadness, still contains the full energy of life. This is one of Tooker's very few paintings about death; compare Tooker's depiction of the dead woman's face against those faces that may be seen as "sleeping" or "watching."

More than fifteen years later Tooker painted another version of this work, albeit with substantial changes. *Meadow II* (1977-79) is a vertical painting, with the emphasis much more on the figure of the man than on the supine figure beside him. There are several other differences. The oak trees are in leaf, and a dandelion plant is present between the figures. It has two stems: one is in full flower, the other has gone to seed – direct references to the cycle of life. It is appropriate that emphasis has been placed upon the living figure. It is the figure of the mourner at the bier or the watcher at the tomb, and, in this painting, that watcher is acknowledged as being

the artist himself.

In late 1973, William Christopher, ill for a number of years, died in Spain, and an intense relationship of twenty-five years came to an end. In the several years following, Tooker painted a loose cycle of paintings that dealt with Christopher's illness and death, and the artist's response to it. *Meadow II*, while a variation of the earlier painting, is one of the works in this cycle. The others will be described in another chapter, but *Meadow II* is placed here because of its direct derivation from the first version of 1959.

With the death of William Christopher and Tooker's conversion to Roman Catholicism in the late 1970s, the paintings of "sleepers" and "watchers"– and of that meditative state of consciousness – almost ceased, and he began to paint pictures whose imagery has its source in the traditional spiritual order and divine organization of his newfound faith.

**MEADOW I** 1960-61.
Egg tempera on gesso panel,
20 x 28 in.

(Opposite)

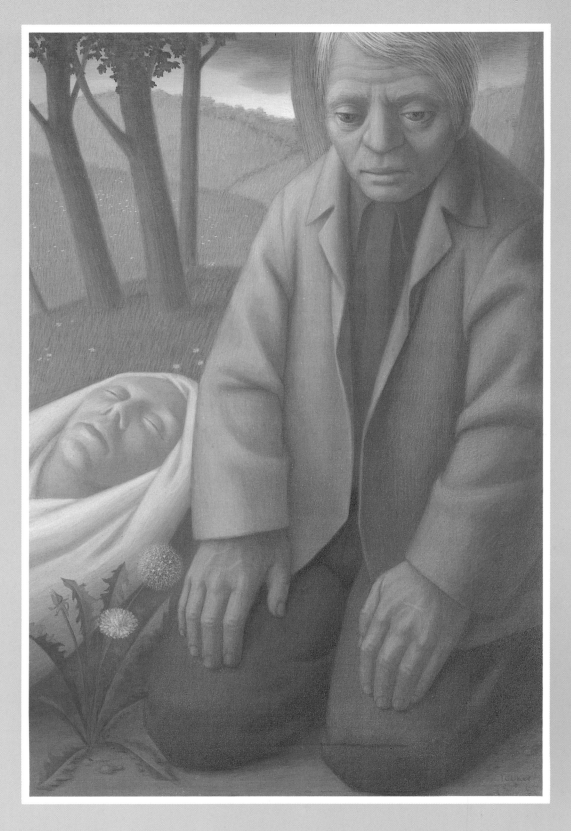

**MEADOW II** 1977-79.
Egg tempera on gesso panel,
21 x 15½ in.

# THE SPANISH PICTURES

In the late 1960s, George Tooker and William Christopher began to find the Vermont winters increasingly arduous and decided to look for a place in southern Europe in which to spend that part of each year. The climate, food, landscape, and most particularly the people convinced them that Málaga, Spain, would be an ideal location. Perhaps Tooker felt so comfortable with the people because in so many ways they embodied a spirit he much admired. The land and people are poor in Málaga, and there is a deep sadness which seems to underlie the Andalusian personality; but, for all that, the Andalusians enjoy their pleasures fully and live their lives with both grace and passion. Simple food fresh from sea or garden, simple objects, pleasure and delight in one's friends, and a certain formality in the conduct of one's life are to be found there, and they are qualities that Tooker requires of himself. It was here that he learned the phrase *de las entrañas*, and its translation, "from the guts," suits him well in either language. It is a phrase he uses often when asked to describe the genesis of many of his images.

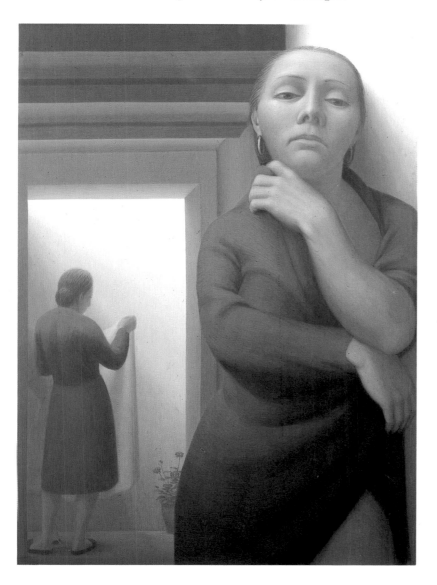

**TWO WOMEN WITH LAUNDRY** 1974.
Egg tempera on gesso panel,
24 x 18 in.

After Christopher's death, Tooker remained in Spain for most of 1974 and did not go back to Vermont until late in the year. His stay in Vermont was brief that year, and he quickly returned to Málaga. Thus, most of the paintings from 1974 and 1975 were done in Spain, and the imagery of his works from that period took on a strongly Spanish character. It was a time of prolific production for Tooker, as painting was a way of mitigating his pain by concentrating on an intense and worthwhile activity to the exclusion of almost all else. He continued to divide his time between Málaga and Vermont until 1981. Since then he has lived in Vermont, save for a few brief visits back to Spain. He sold his apartment in Málaga in 1990.

The Spanish mood carried over into some of the works painted in Vermont during that period, such as *Two Women with Laundry* (1974). While the title may suggest a reprise of an earlier work, the laundry is a very minor part of the composition. The emphasis is placed not on the swags of cloth hung to dry, but rather on the structural geometry of the deep, shadowed passageway through the building to the tiny courtyard beyond. The similarity of dress, stance, and age of the two major figures (a fragment of a third figure is barely visible in the courtyard) suggests that they are manifestations of the same Tooker person. She is the watcher, now tempered by the Spanish experience and Tooker's own personal grief into a persona of humility and sadness. Even the color of her dress, a slate blue, is one that Tooker has used on several occasions as a mark of tragedy and sadness. (A close variant of the same color is used again later in the figure of the "madonna" in *Corporate Decision*.)

Several works of strongly Spanish character, including *Pot of Aloes* (1974), were in fact painted in Spain. *Pot of Aloes* is set in Tooker's traditional window framework, but it is the aloe plant, bathed in bright sunlight on the window ledge, that occupies most of the foreground and commands our attention. The aloe, in a simple but elegant earthenware pot with crimped edges, displays its serrated leaves in a series of arabesques that Tooker has set against the shadowed interior of colorful patterned Andalusian tiles (the Spanish equivalent of New York's pressed tin). At the left just inside from the window, in the coolness of the dimly lit room, stands a woman dressed in black, her hands folded and her face wearing an expression of slight melancholy. She looks out over the plant as if without seeing, while a young boy, barely able to reach the window ledge, peers impishly from behind the right side of the flowerpot, staring directly at us.

Another similar picture *Claveles* (1974), is also recorded as being painted in Spain in the same year. This would be most unusual as the artist almost never painted two similar pictures back to back. Still, Tooker recalls being very interested in potted plants at the time and was intrigued to see that even the poorest household in the *barrio* would invariably have at least one pot of flowers in the window. Claveles is the Spanish word for carnations and these blossoms, spindly but carefully tended, soak up the sun—while we receive a masked but thoughtful glance from the shadows.

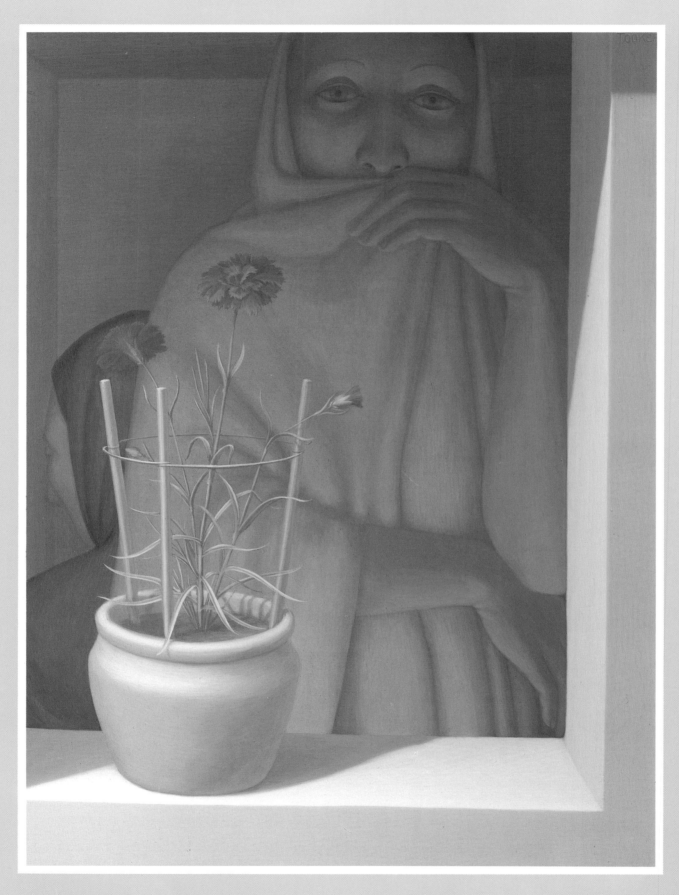

**CLAVELES** 1974.
Egg tempera on gesso panel,
24 x 18 in.

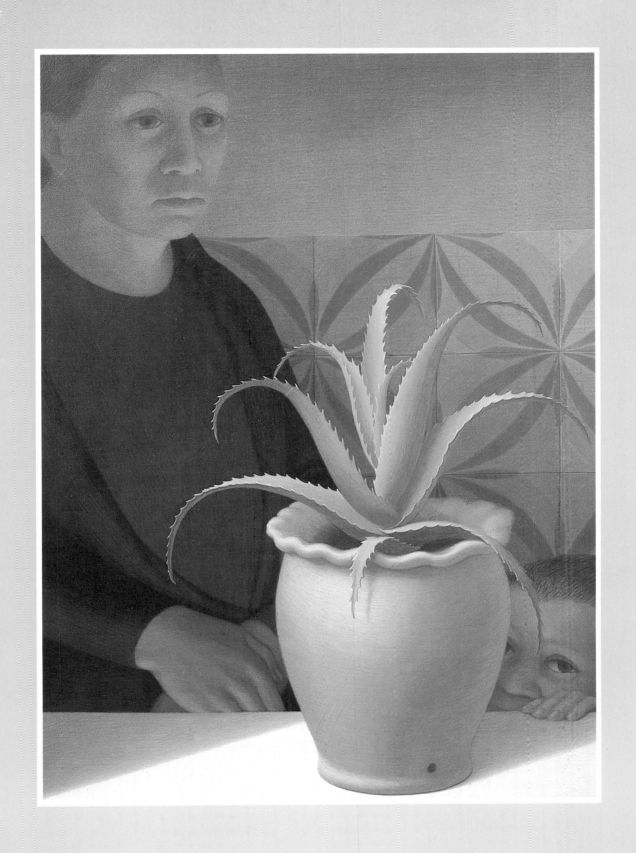

*Sevillanas* (1975-76) was painted in Vermont from drawings started in Spain. Flamenco music appeals to the artist for its emotional intensity, and Sevillanas, literally a person from Seville, is also a style of flamenco singing often accompanied by rhythmic hand clapping. Tooker acknowledges that it is a variant of the painting, *Entertainers*, of fifteen years earlier. As always, odd light sources capture the artist's attention and here the figures are again dramatically lighted from below. Tooker is not so radical this time with the eyes, but these three women in their tight red dresses and compressed circular composition (giving Tooker ample opportunity to study the faces from several angles) suggest sculpture, or even architectural forms.

In *Woman with Oranges* (1977), also painted in Spain, Tooker, displaying a more provocative style, has placed a rather androgynous figure of a woman within a setting that consists entirely of blue-and-white decorative tilework, a tour de force of dramatic form created through pattern. The pyramid of four or five freshly picked oranges is a tribute to the eighteenth-century

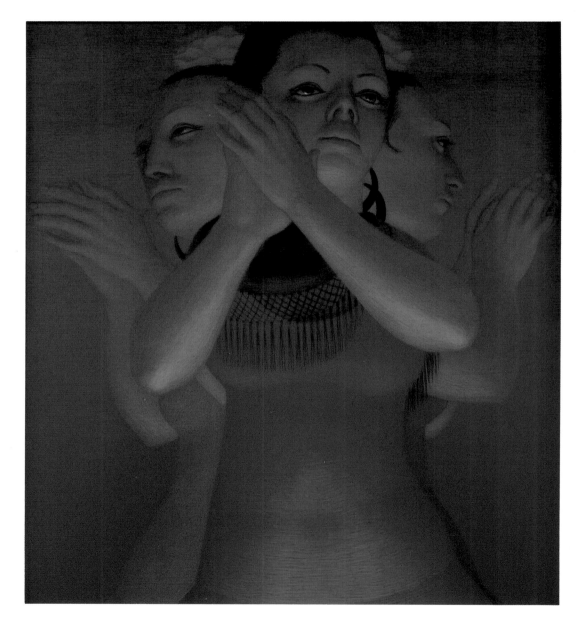

**POT OF ALOES** 1974.
Egg tempera on gesso panel,
24 x 18 in.

(Opposite)

**SEVILLANAS** 1975-76.
Egg tempera on gesso panel,
20 x 18 in.

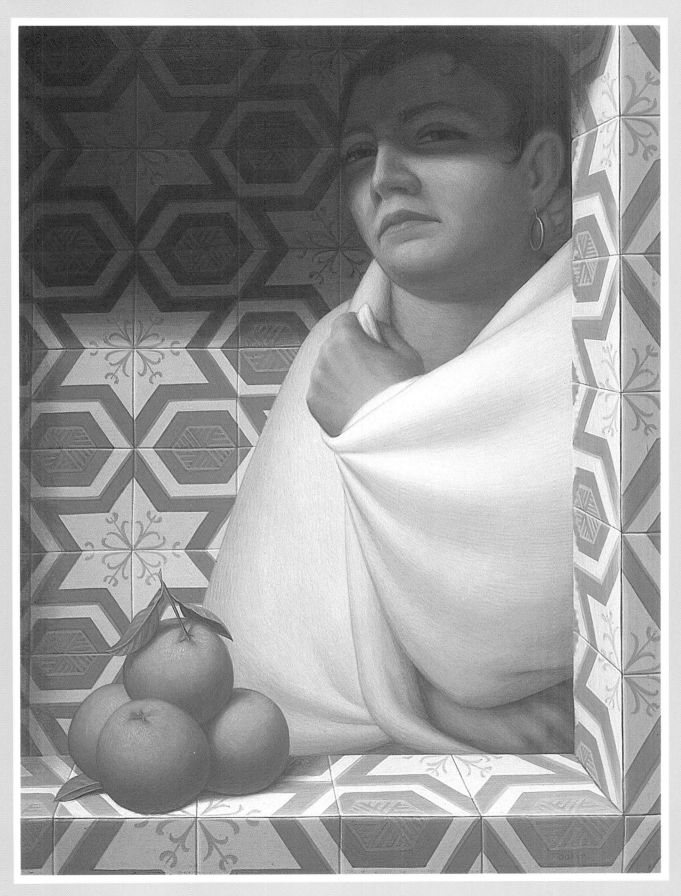

**WOMAN WITH ORANGES** 1977.
Egg tempera on gesso panel,
24 x 18 in.

Spanish still-life painter Luis Melendez. The tilework at the bottom and to the right acts almost as a proscenium, and the pose of the figure (pulling a blanket tightly around herself) and the lighting emphasize the inherent theatricality of the work. Her face is only partially illuminated; her eyes and forehead are in shadow, perhaps as a reminder not only of the glare of the Spanish sun but of the shadowed sorrows of the people of this region.

*Still Life with Oranges* (1980), a work done in Vermont, was painted quickly as a "relaxation piece" following completion of *The Seven Sacraments*. Perhaps a sunny picture was in order to help offset the somber New England winter, but the subject more likely suggested itself because it is a painting of basic geometric forms and volumes, without people, and *The Seven Sacraments* had been a painting filled with figures. He obviously thought well of it, for *Still Life with Oranges* is the only still-life painting to which Tooker

signed his full last name rather than just his initials.

The subject and the structure of this work were directly influenced by Spanish seventeenth- and eighteenth-century still-life painting, which often treated common objects with a simple dignity that borders on the reverential. Again, the artist cited by Tooker as the source of this work was Luis Melendez, particularly his careful, almost geometrically composed arrangements of common foodstuffs in utilitarian, everyday containers. This picture is seemingly rendered without artifice, the composition a bit off balance, with the earthenware jug wedged into a shadowed corner. The organization of the work is handled with Tooker's usual subtlety, however. The structure of the shelf is revealed by the edge of the wooden upright seen to the left, and, within the constructed geometry, the leaves and orange bud and blossom add an element of temporal and physical fragility, a moment of beauty that will quickly fade.

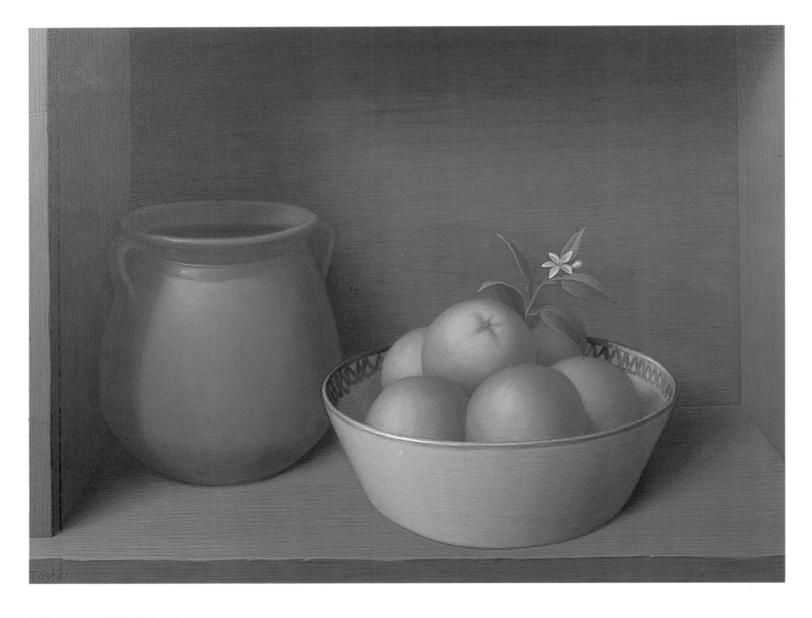

**STILL LIFE WITH ORANGES** 1980.
Egg tempera on gesso panel,
14½ x 19½ in.

# LOVERS

**LOVERS I** 1959.
Egg tempera on gesso panel,
18 x 24 in.

So much emphasis has been placed on a few of Tooker's "public" pictures by virtue of their portentous message and their inclusion in major public collections that it is often assumed that Tooker must be a formidable and rather chilly man. He has been seen as an unsmiling commentator upon a civilization deeply flawed and indifferent to its individual constituents, a person who has no place in his heart for the more tender passions. Yet we have seen another aspect of his painterly personality, that of voluptuary, a painter of sensuality, of pleasure glimpsed through windows, enjoyed without concern for consequences. In addition to these two aspects of humankind – one perfect in its cruelty and indifference, the other glowing in carnal embrace – one must note yet another facet of the

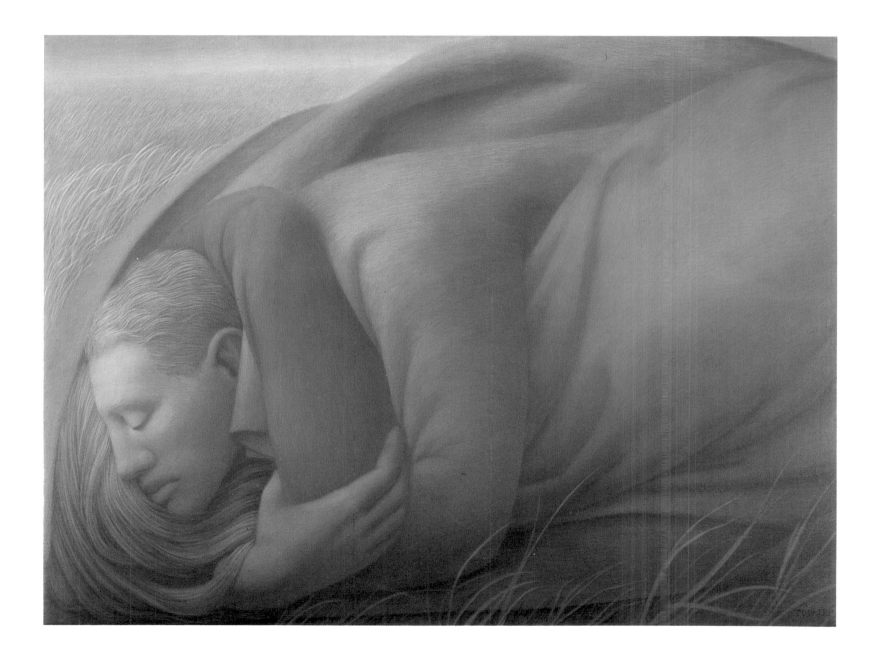

Tooker personality. There is, in an important body of work, a vision of love in a perfected form, built as much upon caring as upon passion. Tooker's lovers exist only for themselves, in magical landscapes or light-filled interiors empty of any distractions.

The earliest painting of this group is *Lovers I* (1958-59). The source of the visual and intellectual imagery for this work remains vivid in Tooker's mind. He was much moved by reading a poem by W. H. Auden, especially one stanza:

*Soul and body have no bounds;*
*To lovers as they lie upon*
*Her tolerant enchanted slope*

**LOVERS II** 1960.
Egg tempera on gesso panel,
22 x 26 in.

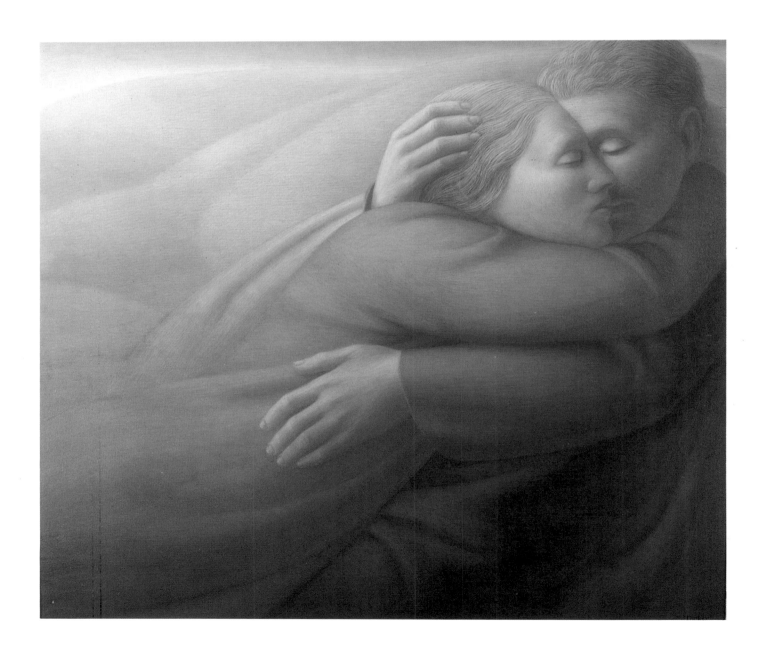

*In their ordinary swoon,*
*Grave the vision Venus sends*
*Of supernatural sympathy,*
*Universal love and hope;*
*While an abstract insight wakes*
*Among the glaciers and the rocks*
*The hermit's sensual ecstasy.*[12]

If the literary source for *Lovers I* was clear to the artist, the imagery with which to illustrate it was not. Tooker began to sketch on a sheet of the thin, white tracing paper he favors for his little "scrappy drawings." A small squiggle suggested what was to become the almost art nouveau flow of hair and grass through which the double helix of the lovers' figures was intertwined. Only the man's face is visible, in profile, circled by the woman's arm and the tresses of her hair; the circle is completed by his hand reaching around her to hold her by the arm, clasping her in a warm embrace. The work is remarkably abstract, and the two figures are in such a shallow, compressed space that their forms appear almost to occupy the same space. Tooker acknowledges the influence on his work of the relief sculpture of Agostino di Duccio, which pressed the imagery to the picture plane rather than attempting an illusion of deep space.

Because Tooker's best-known works are sober in imagery, there has been speculation that *Lovers I* contains some dire portent, that it represents perhaps an emotional last embrace before an eternal parting, an interpretation that is far from Tooker's intent. The imagery of the painting shows lovers and landscape appearing to flow together in perfect unity, a visual equation of Auden's image of

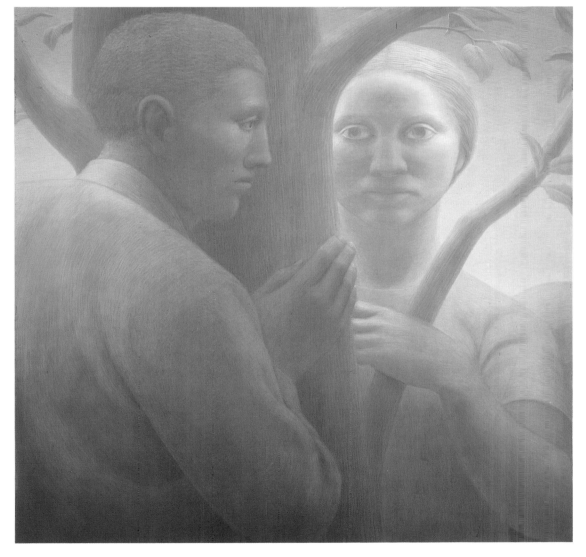

**TREE** 1965.
Egg tempera on gesso panel,
22 x 22 in.

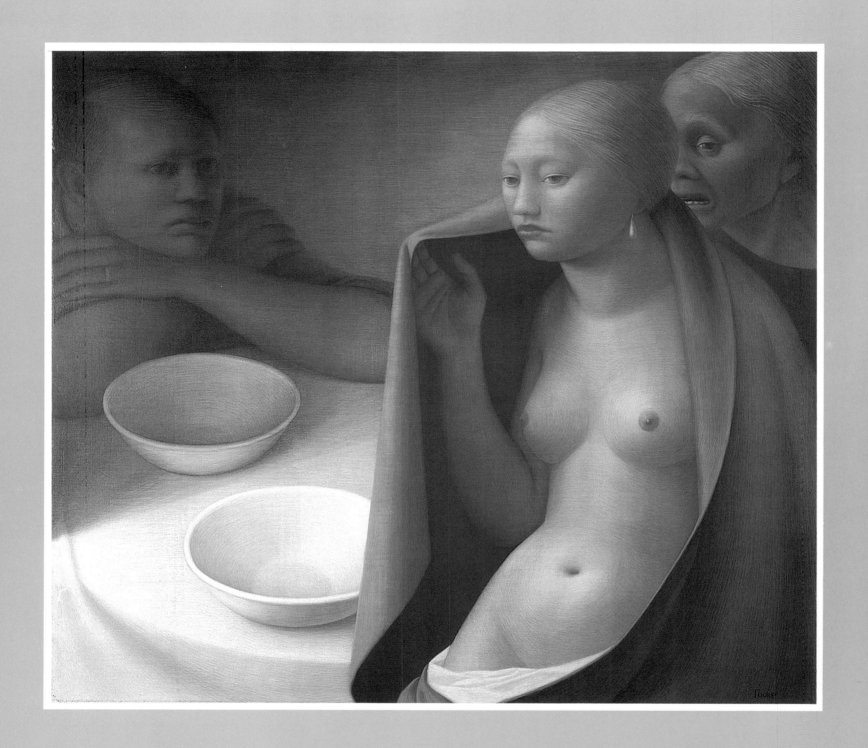

**TABLE** I 1959.
Egg tempera on gesso panel,
24 x 28½ in.

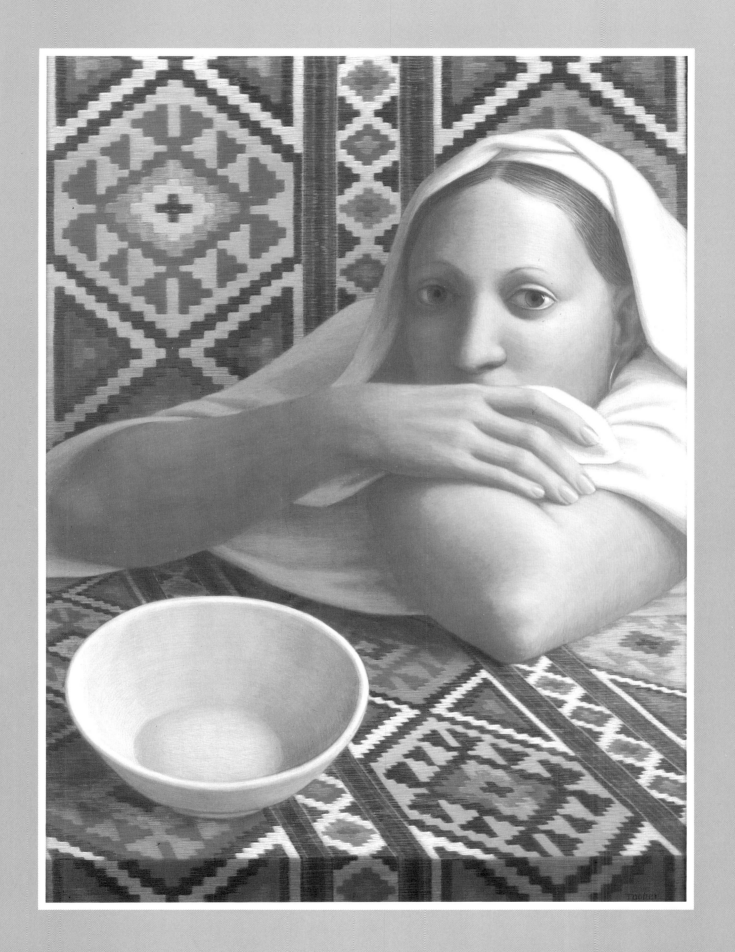

lovers who "lie upon her tolerant enchanted slope in their ordinary swoon," a vision of "universal love and hope."

While *Lovers I* showed only the man's face in its portrayal of a couple embracing, *Lovers II* (1960) shows the faces of both, with the woman's profile superimposed on the man's nearly frontal face, as if the two were merging to form a single face. Similar in composition to the earlier work, *Lovers II* moved the figures from the left to the right side of the painting and reversed the prominence of the man and the woman. Tooker now feels that *Lovers II* is less successful because it is less sculptural and possesses less of the dynamic force conveyed by the sweeping curve and intertwined bodies in *Lovers I*. While that may be true, *Lovers II* extends the figures much more into the landscape in an allegorical way, where they become one with the landscape as well as with each other. The use of figures as landscape has already been seen in several variations of the *Sleepers* picture and in other variations of the *Lovers* theme as well.

*Tree* (1965) certainly warrants inclusion among this group of lovers, but, unlike the other pictures, it shows a different and more ordered aspect of love. The timeless embrace, the desire to be together *always* is replaced by a couple whose relationship to one another is more visual than visceral. Tooker has commented that it is "a light picture," and, indeed, "a formal exercise," but it is important to him nonetheless. The work is painted with very little contrast. The highlights and shadows are very close in intensity, without fortissimo or pianissimo, matching the quiet, relaxed tone of the figures themselves. The two heads, one seen in profile and the other in full face, are classic studies of the Tooker physiognomy, and that seems to suggest another reason for the execution of the painting, a desire to portray the same head from two points of view.

*Table I* (1959) and *Table II* (1981) are among the closest variations Tooker has painted of a single theme, and they are as interesting programmatically and autobiographically as they are visually. *Table I* was painted at a time when the artist was much involved in the painting of semi-nude figures, and the figure of the young woman, draped in her red-lined, blue-gray cloak, is the same type of figure as those seen in *Guitar* (1958) and in *Toilette* (1962) as well as in other window and mirror paintings. The figure of the beautiful young woman came easily, but the rest of the composition took more time. "I wanted to paint her belly, but the other elements just accumulated around her. The old woman came in a flash one day." The psychological derivation of the young man looking at the young woman drape herself, more worshipful than lustful, is "a later version of the man in *The Chess Game*." It is Tooker himself. What had been experienced as terror in the earlier work has now been transmuted into shadowed fascination. Even the older woman, the ever-present reminder that age will inevitably supplant beauty, is not there to threaten the visitor to this table, but is rather a document of the effect of time. The composition is based on circles and arcs of circles. The young woman's head, the curve of the cloak which carries the edge of the table up around the right side of the picture, the convex shapes of belly and breast against the concave

forms of the two empty bowls, all work well together in one of Tooker's best integrated compositions.

*Odalisque* (1967) is a variation on the watching figure of *Night I* (1963). Unlike that work, however, *Odalisque* is more connected to our earthly time and place. It is perhaps the end of a leisurely meal, and this *Odalisque* fixes us with the gaze of her soft brown eyes from across the table. This woman's figure is demurely covered, unlike the usual image of an odalisque (those beautiful quasi-oriental figures used as an artist's rationale for painting the female nude in an exotic setting). The only clear reference to the Orient is found in the startlingly (for Tooker) *trompe l'oiel* rendering of the large kilim rug, based on one Tooker had owned for years. He was thinking of creating a painting on an oriental theme when he composed the work, but the pattern of the wall and table are reminiscent, too, of *Gypsy* and the sets for *The Saint of Bleecker Street*. In compositional terms, Tooker has created a controlling geometry through decorative pattern, and it is one of the most remarkable bits of *trompe-l'oeil* painting in his entire *oeuvre*.

The bowl, however, brings us back to the present. It is Ohio ironstone, the model for which remains in daily use in Tooker's kitchen. It was purchased long ago at a flea market and, because of its very satisfying shape, it is occasionally taken from the pantry and incorporated into his work. It has been used in *Odalisque*, *Table I* and *II*, and *Supper*. It forms a focal point here, for he uses the almost uninflected volume in the white-on-white interior of the anonymous commercial bowl as a contrast to the complex middle-eastern patterns of the kilim and as a balance to the weight of the figure.

Three paintings, all variations on the embracing couple, relate directly to the earlier images of lovers. They portray love as enduring and fundamental, a necessary sustenance to the human race. *Embrace I* (1979) was painted very shortly before the artist was to begin the planning for the major cycle of *The Seven Sacraments*. It is the prototype for the embrace of brotherhood in the panel depicting reconciliation in that large work. This embrace is an embrace of agape, the hug of God, not of carnality. The couple's strong embrace tilts the woman's head back and allows the pale, almost shadowless twilight to fall full upon her face, illuminating the bridge of the nose and the arch of the eyesocket in a way that most pleases the artist. (Tooker has acknowledged that he rarely paints eyebrows, or at least minimizes them, because they are, to his mind, a rather fuzzy decoration that tends to obscure the true structure of the forehead and eyesocket.) As in *Lovers II*, this embracing couple is placed directly within the landscape. They appear to be standing in a little bower of ferns, and the rolling moors, devoid of trees or bushes, echo the back and head of the man as he holds the young woman warmly. Even his hair, sandy blond, conforms to the coarse texture of the grass on the distant hillside.

*Embrace II* (1981) is a close variation of *Embrace I*, although it is more expansive and more sculptural. The horizontal format permits an extension of the figures into a wider space. There are

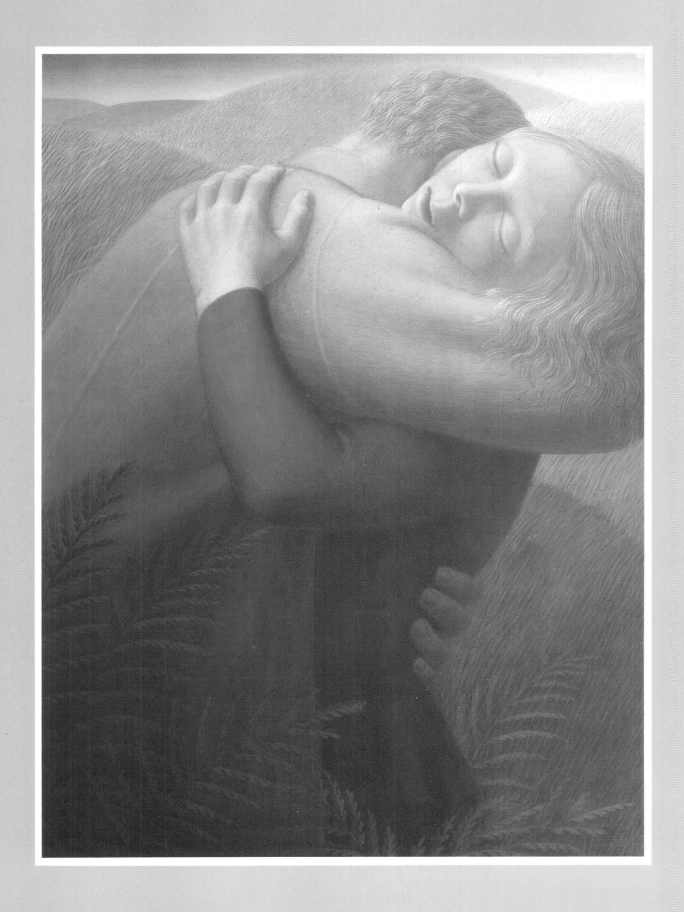

**EMBRACE I** 1979.
Egg tempera on gesso panel,
24 x 18 in.

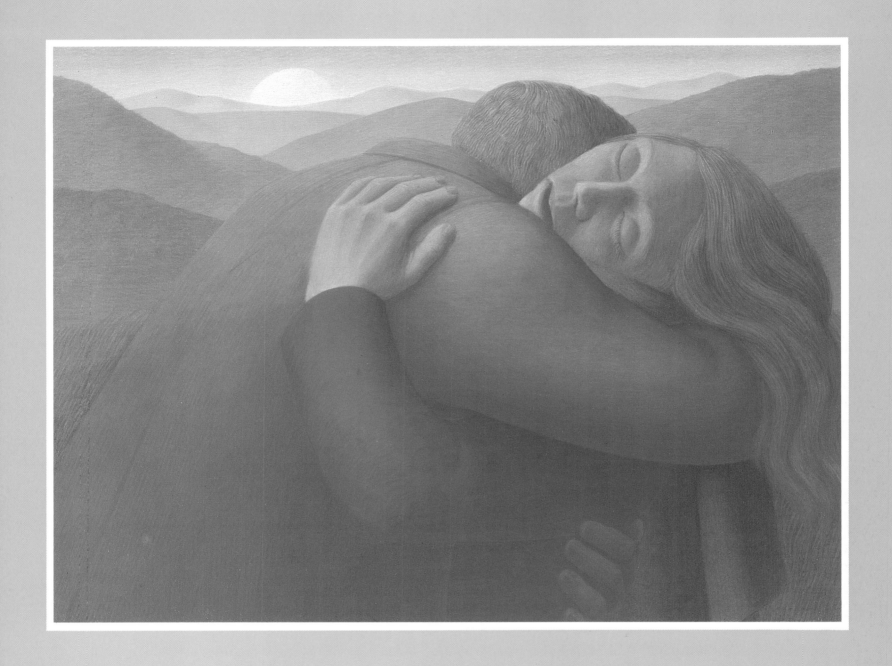

**EMBRACE II** 1981.
Egg tempera on gesso panel,
18 x 24 in.

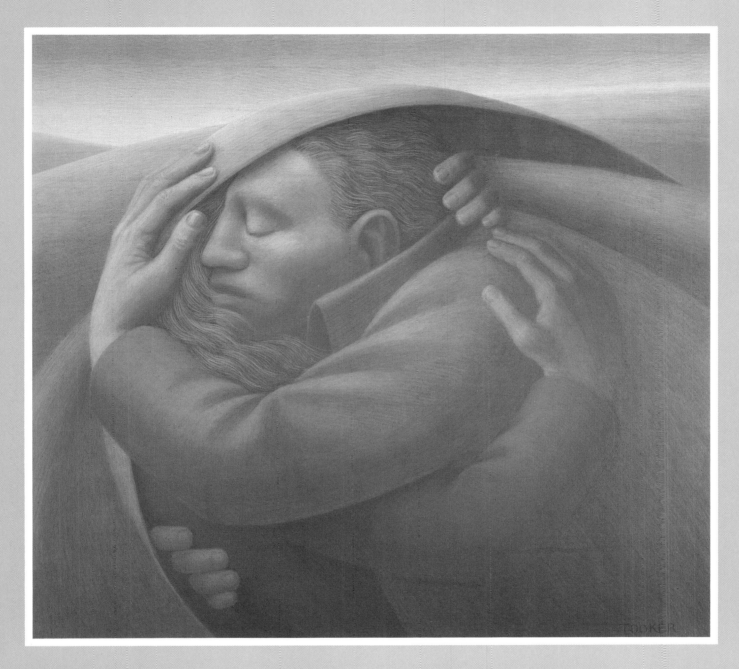

**EMBRACE III** 1983.
Egg tempera on gesso panel,
16 x 19 in.

**GARDEN WALL** 1990.
Egg tempera on gesso panel,
15¼ x 23¼ in.

(Opposite)

more planes of hills in this backward extension of space, and the figures may be read from their bulk and shape as the first of the row of those hills.

*Embrace III* (1983) is the most abstract of the group. It was one of the first works Tooker created in the small house he had purchased on the south shore of Long Island a couple of years previously and which was his home for most of that winter. He continued to use it as a winter home and studio off and on until 1991. The figures, which bear an unmistakable resemblance to the pair in *Lovers I*, are treated rather as a bas-relief medallion that appears to be cut from the landscape just as the landscape flows around it. The landscape itself is treated in a remarkably fluid manner, rather as a cloak of heavy fabric which partially protects this couple, then opens out into treeless hills. The man's coat, almost the same color as the loden green of the landscape, only emphasizes the oneness of the figures with the site. The hands of the two figures are each

placed approximately in the center of a quadrant of the medallion, emphasizing their centrifugal, swirling form. It is a simple but very potent work, almost entirely constructed from light, suffused with a pale, translucent sfumato that softens and distances this image.

There is warmth of feeling between the figures in *Garden Wall* (1990) that is more akin to siblings than lovers. Tooker regards the picture as an emotional if not physical reprise of *Builders*. While the most recognizable element from an earlier work is the gazing figure from *Table I*, the theme is that of telepathic and respectful guidance first articulated in *Builders*, nearly 40 years earlier. The two males are receiving instruction from the woman, less oracular in appearance now than in 1952, but all the figures focus their eyes in the distance and the lesson that is being taught is passing wordlessly but respectfully between them. It is worth noting that both paintings deal with growth, one of a human-made object, the other of objects in nature.

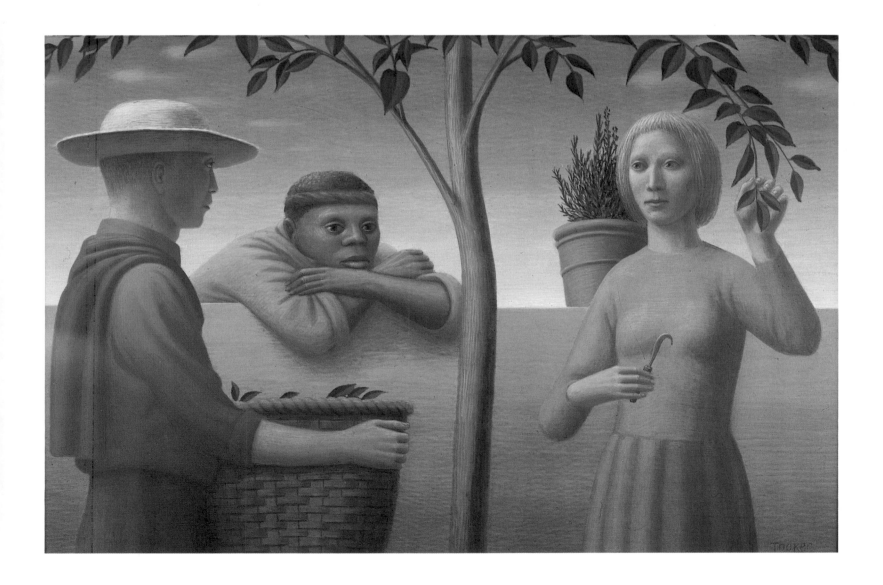

**DEATH**    As has been discussed, first the illness and then the death of William Christopher strongly affected some of Tooker's paintings.

In September, 1973, when I first visited George Tooker in Hartland to gather information for his 1974 exhibition at the Fine Arts Museums of San Francisco, *Standing Figures* was nearing completion. In the catalogue for that exhibition, *Standing Figures* was identified as one of the artist's "public" paintings. The artist acknowledges it now as a response to his private pain. The comments made in the 1974 catalogue, however, still seem appropriate:

> *Standing Figures . . . is marked by a nadir of energy. The figures and forms mold into one another . . . . The bodies (perhaps shades is a better word) seek these block-like forms for protection, hiding within their shadow. Geometry wins, yet these blocks now contain nothing. Their monumentality shields rather than clarifies. What is going on here? Shall we come to the point of willingly accepting that which we once so feared?*[13]

Truly, as the decades since have borne out, Tooker was at a nadir of his energy and may have been falling into a bleak, trance-like state brought on by continuing depression in which nothing really mattered. He now remembers often humming, as he worked, a few lines from a Joan Baez song about living one day at a time and dreaming one dream at a time.

*Standing Figures* (1973) may be Tooker's most monochromatic painting. The atmosphere is suffused with that gray-white dust which indicates fluorescent lighting, and there are no touches of color anywhere, only a hint here and there of warm underpainting obliterated by a gray despair as pervasive as volcanic ash.

*Woman at the Wall* (1974), the first painting completed after Christopher died, must be one of the most unselfconscious depictions of despair in twentieth-century painting. It is a work without obvious artifice but with some subtleties worth noting. A burst of light streaks the wall above this figure of a woman grieving, who is submerged into the pale shadow below it. The grieving woman is modeled after the central figure of *Standing Figures* and is closely related to figures in several other paintings, *Voice I* and *Door* among them. In those paintings, however, the figures are activated by some external force, while the figure in *Woman at the Wall* is consumed by an internal despair.

After depression came anger, and the painting that followed, *The Lesson* (1974), was filled with it. The two figures in *The Lesson* are separated by a wall, as in *Voice I*, but the barrier here is now a means of protection for the figure on the left (an acknowledged representation of the artist, although not a direct portrait). The other figure is that of a "galvanized corpse," and her purpose is clear. In Tooker's own words, "She is teaching a lesson, and the man is an attentive student—learning some very unpleasant facts. This is what we all come to." The figures are created in an almost mono-chromatic umber tonality, like that of a faded sepia photograph, which is offset by a Spanish funeral wreath of intensely red artificial carnations. It is a resurgence of Tooker's "passionate red" in an odd yet appropriate place, for the Spanish understand the passion that accompanies this most finite of temporal and spiritual transitions.

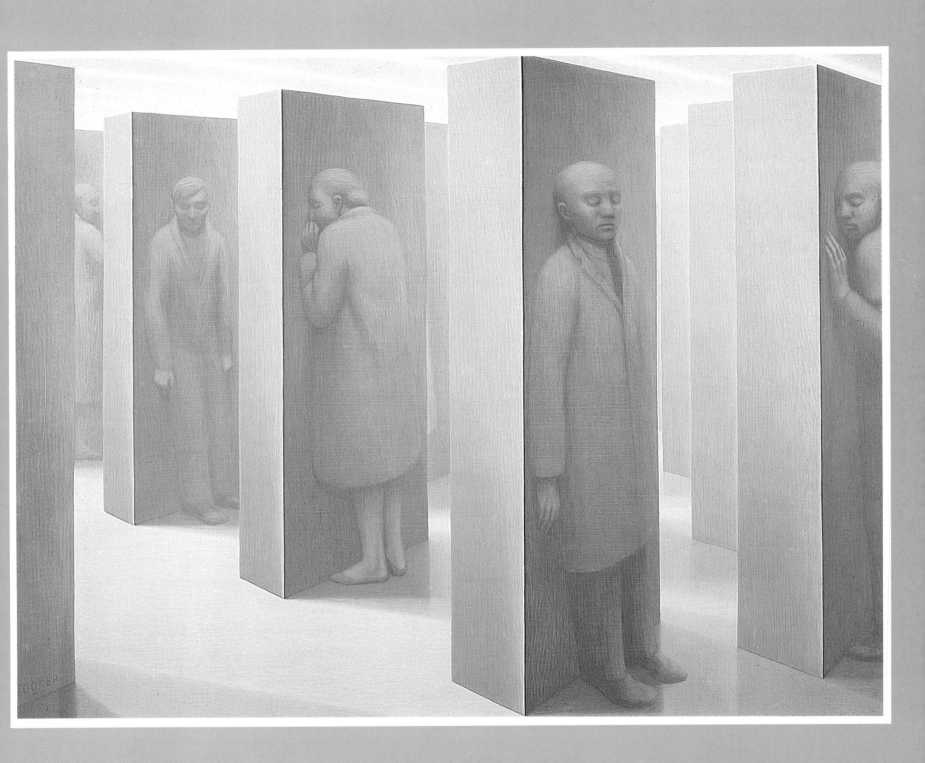

**STANDING FIGURES** 1973.
Egg tempera on gesso panel,
18 x 24 in.

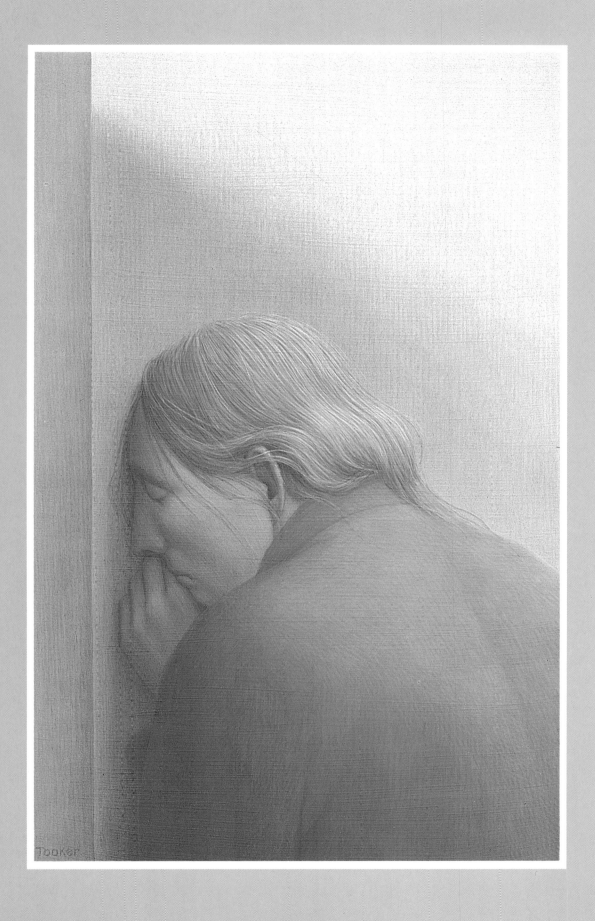

**WOMAN AT THE WALL** 1974.
Egg tempera on gesso panel,
18 x 11½ in.

**THE LESSON** 1974.
Egg tempera on gesso panel,
21 x 14 in.

(Opposite)

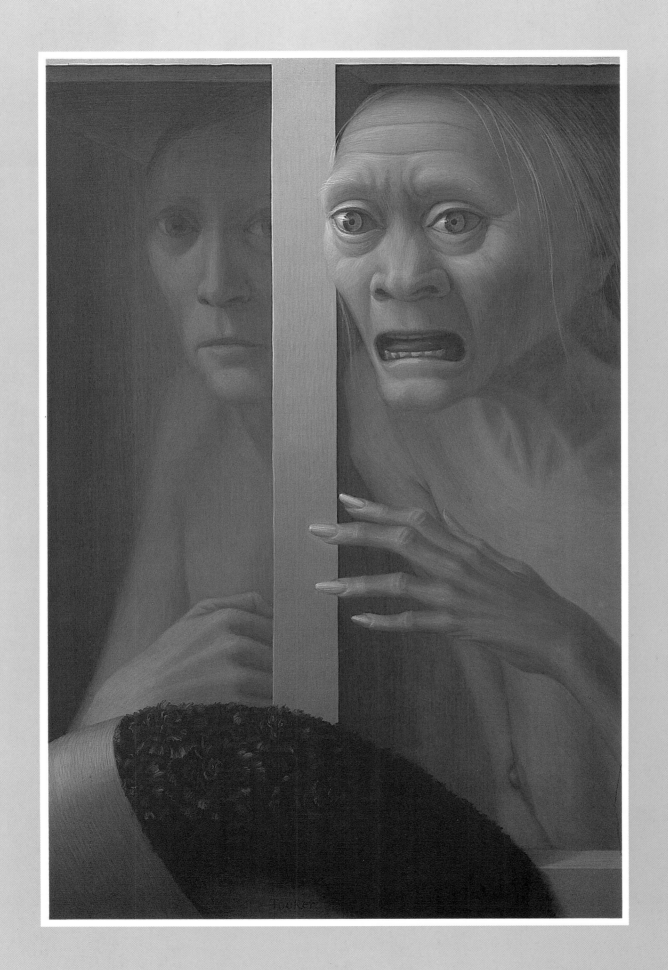

## RESURRECTION

**G**eorge Tooker has always been a deeply believing man, and the treatment of humankind in his work as a whole demonstrates that, no matter how bleak any one picture may be. His churchgoing waxed and waned over the years, but his fundamental faith in God as a universal force and spirit has never been shaken. He was baptized an Episcopalian, and, during the years at Hartland, attended the Episcopal church there, but in Spain he would often go to Roman Catholic Mass. In September 1976, in Vermont, Tooker was confirmed a Catholic.

That Tooker had a strong sense of faith and belief long before his conversion to Roman Catholicism should be adequately clear by now, and *Supper* (1963) is the first of his paintings that might be described as directly religious in intent. In the early 1960s, Tooker and Christopher attended a memorial service in Selma, Alabama, for an Episcopal minister and another civil rights worker who had been murdered there. Dr. Martin Luther King, Jr. spoke at that service, and the assembly then marched to the Selma Courthouse to place a wreath in memory of the two men. It was an intensely moving experience. "*Supper* is not a depiction of – but an allusion to – the supper at Emmaus and was painted because I was very moved by Dr. King." It is, of course, a depiction, too, of the races seated together at a simple, communal supper of bread and wine, that moment of quiet reflection and prayer before the breaking of bread. And it is to the artist's credit that in this and the other religious works that followed he was able to deal with subject matter that has seemed to confound most artists of the latter twentieth century and to do so without mawkishness.

What *Supper* and other works that followed on this same general theme demonstrate is not that Tooker is capable of painting an unselfconscious painting with a religious subject, but that so many of his paintings are fundamentally religious in nature. The figures at a table and use of the ironstone bowl in *Supper* recall *Table I* and *II* and *Odalisque*, which (despite the depiction of the nude figure in *Table*) are reverential and respectful portrayals of the subject, not erotic ones.

*Magdalene* (1976) is the first of the paintings made at the time of his conversion to Catholicism and was painted while he was receiving instruction in the faith. While Tooker does not compare himself directly to Mary Magdalene, the parallel between the profound changes each of them underwent after their respective conversions was obvious to him. Unfortunately, the painting has suffered some deterioration of the flesh tones, which mars an otherwise very strong picture, but the drawing for the work is illustrated here.

Traditionally, the delight in the temporal and fleshly pleasures of the Magdalene's former life are indicated not only by the skull as a vanitas image, but by jewels and other objects of adornment. Tooker has used the skull but replaced the baubles with several sprigs of eglantine – the lowly sweetbrier which is found in so many rural dooryards, Tooker's included. The use of flowers is apt, for the vase is one of the symbols of St. Mary Magdalene. The skull and

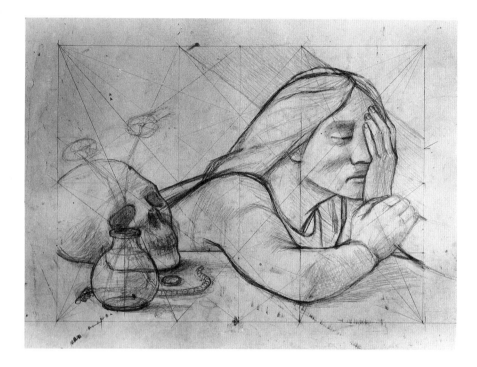

Study for MAGDALENE, 1976.
Pencil, 18 x 24

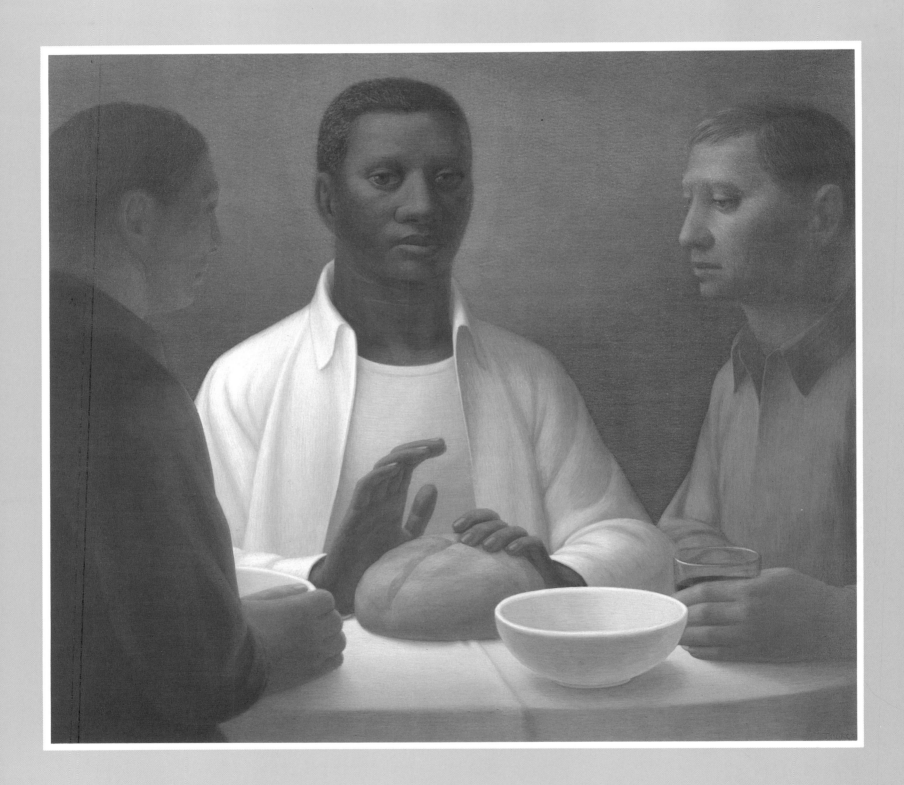

**SUPPER** 1963.
Egg tempera on gesso panel,
20 x 24 in.

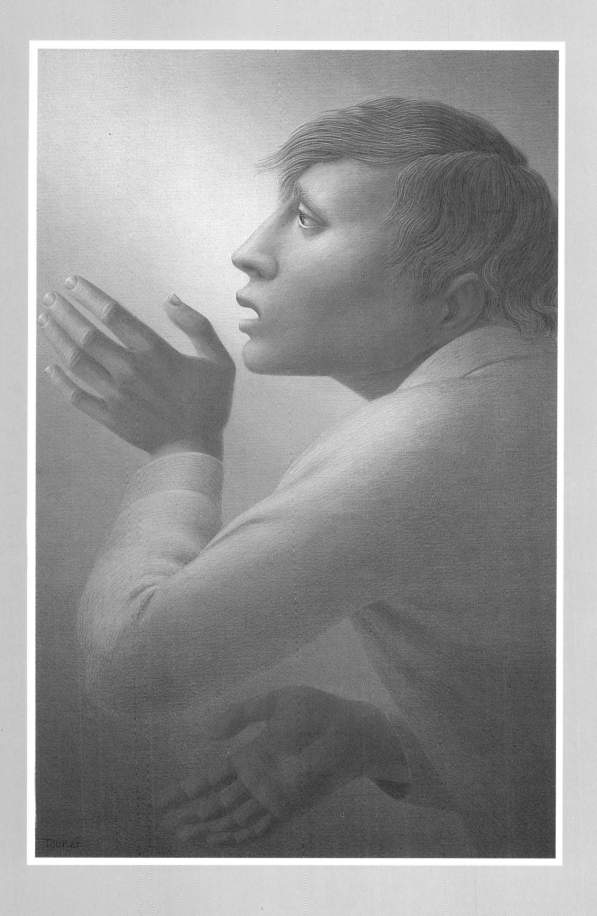

**ORANT** (APPLAUSE) 1977.
Egg tempera on gesso panel,
23½ x 15½ in.

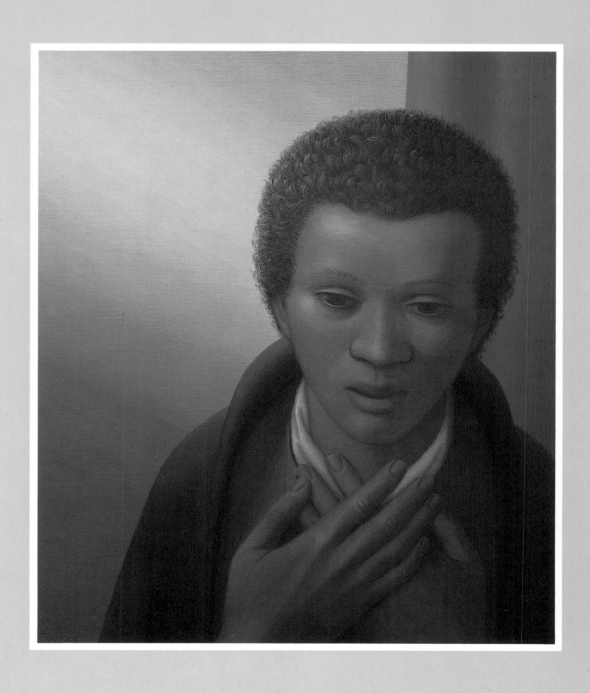

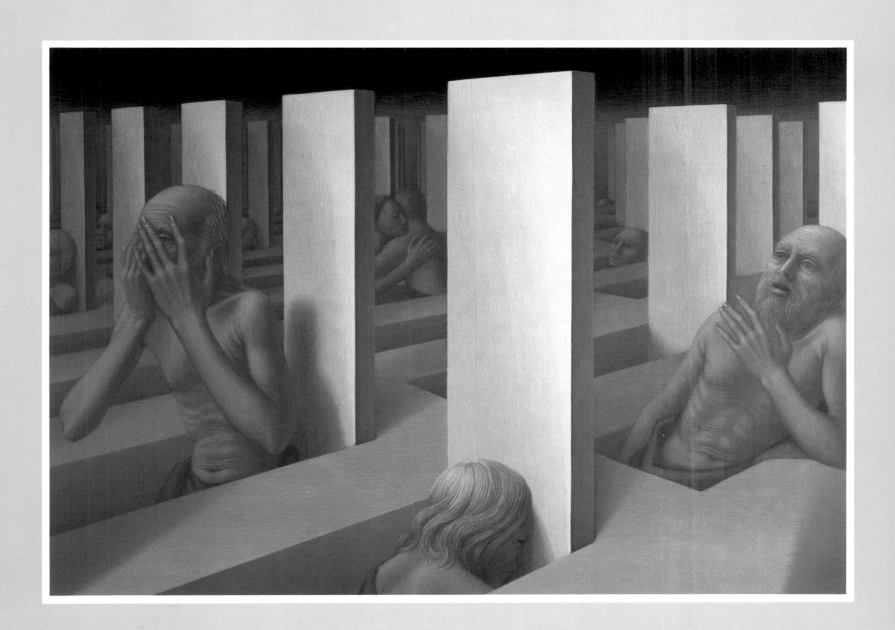

**LANDSCAPE WITH FIGURES II** 1985.
Egg tempera on gesso panel,
22¼ x 32¼ in.

**EMBRACE OF PEACE I** 1986.
Egg tempera on gesso panel,
15½ x 25¼ in.

(Opposite)

flowers as metaphors of temporal fragility are ones that the artist has often used, but their combination into a miniature still life is in strong contrast with the head of the Magdalene who has turned so sharply away from it. The objects of life (and death) and the figure turning from them strongly bisect the composition. One's eye flickers between the brightly lighted flowers set against a rather ominous background and the head in semi-shadow, so obviously engaged in a monumental internal struggle.

*Orant* (1977) and *Girl Praying* (1977) were both painted in Spain shortly after Tooker's conversion, and both pictures certainly demonstrate the strong early enthusiasm and spirit the newly minted convert felt for his faith. Of the two, *Orant* is surely the stronger picture, although each shows a different aspect of prayer – one of ecstatic rejoicing, the other of quiet contemplation.

The word "orant," which derives from the same root as "orate" and "oracle," describes a figure, usually a woman, with hands outstretched in active prayer. The image is frequently found in wall paintings in early Christian catacombs. Tooker has modified the traditional figure, making it a male, but emphasizing the active and participatory quality of this prayer. It is certainly one of Tooker's most active paintings, not only in the stance of the figure, but in the very strong connection of the young man with something beyond the field of the painting. Tooker very rarely casts a figure with so much animation, particularly when the reasons for that animation and intensity are not visible. Only *Watchers* may compare to *Orant* in this regard, but the figures in *Watchers* are numbed with despair or disbelief, not energized by ecstasy.

*Girl Praying*, which Tooker recalls painting immediately after *Orant*, is reminiscent of female figures seen full-face forward in earlier paintings; but while those faces (for example, *Window I* or *Gypsy*) expressed anguish or little emotion at all, *Girl Praying* reflects Tooker's renewed feelings of joy and his new-found religious faith.

*Landscape with Figures II* (1985) is not a reprise of the first painting to share this title. More properly, it is an extension of the imagery in *Standing Figures*, albeit with many significant changes.

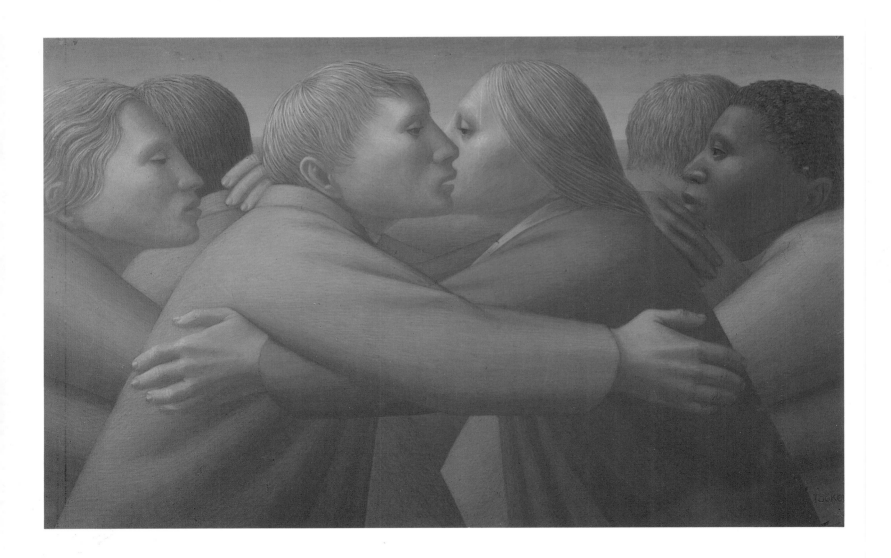

While *Standing Figures* documented the living dead, *Landscape with Figures II* documents the dead called to life again at the last trumpet. It was painted after his survey exhibition at the Marisa del Re Gallery in New York in 1985. Seeing so much of his earlier work again had a profound effect on Tooker. He has recalled a number of these earlier pictures in this painting which contains references to images from all decades of his career. Tooker comments about the figures' startled expressions that, "resurrection is a change of state, as traumatic a time as birth or death." Yet this is not a document of either fear or despair and if some of the figures seem startled, others, such as the couple in the distance, are obviously pleased at being able to see and embrace each other again. *Landscape with Figures II* contains one element which is unusual in Tooker's *oeuvre*, two figures that are conspicuously old. Tooker looked at reproductions of historical paintings of St. Jerome and acknowledges that the figure on the right is an amalgam of St. Jerome as painted by the Baroque painters Domenichino and Zurbaran and the British mystic, William Blake. This is a homage both to art history and to age.

The following year, Tooker drew directly upon an image from *The Seven Sacraments* (see following chapter) in creating *Embrace of Peace I* (1986). Unlike the earlier "embrace" pictures, this one directly documents a moment in the Mass, a moment that Tooker turns into a universal symbol of love. Following the consecration of the Host, but before sharing the bread and wine, parishioners offer "greetings of peace," turning to each other and those nearby, to exchange a handshake or embrace. For Tooker the embrace symbolizes the community he has found in the Church, and the community he hopes to find in paradise. The painting is thus a visual rendering of heaven and Earth where the sexes and races mix harmoniously. It is, as he says, "where we should be."

*The Dream* (1991-92) is Tooker's interpretation of the dream of St. Joseph, in which he is told by an angel that Mary, his wife, will bear not his child but Jesus Christ, the Son of God. The idea for the painting is not taken from scripture and Tooker recalls the story of the Dream of Joseph as appearing first in the Middle Ages. The figural references are obvious; the figure of Joseph is in partial shadow in the foreground while the blond angel, mysteriously lighted, appears at the window. The painting does have another message, however, that of acceptance. Joseph accepts the message of the dream—that the child his wife is about to bear is not his own but the Son of God.

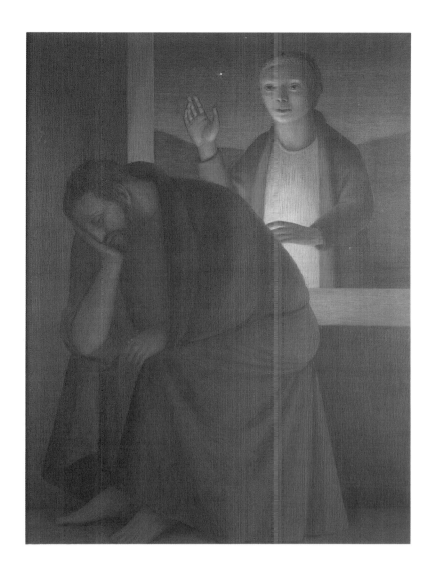

**THE DREAM** 1992.
Egg tempera on gesso panel,
24 x 18 in.

# THE SEVEN SACRAMENTS

*"God doesn't make junk. He makes perfection and he makes it beautiful."* [14]

**W**indsor, Vermont, situated on the west bank of the Connecticut River, is about four miles south of Hartland and perhaps eight miles from Tooker's house. It is a town of a few thousand souls through which tourists pass on their way to the over-restored elegance of Woodstock, Vermont, a few miles north, or the Augustus St. Gaudens Memorial, the sculptor's home and studio, maintained as a museum, across the river in New Hampshire. Once a prosperous manufacturing center with a number of small companies making machine tools and precision machinery, Windsor today is in an economic holding pattern. The big rubber company has closed, and the last of the tool companies is heading the same way. Only a group of tiny manufacturing and service companies remain, providing sketchy and erratic employment, too little for many of the small retail stores which once lined Windsor's main street. Now many of them have closed.

St. Francis of Assisi Church was originally housed in a handsome, if small, carpenter gothic building about a block or so west of Windsor's main street. Shortly after World War II, a time indifferent to historic preservation, a decision was made by the parish to build a bigger church, and the little wooden one was pulled down. It was replaced by a building typical of that time, constructed of light brick interspersed with darker bricks at odd intervals, giving it a distinctly piebald look. On December 22, 1977, that church was destroyed by fire.

While disasters test the mettle of everyone they touch, it is the strongest individuals who respond most strongly to them. Father Forrest Rouelle had been sent to Windsor a few years earlier to revive a dwindling parish, and he took the fire as an opportunity to rebuild the parish as it rebuilt the church.

One must understand a bit about Forrest Rouelle, for it was the dynamic relationship between him and Tooker that created the largest work the artist has ever attempted. Father Rouelle is a charismatic man who, in adopting the promulgations of Vatican II, was as intensely involved in and committed to the daily lives of his parishioners (and to the town of Windsor) as he is to the bedrock beliefs of the Roman Catholic faith. He was born in Vermont of French stock, grew up there, and is a strong force in the Church in Vermont. The parish of St. Francis required dynamic leadership, and Forrest Rouelle provided it in abundance until he was called to serve another needy parish on Vermont's border with Canada.

When Tooker returned from Spain in 1978 the church was gone, but planning for the new one was well under way. Father Rouelle had resisted the pleas of some parishioners and church administrators to hurry the rebuilding so that the parish could carefully consider just what form the new building should take. The planning stage lasted the better part of a year before Peter Kosinski, an architect from New Haven, Connecticut, was finally engaged. The resulting building is simple and handsome, vaguely post-modern in

its massing and use of oversize details, but based, at its heart, on early Christian prototypes. Placed close to the street, it is a two-story structure, almost square, constructed of deep red brick with touches of red tile and a strongly sloping roof. The sanctuary rises to the full height in the center of the building, and on the second floor classrooms open off from a balcony that surrounds the sanctuary on three sides. Below, on the ground floor, a small chapel (where daily masses are held), the sacristy, offices, and church community room surround the sanctuary. It is an open plan building, and the community room opens directly into the back of the sanctuary. The use of the dark red brick is repeated inside the sanctuary, community room, and corridors as well. The furniture is simple and sturdy, with movable wooden chairs replacing fixed pews, and the space is often used for functions other than religious services.

All of the art in the building, stained glass and flat work as well, is original. While the style and quality of each object varies considerably, there are no reproductions or "plaster saints" to be seen here. Tooker's painting, *The Seven Sacraments* (1980), often unofficially subtitled "A Celebration of Life," is installed at one end of the community room over the altar and ambo that survived the fire in the former church.

The development of *The Seven Sacraments* came about almost by accident. Tooker made a contribution to the church building fund, but, at dinner one evening in October 1979, as rebuilding was just getting under way, Father Rouelle asked him if he wouldn't also contribute a painting which might be sold to benefit the reconstruction. Tooker demurred, proposing instead that he paint a major work for the new building. Father Rouelle agreed at once, and at that dinner they discussed what the picture might depict. Father Rouelle now recalls saying that "the theme of the Church is 'celebrating life,' so how about painting the seven sacraments." Tooker responded that he didn't know if he was worthy, but Father Rouelle, pressing on, said, "George, the fact that you can say that makes you worthy." Shortly thereafter Tooker left for Spain, where he began his investigations into the preparation of a painting that would illustrate all of the seven sacraments.

The seven sacraments – Baptism, Confirmation, Reconciliation (formerly Penance), the Eucharist (Communion), Marriage, Anointing of the Sick (formerly Extreme Unction), and Holy Orders – are obviously difficult to represent within a single unified image. During the months in Spain, Tooker cast some ambitious plans and modified them substantially. Gradually, from the early studies, the final design evolved: seven panels, six of them three feet high flanking the central panel of the Eucharist, which is six inches higher. The panels also increase in width as they progress toward the center. The outside panels are fifteen inches wide, the width of each succeeding pair increasing by three inches, with the central panel being twenty-five inches wide.

When Tooker returned to Hartland in April 1980, the preliminary drawings of the final work had been substantially completed, and the artist submitted them to Father Rouelle for review. After studying them, he commented, "George, your theology is perfect," and work on the panels began at once, in a burst of ecstatic energy that was to condense the equivalent of three years' production into one. Even though there are seven individually framed panels, the work is planned rather as a single if discontinuous image into which the applied architecture of the frames acts as "windows," separating each element without isolating any individual image from the whole composition. Tooker's careful attention to Agostino di Duccio's relief sculpture, those figures strongly set in architectural enframements, obviously served him well here.

*The Seven Sacraments* is set in that place and time we have come to recognize as "here" and "today," although Father Rouelle has accurately observed that "George has always painted in parables. He kept the universal man, but gave life and hope to the painting. He knew what he was doing – he was embracing his whole

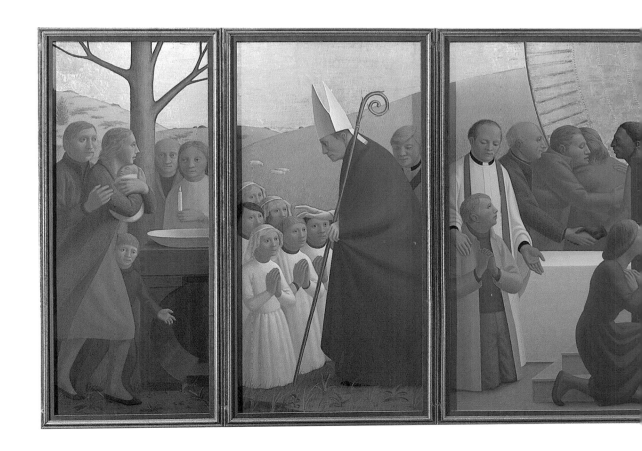

concept of faith in that painting." The long horizontal structure of the polyptych is dominated by the sky of burnished and incised gold and by the open pastoral landscape which flows between panels beneath that golden sky. The use of gold, and of the concentric halos of light that pulse out from the Eucharist held aloft in the very center of the middle panel, is the traditional symbol of the presence of God in the universal Church, and Tooker himself claims that "the subject matter is the centrality of the Eucharist among the sacraments in the Church."[15]

The gold ground dominates the central panel of the Eucharist as the celebrant holds the Host aloft after consecration before offering it to the communicants below. It is the most profound moment of the Mass, and the priest faces the congregation from behind the altar, alone and surrounded by the glory of God. This is both the most literal and most allegorical passage in the painting. It is literal in that the priest consecrating the Host is a direct portrait of Father Rouelle, and even the altar at which he stands is the one

**THE SEVEN SACRAMENTS**
(A CELEBRATION OF LIFE), 1980.
Egg tempera on gesso panel,
42 x 132 in.

(Detail opposite)

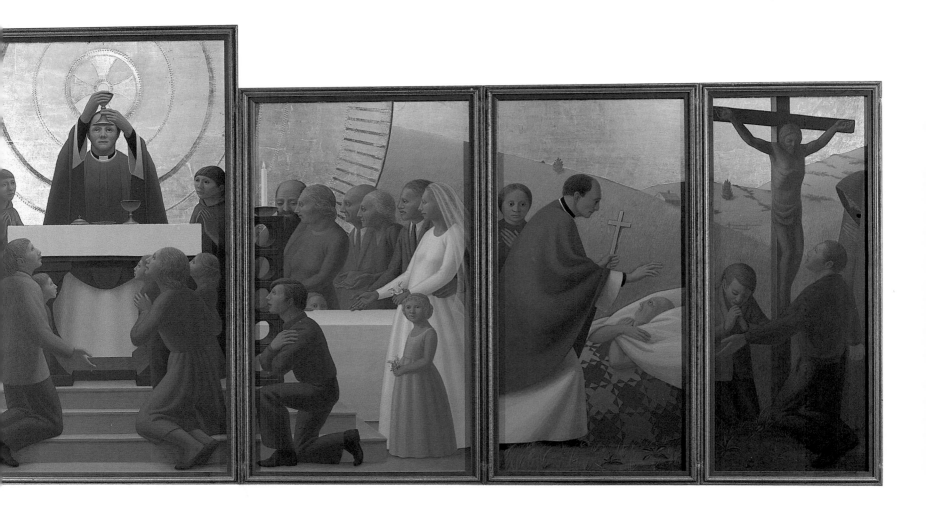

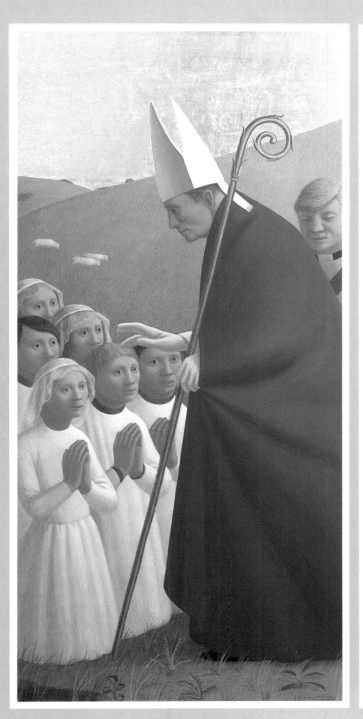
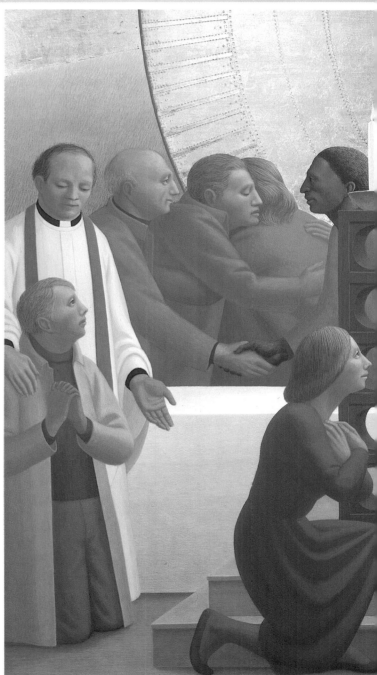

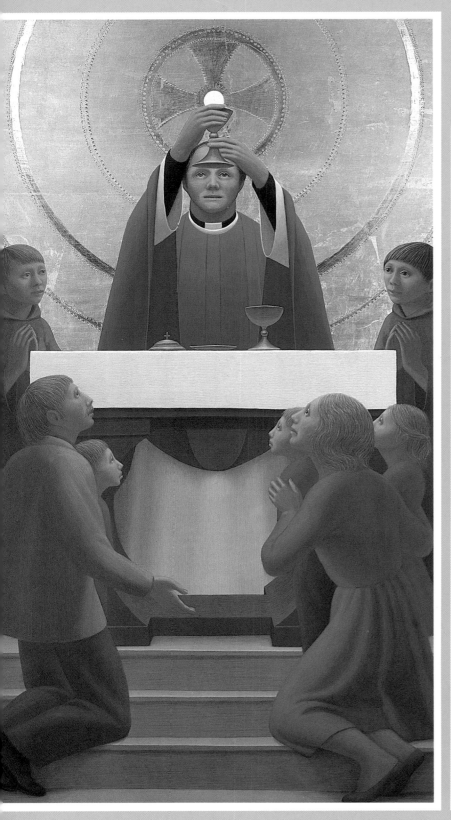

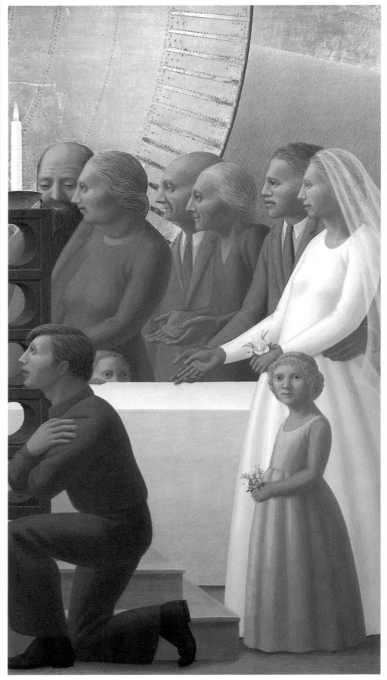

designed for and used in St. Francis of Assisi at present. (Tooker went to the cabinet shop where the church furniture was being fabricated to verify its appearance.) Yet the gold ground and radiating light mark the image also as an allegory of the universal Church, dominated not by individuals but by radiant faith.

That radiance is expressed directly in the subtle shifts of color and light that occur between panels. The light from the Host is as palpable as it is spiritual. The illumination of all the figures comes directly from this glowing source, so radiantly warm in the central panel, then gradually fading to a cooler, grayer luminescence at either end.

The sacraments are arranged, with one exception, to follow the cycle of life. Baptism is to the extreme left, and the barren tree in that panel is a reference to humanity's fall from grace, but the somewhat somber atmosphere of the landscape is offset by the warm light that falls on the faces of the young family with its new baby, come to be baptized, "to be washed in the waters of life." One of the witnesses to the baptism holds a candle, another reference to the light of the divine presence.

The rolling New England landscape behind these figures flows into the sacrament of Confirmation, uniting the panels through the shared horizon line. The sacrament of Confirmation is set directly in the meadow landscape. A half-dozen young confirmants dressed in spotless white gaze up in anticipation at the bishop as he blesses them. The bishop's crozier takes on a direct significance here. Tooker has emphasized the metaphor of the Church's responsibility to its parishioners as the shepherd has responsibility to his flock, for several sheep graze quietly in the luxuriant landscape directly behind the children.

The sacrament of Reconciliation, perceived traditionally as the confession of one's sins and expiation of them through required prayer or performance of good works, underwent a substantial transformation following Vatican II. Even the name was changed, and here Reconciliation is illustrated "not with the confessional but with a communal breaking down of hatred and prejudice. Black reaches out to white, man embraces woman. The penitent does not look down in shame, but looks hopefully at the Eucharist."[16] Tooker has painted himself as the kneeling penitent, and Father Rouelle, again, appears as the priest who stands behind ready to help him rise.

The artist has employed an interesting unifying device in the two panels that flank the central one. The altar platform, so obvious in the central panel, has been extended into each of these flanking panels, forming a pyramid of steps and giving the altar more prominence than could be achieved if it were confined to just one panel. Behind the steps on the flanking panels are two cloth-covered tables, and in the panel of Reconciliation this table separates the priest, the penitent, and a kneeling woman who faces the Eucharist from those behind. In one gesture, Tooker has expanded the perceived depth of the work at a point where the larger number of people require more room to eliminate any impression of crowding, while at the same time isolating those kneeling in prayer from the more active figures behind. In a further subtle development of the space and of the whole concept of inside and outside, all three of the central panels are set in a floored space rather than the natural earth of the outer four panels; the altar steps would surely have seemed odd if they were set directly on the grass.

The four figures behind the table in the panel of Reconciliation form one of the finest passages in the painting. The embrace is that of agape, not carnal love, and is an image of faith and passion, which Tooker has subsequently repeated several times in smaller versions. The profiles of the white man, light against darker ground, and the black man, dark against the dazzling gold ground, are warm and individual restatements of Italian fifteenth-century portraiture brought up to date.

The sacrament of Marriage, to the right of the Eucharist panel, is also filled with figures. The principal performers, the young couple being married, stand in front of the table, not looking at each other but rather toward the central panel, their hands outstretched, waiting to receive the Eucharist. Of all the faces in this expansive painting, these are the most racially mixed combination, their bone structure and skin tones suggesting elements of all of the races. Behind the table two other couples, obviously partners of many years, are enjoying the ceremony, through which they appear to be reaffirming their own faith.

Another warm touch in this panel are the figures of the two children: the little boy peeping over the edge of the table and the young girl dressed in pink. The head of the little boy, seen before in *Pot of Aloes*, was not in the original drawing for this panel. Tooker added it spontaneously while painting it, and it is one of those gestures that soften and humanize the majesty of this picture. The charming young girl is one of the wedding attendants, but she has been distracted and gazes out at us. She and a young boy in the first panel, who peers out from behind his mother's skirt, are the only two figures who are not watching someone or something within this complex structure. They are watching us, and in that simple gesture of awareness they seem to invite our participation.

Anointing the Sick is another of the sacraments to undergo substantial change as a result of Vatican II. The emphasis is now less on offering forgiveness and redemption at the last moment before death, but rather on making peace with God as the end of one's life approaches. The composition, again set within a grassy meadow, is a mirror image of Confirmation, with the priest and witness behind him blessing an elderly man whose face is lighted with the radiance of the Eucharist. The man lies in a simple bed, and the patchwork quilt is a homely touch, a natural part of the New England setting. It is also a bit of geometric painting of the sort Tooker so much enjoys.

The final panel, Holy Orders, is not depicted by Tooker by the laying on of hands, as it often is. A young man, his gesture imitating the *Orant* figure, and indeed that of the crucifix itself, is dropping to his knees to offer his life to the Church. Tooker feels he is unable to paint the living body of Christ, and so the image of the crucifixion has been changed to a crucifix. The theme of the panel is taken from Jesus's presentation of John to Mary: "While on the cross, Jesus said to his mother, who was standing with the disciple, John, 'Woman, behold your son!'"

In the selection of this passage, Tooker points out that "the priesthood carries with it the weight of the Cross – a tree quite different from the barren tree in the first panel, since this is the tree of redemption."[17]

*The Seven Sacraments* was dedicated on Epiphany, January 6, 1981, in the church community room, which was crowded with parishioners. Each panel was unveiled individually, preceded by an appropriate reading, and Father Rouelle reported that the work was received "with absolute silence for the unveiling, and then a burst of applause at the end."

Of *The Seven Sacraments*, Tooker has observed that he constructed it to be simple in form and clearly narrative. The bilateral balance and repetitive forms reinforce the central belief in the rituals of the church. Tooker himself has described the work in one short and pithy sentence: "It's a pretty primitive work." In its unselfconscious simplicity it possesses the qualities that mark the best of Tooker's work, bold forms, light from an invisible or unique source, emotional certitude and honesty and, in the case of this work, monumental and unembarrassed dignity. It dominates the not terribly congenial space of the church community room because it possesses such an enormous presence. It is no wonder that the parishioners of St. Francis of Assisi were first silent, then applauded their approval upon its presentation to them. It has produced the same effect on nonbelievers as well.

After completion of *The Seven Sacraments*, Tooker accepted another request from his church, to paint the *Stations of the Cross* (1984). In these fourteen small panels one does not see the figure of Christ. Because Tooker feels he is unworthy to paint Him, he shows only His hands. These panels are remarkable for the research Tooker has put into the Christian symbols that form the backgrounds to the paintings. These symbols may be arcane but they have a strong tradition in the church and form a powerful graphic background to the images. The cycle combines Tooker's sure sense of graphic description with his strong sense of ambiguity and fantasy to tell a story that will leave much to the individual imaginations of those following the path.

One Sunday afternoon, Father Rouelle talked a bit about his reticent friend, George Tooker. "Coming to know the community of faith has given George a much greater awareness of who he is. Previously his life was solely in his art, and his friends were artists, but now he has come into a much broader community. His spirituality has crystallized. It permeates him. It was deep in him, but just not allowed to come out. I just praise God that George Tooker crossed my path. He's a great contribution to society."

Since words of praise are something of an embarrassment to this quiet man, although they warm him deeply, let the words of W. H. Auden, a poet George Tooker so greatly admires, supply the final thought:

> *His aging nature is the same*
> *As when childhood wore its name*
> *In an atmosphere of love*
> *And to itself appeared enough:*
> *Only now, when he has come*
> *In walking distance of his tomb,*
> *He at last discovers who*
> *He had always been to whom*
> *He so often was untrue.*[18]

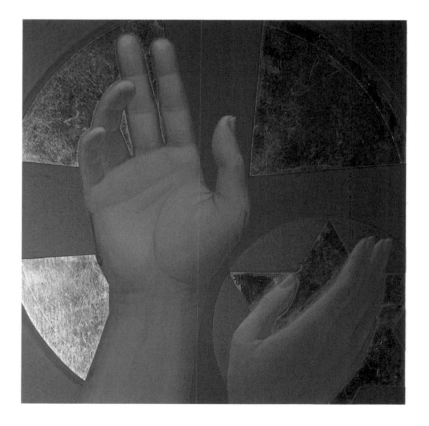

**THE FOURTH STATION OF THE CROSS:**
**JESUS ENCOUNTERS HIS HOLY MOTHER** 1984.
Egg tempera on gesso panel,
11¾ x 11¾ in.

## NOTES

Unless otherwise noted, George Tooker's remarks have come from several long interviews with the author in September, 1973, August and November 1983 and February, 1988.

Numbers in boldface refer to page numbers in text; numbers in roman (in sequence) are footnote numbers.

**9** 1. Although Tooker did not have a one-person show in New York from 1967 to 1985, he was the subject of exhibitions in other cities (in 1974-1975) and was included in several important museum exhibitions during this period. Since 1985, there have been a number of one person exhibitions and group exhibitions that have included his work. See the list of exhibitions, pages 160-161.

2. William C. Seitz, in the catalogue for *São Paulo Bienal 9*, National Collection of Fine Arts, Washington, D.C., 1967, p. 19.

**10** 3. Lincoln Kirstein, Introduction to *Symbolic Realism in American Painting, 1940-1950*, exhibition catalogue, Institute of Contemporary Art, London, July 18-August 18, 1950, pp. 3-6. This group of artists included Tooker, Paul Cadmus, Jared French, Edward Hopper, Walter Murch, Alton Pickens, Ben Shahn, and Andrew Wyeth, among others. (Note: The London exhibition was preceded by a New York gallery show, "Symbolic Realism," Edwin Hewitt Gallery, April 3-22, 1950.)

4. Seldin Rodman, *Conversations with Artists* (New York: Devin-Adair, 1957), p. 209.

**27** 5. W. H. Auden, "The Sea and the Mirror: A Commentary on Shakespeare's *The Tempest*," *The Collected Poetry of W. H. Auden* (New York: Random House, 1945), p. 402; reprinted in *W. H. Auden: Collected Poems*, edited by Edward Mendelson (New York: Random House, 1976), p. 340.

**30** 6. George Tooker, in a questionnaire concerning his painting *Subway*, in the artist's file at the Whitney Museum of American Art, New York, dated January 30, 1951 (quoted in *Realism and Reality: The Other Side of American Painting, 1940-1960*, exhibition catalogue, Rutgers University Art Gallery, New Brunswick, N.J., 1982, catalogue introduction by Greta Berman and Jeffrey Wechsler).

**48** 7. Lloyd Goodrich, in his essay for *Georgia O'Keeffe*, exhibition catalogue, Whitney Museum of American Art, New York, 1970. (The gender in the quote has been changed by the author.)

**88** 8. Kirstein, *Symbolic Realism*, pp. 3.

9. Ibid., p. 4.

10. Ibid., p. 3.

**90** 11.     Only from the long line of spray
            Where the ebb meets the moon-blanch'd sand,
            Listen! you hear the grating roar
            Of pebbles which the waves draw back, and fling,
            At their return, up the high strand,
            Begin, and cease, and then again begin,
            With tremulous cadence slow, and bring
            The eternal note of sadness in.
"Dover Beach," second stanza, *The Poems of Matthew Arnold, 1840-1867* (London: Oxford University Press, 1909); reprinted in *Poetical Works* (1950, reprinted 1969), p. 211.

**110** 12. W. H. Auden, "Lullaby (Lay your sleeping head, my love)," second stanza, *The Collected Poetry of W. H. Auden*, pp. 208-9; reprinted in *W. H. Auden: Collected Poems*, p. 131.

**118** 13. Thomas H. Garver, Introduction to *George Tooker: Paintings 1947-1973*, exhibition catalogue, The Fine Arts Museums of San Francisco, California Palace of the Legion of Honor, July 13-September 2, 1974, n.p.

**129** 14. Father Forrest Rouelle, in his homily, St. Francis of Assisi Church, Windsor, Vermont, Sunday, August 28, 1983. Other quotes attributed to Father Rouelle, unless otherwise noted, are taken from an interview with him later that day.

**131** 15. Mark D. Lombard, "Artist Convert Paints Celebration of Joy," *The Vermont Catholic Tribune* 25, no. 2, January 23, 1981, p. 24.

**134** 16. Ibid.

**135** 17. Ibid.

18. W. H. Auden, "True Enough (His aging nature is the same)," *The Collected Poetry of W. H. Auden*, p. 54; reprinted in *W. H. Auden: Collected Poems*, p. 231.

**156** 19. Lincoln Kirstein, "The Saint of Bleecker Street," published in *Center: A Magazine of the Performing Arts* 1, no. 7 (December 1954): 3-8. All quotes attributed to Kirstein in this section are drawn from this article.

## ABOUT THIS REVISED EDITION

It has been a pleasure to know George Tooker over many years and to record his life's work. This new edition of the catalogue raisonné includes all the paintings and prints completed by Tooker in the last ten years, as well as a number of earlier paintings discovered since the 1992 edition. Chameleon Books and DC Moore Gallery have worked together to update the location of as many paintings as possible. Information in the sections devoted to Solo and Group Exhibitions, Selected Bibliography, Selected Reviews, Public Collections, and Awards has also been expanded. George Tooker continues to live and work in the hills of Vermont. As we go to press he is creating a new lithographic print, which will be included in a future edition of this volume.

—Arnold Skolnick

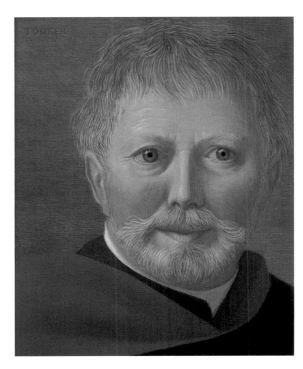

**SELF PORTRAIT** 1994.
Egg tempera on gessoed panel,
14 x 12 in.

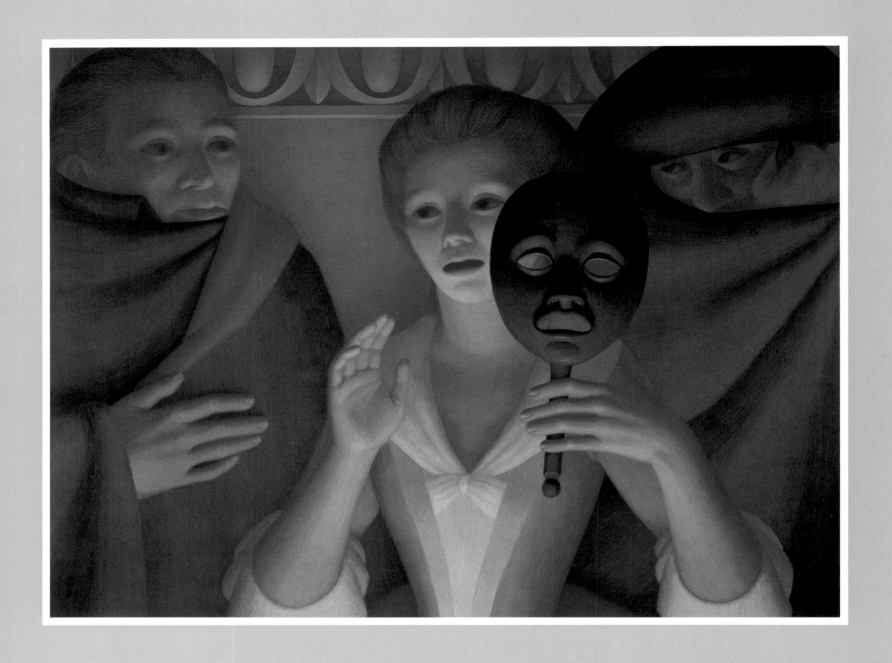

**UN BALLO IN MASCHERA** 1982.
Egg tempera on cardboard,
22 x 30 in.

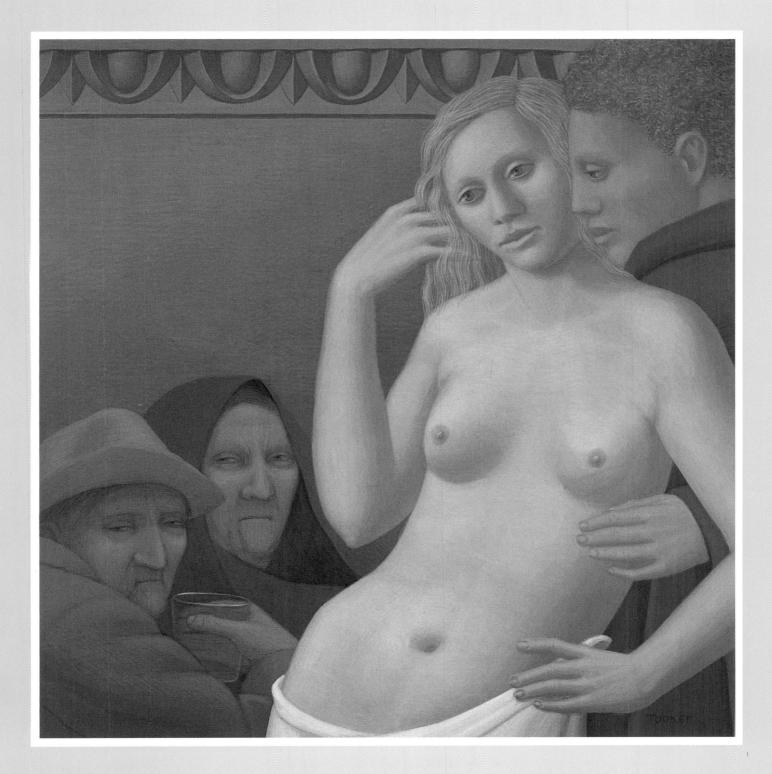

**THE COUPLE** 1993.
Egg tempera on gesso panel,
18 x 17³/4 in.

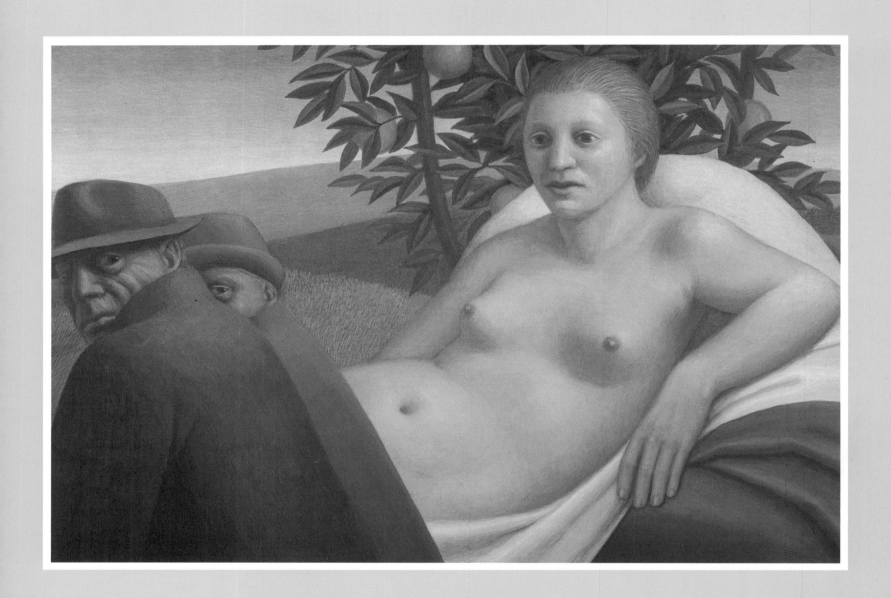

**LANDSCAPE WITH FIGURES IV** 1999.
Egg tempera on gesso panel,
19$^{1}$/$_2$ x 29$^{1}$/$_4$ in.

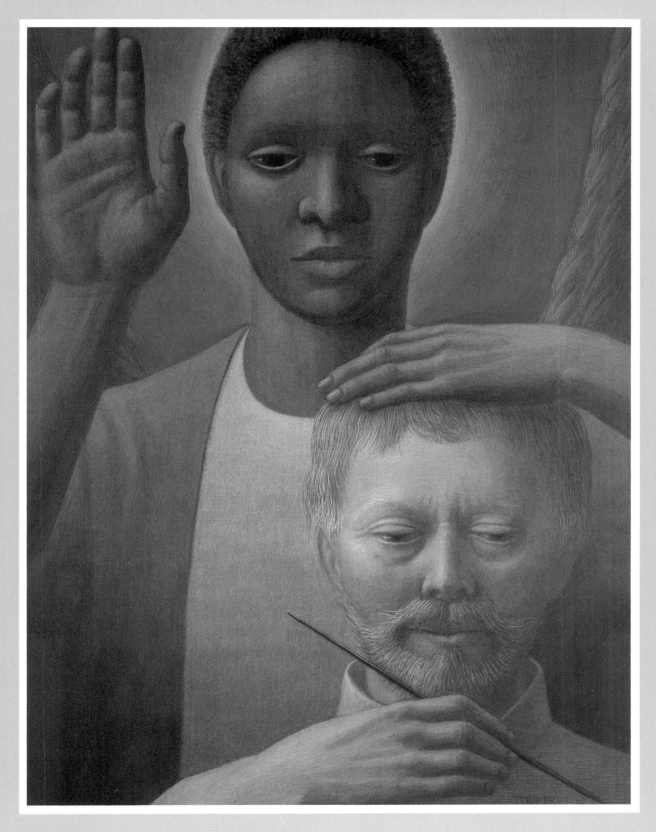

**DARK ANGEL** 1996.
Egg tempera on gesso panel,
22 x 30 in.

**WINDOW XI** 1999.
Egg tempera on gesso panel,
22 x 30 in.

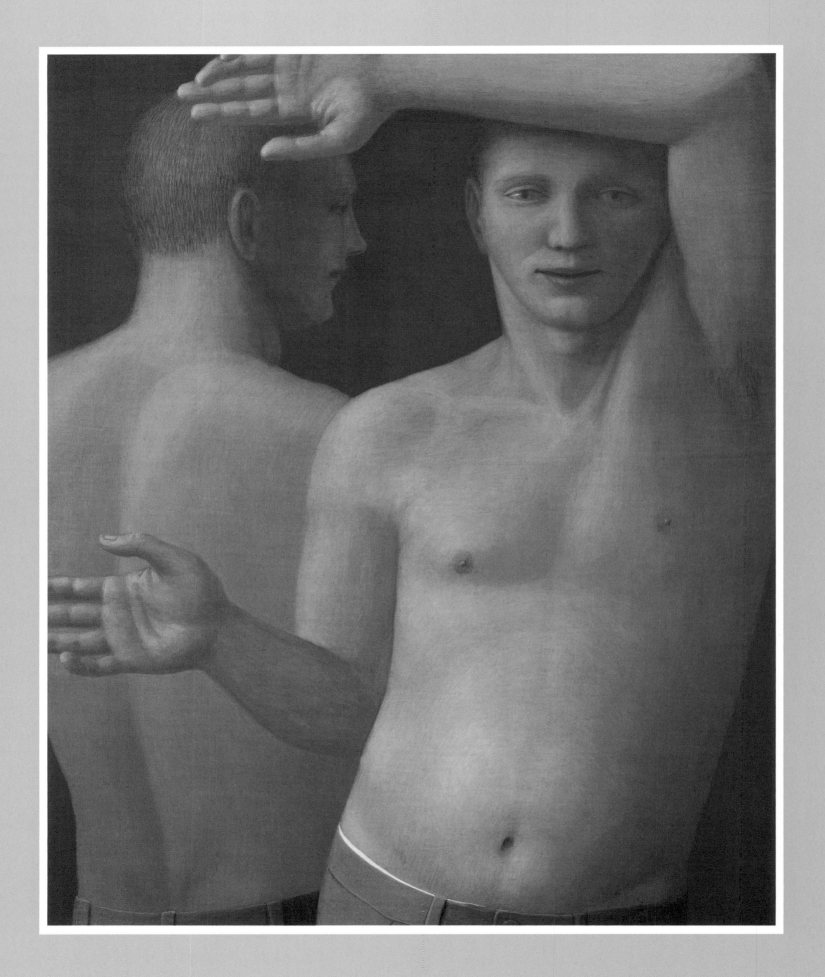

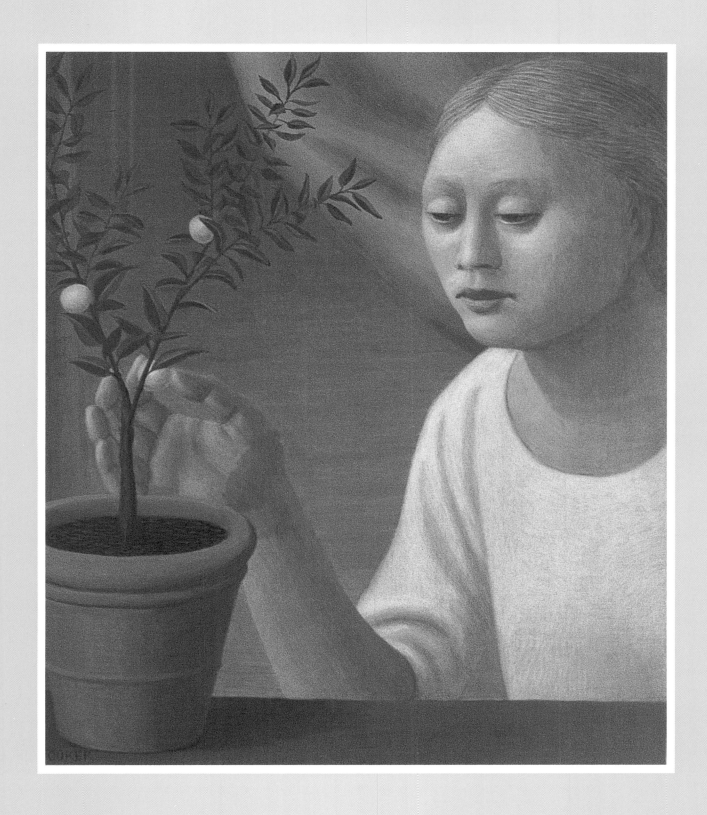

**POTTED ORANGE TREE** 1997.
Egg tempera on gesso panel,
18 x 16 in.

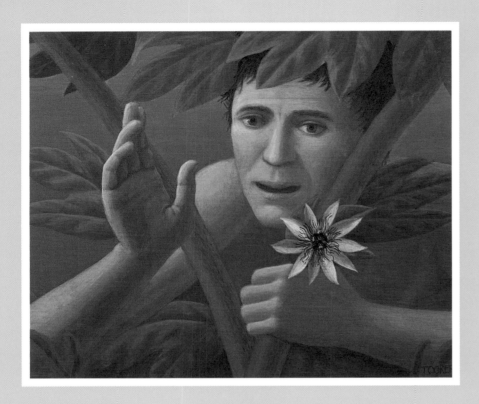

**MAN IN A TREE** 1998.
Egg tempera on gesso panel,
14 x 17 in.

**MOON RISE** 1997.
Egg tempera on gesso panel,
22 x 30 in.

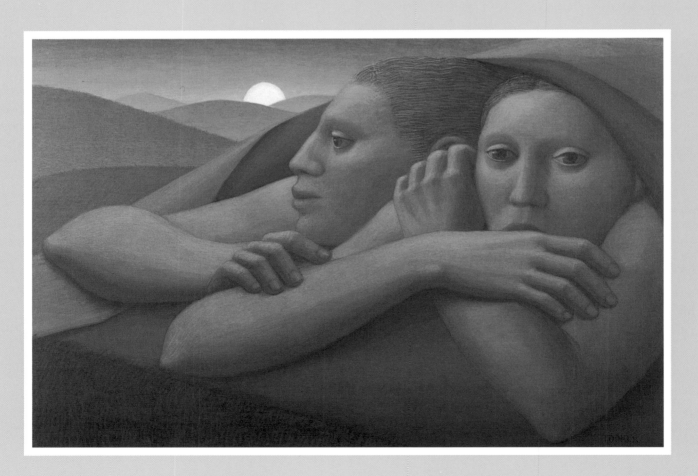

# CATALOGUE RAISONNE OF PAINTINGS 1945–2002

Unless otherwise noted, the medium of all paintings is egg tempera on gesso panel.

The problem of dating Tooker's paintings is a knotty one and may not be entirely resolved here. Early in his career, at the suggestion of a dealer, Tooker made a practice of not dating his paintings. The dealer encouraged him in this practice because, as a young artist, the works most often sold were the most recent, and neither the artist nor the dealer wanted to be caught with "stale" paintings on hand. There was also concern that Tooker, a slow worker, might miss the opportunity of having work included in the many annual and biennial exhibitions organized by a number of musums in the United States. These were the major salons of the late 1940s and early '50s where new work and new artists often made their debut. The organizers of some of these exhibitions were apparently concerned that only very recent work should be included in them and a dated work might be ruled out as having been executed before the time permissible by exhibition regulations. Tooker wanted to avoid this problem. Both concerns were groundless, of course, but with one or two exceptions Tooker has never dated his work.

After about 1949 he also left the inventorying of his production to his successive dealers. Unfortunately, these records have been lost and the dates listed here must be assumed to be approximate—that is, accurate to within one year either way.

Much information has been assembled from the checklists of his various one-person gallery exhibitions in New York in 1951, 1955, 1960, 1964, and 1967. These shows determine dates of paintings to within one or two years, but the precise order of his output becomes more confused after 1967. There were no dealer exhibitions after this date until 1985, and the records of the Rehn Gallery—his dealer from the late 1960s to the early '80s—were destroyed following the death of John Clancy, its owner.

Information has also been drawn from the exhibition records of museums that organized major American exhibitions in which Tooker's work had been included. Dating of the paintings, however, becomes particularly problematic during the period from the early 1970s to the early '80s. Tooker can always recall where he painted a picture but not when he painted it. Thus, certain "Spanish" pictures or "Vermont" pictures have been assigned to certain years based in part on what works have preceded them and what visual and emotional issues were occupying Tooker's attention at the time.

In certain cases, titles have also been slightly adjusted. Such title changes have been made at the artist's request and are the titles he now prefers.

In organizing this catalogue I have relied heavily on a master's thesis, "The World of George Tooker: Surreal or Real?", written in 1982 by Ms. Heidi D. Shafranek for the Department of Art History at the University of Delaware. Ms. Shafranek has done meticulous research on dates of paintings, but unfortunately she has been confused in several instances by misinformation in published catalogues. In some cases the artist himself has supplied her with one date and myself with another. Discussion with the artist has helped to resolve these problems—to a degree.

## 1945

**AUDIENCE**
9 x 12 in.
Collection of Roberto Giannotta, Rome
Illustration, p. 11

## 1946

**CHILDREN AND SPASTICS**
24$^{1/2}$ x 18$^{1/2}$ in.
Museum of Contemporary Art, Chicago
Gift of the Mary and Earle Ludgin Collection
Illustration, p. 14

**DANCE**
13 x 20$^{1/2}$ in.
Collection of John P. Axelrod, Boston, MA
Photo courtesy of Christie's
Illustration, p. 13

**THE ISLAND**
15$^{1/4}$ x 18$^{1/2}$ in.
Whereabouts unknown

## 1947

**THE CHESS GAME**
30 x 15 in.
Collection of Mr. Barney A. Ebsworth
Illustration, p. 15

**THE GROPING HAND**
Egg tempera on watercolor paper
3$^{1/2}$ x 2$^{3/4}$ in.
Collection of Nicholas Miles Pentecost

**SELF-PORTRAIT**
16$^{1/2}$ in. diameter
The Regis Collection, Minneapolis, MN
Illustration, p. 17

**THE SWING**
7 x 7 in.
Whereabouts unknown

## 1948

**CONEY ISLAND**
19 x 26 in.
Whereabouts unknown
Illustrations, pp. 18, 19

**BIRD WATCHERS**
26$^{1/2}$ x 32$^{1/2}$ in.
New Britain Museum of American Art
Gift of Olga H. Knoepke
Illustration, p. 22

**FESTA**
21$^{1/2}$ x 17$^{1/4}$ in.
Collection of Leslee and David Rogath
Illustration, p. 21

## 1948–49

**HOW DO YOU DO?**
20 x 15 in.
Whereabouts unknown

## 1949

**MARKET**
22 x 22 in.
Collection of John P. Axelrod, Boston, MA
Illustration, p. 25

**CORNICE**
24 x 16 in.
Columbus Museum of Art, Ohio
Museum Purchase, Howald Fund II
Illustration, p. 26

**VENUS**
Egg tempera on ivory
1$^{3/4}$ x 1$^{1/4}$ in. oval
The New York Historical Society, New York City

## 1950

**BATHERS** (BATH HOUSES)
20$^{1/4}$ x 15$^{1/4}$ in.
Private collection
Illustration, p. 75

**FOUNTAIN**
24 x 24 in.
Michigan Collection
Illustration, p. 89

**GLASS OF WATER**
Dimensions and whereabouts unknown
Illustration unavailable

**SCRAPS OF PAPER**
22$^{3/4}$ x 8$^{1/2}$ in.
Collection of Howard Perry Rothberg II
Illustration unavailable

**THE SUBWAY**
18 x 36 in.
Whitney Museum of American Art
Juliana Force Purchase
Illustrations, pp. 29, 30, 31

## 1950–52

**ACROBATS**
24 x 16 in.
Collection of Leslee and David Rogath
Illustration, p. 77

## 1951

**CUPBOARD I**
12$^{1/4}$ x 22$^{1/4}$ in.
Courtesy DC Moore Gallery, NYC

**GYPSY**
23 x 1$^{1/2}$ in.
Collection of Linda Eder Storrow
Illustration, p. 49

**LETTER BOX**
17$^{3/4}$ x 24 in.
Hirshhorn Museum and Sculpture Garden,
Smithsonian Institution
Museum Purchase, 1993

**SLEEPERS I**
18 x 30 in.
Whereabouts unknown
Illustration, p. 90

**WHITE CURTAIN**
17½ x 13½ in.
Private collection
Illustration, p. 50

1952

**BUILDERS**
16 x 16 in.
Lent by Wayne County
Public Library, Inc.,
Goldsboro, NC, Elizabeth
Rosenthal Collection
Illustration, p. 55

**DIVERS**
12 x 18 in.
Private collection
Courtesy of Sotheby's
Illustration, p. 76

**GARDEN PARTY**
18 x 11¾ in.
Private collection
Illustration, p. 78

**LAUNDRESS**
Oil on panel
23½ x 24 in.
Collection of John Horton

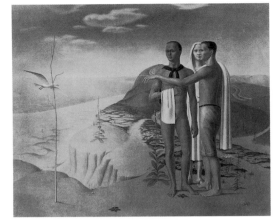

**THE ISLAND** 1946

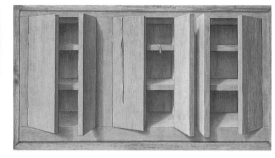

**CUPBOARD I** 1951

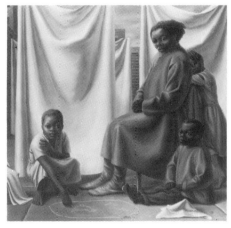

**LAUNDRESS** 1952

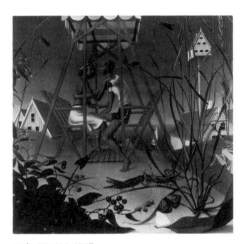

**THE SWING** 1947

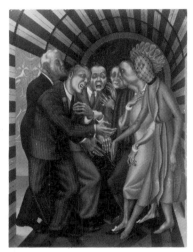

**HOW DO YOU DO?** 1948-49

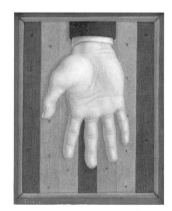

**THE GROPING HAND** c. 1947

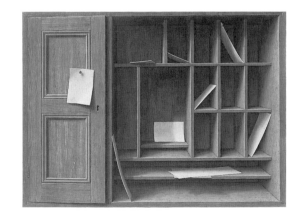

**LETTER BOX** 1951

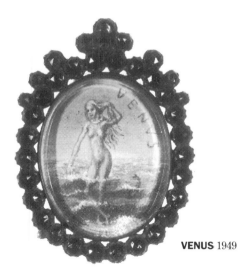

**VENUS** 1949

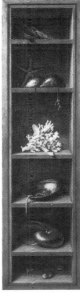

**CABINET** 1954

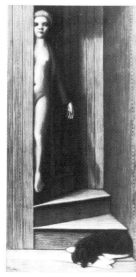

**THE STAIRWAY** 1956

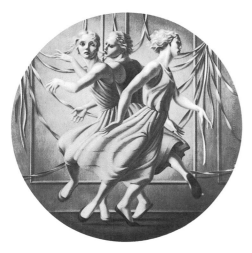

**DANCERS** 1954

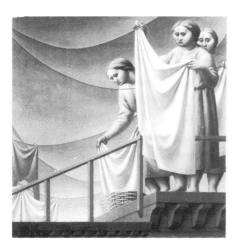

**LAUNDRESSES** 1959

## 1953

**DOORS**
12¹/₂ x 17¹/₂ in.
Virginia Museum of Fine Arts, Richmond
The Adolph D. and Wilkins C. Williams Fund
Illustration, p. 54

**HIGHWAY**
23 x 18 in.
Terra Museum of American Art, Chicago
Daniel J. Terra Collection
Illustration, p. 38

**JUKEBOX**
21 x 14 in.
Private collection
Illustration, p. 52

**RED CARPET**
16 x 20¹/₄ in.
Collection of Nananne Porcher
Illustration, p. 53

## 1954

**CABINET**
32 x 8 in.
Courtesy DC Moore Gallery, NYC

**CUPBOARD II**
Dimensions and whereabouts unknown
Illustration unavailable

**DANCERS**
24 in. diameter
Private collection
Courtesy DC Moore Gallery, NYC

**SHELLS**
Dimensions and whereabouts unknown
Illustration unavailable

**THE SAINT OF BLEECKER STREET**
Four stage set designs
Collection of Gian Carlo Menotti
Illustration, p. 157

## 1955

**THE ARTIST'S DAUGHTER**
24 x 12¹/₂ in.
Private collection
Illustration, p. 94

**FIG TREE**
18 x 24 in.
Collection of Richard Artschwager
Illustration, p. 95

**WINDOW I**
23³/₄ x 16¹/₂ in.
Walker Art Center, Minneapolis, MN
Gift of the T. B. Walker Foundation
Illustration, p. 57

## 1956

**GOVERNMENT BUREAU**
20 x 30 in.
Metropolitan Museum of Art
George A. Hearn Fund, 1956
Illustration, p. 32

**WINDOW II**
24 x 18 in.
Collection of James and Barbara Palmer
Illustration, p. 58

**THE STAIRWAY**
15³/₄ x 8 in.
Private collection

## 1957

**GUITAR**
18 x 24 in.
Private collection
Illustration, p. 60

## 1958

**IN THE SUMMER HOUSE**
24 x 24 in.
National Museum of American Art,
Smithsonian Institution
Gift of the Sara Roby Foundation
Illustration, p. 79

**MEN AND WOMEN FIGHTING**
24 x 30 in.
Michigan Collection
Illustration, p. 39

**WINDOW III**
24 x 18 in.
Arizona State University Art Museum, Tempe
Gift of Jerome H. Loucheim, Jr.
Illustration, p. 59

## 1959

**LAUNDRESSES**
24¹/₂ x 23¹/₂ in.
Private collection

**LOVERS I**
18 x 24 in.
Private collection
Illustration, p. 108

**TABLE I**
24 x 28¹/₂ in.
Private collection
Illustration, p. 111

**SLEEPERS II**
16¹/₈ x 28 in.
The Museum of Modern Art, New York
Larry Aldrich Rockefeller Fund
Illustration, p. 91

**THE WAITING ROOM**
24 x 30 in.
National Museum of American Art,
Smithsonian Institution
Gift of S. C. Johnson & Son, Inc.
Illustration, p. 33

**1959–60**

**ENTERTAINERS**
20 x 24 in.
The Regis Collection, Minneapolis, MN
Illustration, p. 96

**THREE WOMEN**
23 1/2 x 17 1/2 in.
Private collection
Illustration, p. 98

**1960**

**WINDOW IV**
15 x 21 1/2 in.
Collection of Mary Alice Baunberger

**LOVERS II**
22 x 26 in.
Collection of Leslee and David Rogath
Illustration, p. 109

**1960–61**

**MEADOW I**
20 x 28 in.
Collection of Elisabeth and
William M. Landes, Chicago
Illustration, p. 100

**1961–62**

**SINGER**
20 x 16 in.
The Brooklyn Museum of Art
Gift of Mr. and Mrs. Hollis K. Thayer

**1962**

**MIRROR I**
20 x 18 in.
Private collection
Illustration, p. 69

**TOILETTE**
20 1/2 x 17 1/2 in.
Collection of Linda Lichtenberg Kaplan
Washington, DC
Illustration, p. 68

**WINDOW VI**
24 x 18 in.
Private collection
Illustration, p. 61

**1962–63**

**WATCHERS**
26 x 20 in.
Whereabouts unknown
Illustration, p. 99

**1963**

**CARTON OF EGGS**
7 1/2 x 9 1/2 in.
Private collection

**MIRROR II**
20 x 20 in.
Addison Gallery, Phillips Academy, Andover, MA
Gift of R. H. Donnelly Erdman
Illustration, p. 70

**NIGHT I**
14 1/2 x 17 1/2 in.
Private collection
Illustration, p. 92

**SUPPER**
20 x 24 in.
Collection of Mr. and Mrs. John Elliott, Jr.
Illustration, p. 123

**VOICE I**
19 1/2 x 17 1/2 in.
Private collection
Illustration, p. 83

**WINDOW VII** (DESDEMONA)
24 x 21 in.
Terra Museum of American Art, Chicago
Daniel J. Terra Collection
Illustration, p. 62

**1964**

**SLEEP**
18 x 24 in.
Collection of Joann and David Honigman
Photo courtesy of Christie's
Illustration, p. 93

**LUNCH**
20 x 26 in.
The Collection of Philip J. and Suzanne Schiller,
American Social Commentary Art, 1930–1970,
Highland Park, IL
Illustration, p. 40

**1964–65**

**WHITE WALL**
24 x 18 in.
Delaware Art Museum, Wilmington,
F. V. du Pont Acquisition Fund, 1991
Illustration, p. 84

**1965**

**TREE**
22 x 22 in.
Private collection, Canada
Illustration, p. 110

**1966**

**FAREWELL**
24 x 24 in.
Hood Museum of Art,
Dartmouth College, Hanover, NH
Gift of Pennington Haile, Class of 1924
Illustration, p. 85

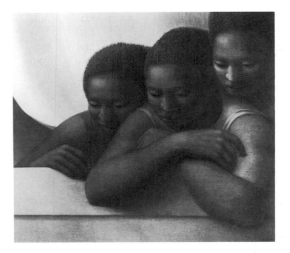

**WINDOW IV** 1960

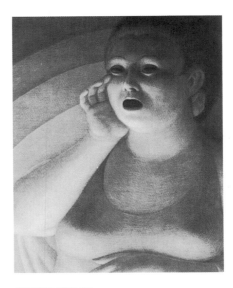

**SINGER** 1961-62

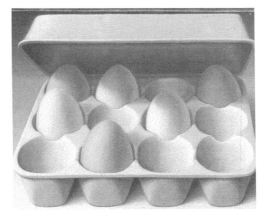

**CARTON OF EGGS** 1963

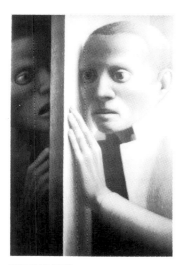

**VOICE II** 1970

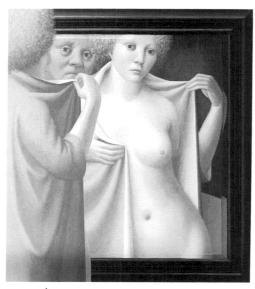

**MIRROR III** 1970-71

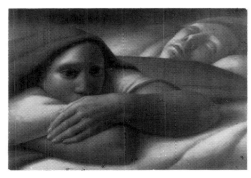

**NIGHT II** 1972

**LANDSCAPE WITH FIGURES**
26 x 30 in.
Private collection
Illustration, p. 36

**TWO HEADS**
12 x 16 in.
Private collection
Illustration, p. 84

**WINDOW VIII**
24 x 20 in.
Private collection
Illustration, p. 63

### 1967

**MAN IN THE BOX**
20 x 24 in.
Collection of Dr. and Mrs. Fouad A. Rabiah
Illustration, p. 87

**ODALISQUE**
24 x 18 in.
Private collection
Illustration, p. 112

**TELLER**
23$^{1/2}$ x 15$^{1/2}$ in.
Collection of Merrill C. Berman
Illustration, p. 41

**THREE HEADS**
Dimensions and whereabouts unknown
Illustration, p. 97

### 1968

**GYPSIES**
23 x 23 in.
Collection of Mr. and Mrs. Joel Wm. Harnett
Illustration, p. 50

**WINDOW IX**
24 x 22 in.
Private collection
Illustration, p. 64

### 1969

**SELF-PORTRAIT**
24 x 19$^{1/2}$ in.
National Academy of Design, New York
Frontispiece

### 1969–70

**DOOR**
20 x 18 in.
New Britain Museum of American Art
Gift of Olga H. Knoepke
Illustration, p. 84

### 1970

**VOICE II**
18 x 12 in.
National Academy of Design, New York

### 1970–71

**MIRROR III**
24 x 20 in.
Whereabouts unknown

**WARD**
19$^{3/4}$ x 29$^{1/2}$ in.
Private collection
Illustration, p. 42

### 1972

**NIGHT II**
12$^{1/2}$ x 20$^{1/2}$ in.
Private collection, New York

### 1973

**STANDING FIGURES**
18 x 24 in.
Private collection
Illustration, p. 119

**SUPERMARKET**
23 x 17$^{1/4}$ in.
The Regis Collection, Minneapolis, MN
Illustration, p. 37

### 1974

**CLAVELES**
24 x 18 in.
New Britain Museum of American Art
Gift of Olga H. Knoepke
Illustration, p. 103

**EL BOTIJO**
18 x 24 in.
Whereabouts unknown

**THE LESSON**
21 x 14 in.
Collection of Henry Crapo, Paris
Illustration, p. 121

**POT OF ALOES**
24 x 18 in.
Private collection
Illustration, p. 104

**TWO WOMEN WITH LAUNDRY**
21 x 18 in.
Private collection, New York
Illustration, p. 102

**WOMAN AT THE WALL**
18 x 11$^{1/2}$ in.
New Britain Museum of American Art
Gift of Olga H. Knoepke
Illustration, p. 120

### 1975

**SIBYL**
23 x 17 in.
Private collection

**DREAMERS**
12¹/₂ x 15¹/₂ in.
Collection of Frank Mainzer

**1975–76**

**SEVILLANAS**
20 x 18 in.
Collection of Leslee and David Rogath
Illustration p. 105

**SLEEPERS III**
11¹/₂ x 20¹/₂ in.
Private collection

**1976**

**MAGDALENE**
18 x 24 in.
Whereabouts unknown

**1976–79**

**MIRROR IV**
24 x 20 in.
Collection of Leslee and David Rogath
Illustration, p. 71

**1977**

**GIRL PRAYING**
17 x 15 in.
Private collection
Illustration, p. 125

**LANTERN**
18 x 16 in.
Private collection
Illustration, p. 80

**ORANT** (APPLAUSE)
23¹/₂ x 15¹/₂ in.
Private collection
Illustration, p. 124

**WARD II**
24 x 18 in.
Private collection, New York

**WOMAN WITH ORANGES**
24 x 18 in.
Private collection
Illustration, p. 106

**1977–79**

**MEADOW II**
21 x 15¹/₂ in.
Private collection
Illustration, p. 101

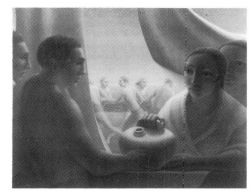

**EL BOTIJO** 1974

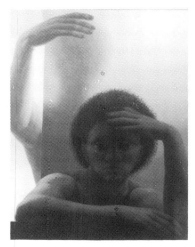

**SIBYL** 1975

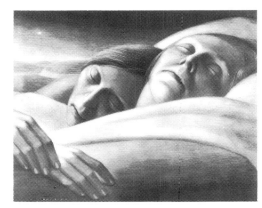

**DREAMERS** 1975

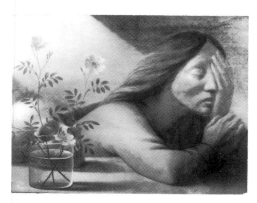

**MAGDALENE** 1976

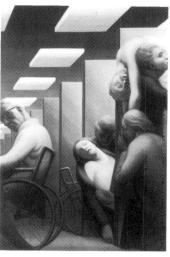

**WARD II** 1977

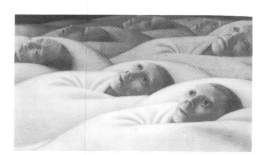

**SLEEPERS III** 1975-76

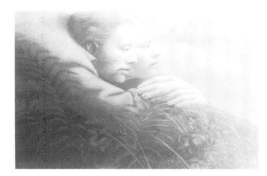

**HILL** 1978

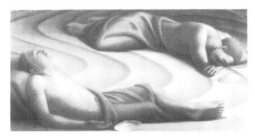

**SLEEPERS IV** 1978

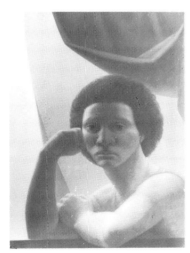

**GIRL IN THE WINDOW** Late 1970s

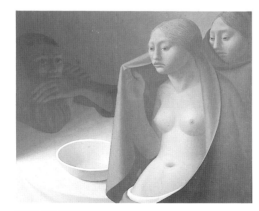

**TABLE II** 1981

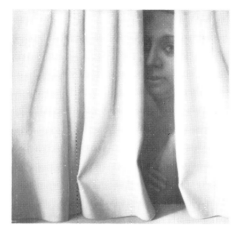

**WHITE CURTAIN II** 1978

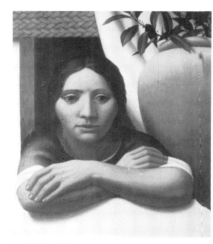

**LAUREL** 1979

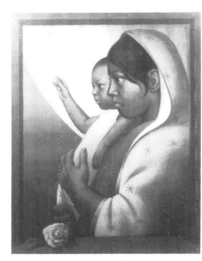

**MOTHER AND CHILD** 1982

1978

**HILL**
16 x 24 in.
Whereabouts unknown

**SLEEPERS IV**
12 x 24 in.
Private collection

**WHITE CURTAIN II**
17¹/₂ x 17¹/₂ in.
Collection of Leon & Irma Rudin, Princeton, NJ

1979

**EMBRACE Î**
24 x 18 in.
Collection of Anka K. Palitc
Illustration, p. 114

**LAUREL**
20 x 18 in.
Private collection

Late 1970s

**GIRL IN THE WINDOW**
24 x 18 in.
Collection of John P. Axelrod, Boston, MA

1980

**STILL LIFE WITH ORANGES**
14¹/₂ x 19¹/₂ in.
Private collection
Illustration, p. 107

**THE SEVEN SACRAMENTS**
(A CELEBRATION OF LIFE)
42 x 132 in.
St. Francis of Assisi Church, Windsor, VT
Illustrations, pp. 130–133

1981

**EMBRACE II**
18 x 24 in.
Collection of Kitty and Herbert Glantz
Illustration, p. 115

**TABLE II**
24 x 30 in.
Private collection

1982

**MOTHER AND CHILD**
20 x 18 in.
Private collection

**WAITING ROOM II**
19 x 37 in.
Private collection
Illustration, p. 44

**UN BALLO IN MASCHERE**
22 x 30 in.
Egg tempera on cardboard
Collection of Mark L. Brock
Illustration, p. 137

1983

**EMBRACE III**
16 x 19 in.
Private collection
Illustration, p. 116

**CORPORATE DECISION**
18 x 24 in.
Collection of Frank Mainzer
Illustration, p. 45

1984

**EMBRACE IV**
16 x 19¼ in.
Private collection

**STATIONS OF THE CROSS**
Fourteen panels,
each 11¾ x 11¾ in.
St. Francis of Assisi Church,
Windsor, VT
Illustration, p. 135

**WOMEN AT THE WALL**
23½ x 19½ in.
Private collection

1985

**LANDSCAPE WITH FIGURES II**
22¼ x 32¼ in.
Courtesy DC Moore Gallery, NYC
Illustration, p. 126

1986

**EMBRACE OF PEACE I**
15½ x 25¼ in.
Whereabouts unknown
Illustration, p. 127

**LANTERNS**
22 x 26 in.
Collection of Leslee and David Rogath
Illustration, p. 81

**TERMINAL**
21 x 39 in.
Private collection
Illustration, pp. 46–47

1987

**WINDOW X**
23½ x 17¼ in.
Whereabouts unknown
Illustration, p. 65

1987–88

**GIRL WITH BASKET**
24 x 18 in.
Collection of James Francis Trezza
Illustration, p. 73

1988

**EMBRACE OF PEACE II**
18 x 30 in.
Private collection

**WOMAN WITH ROSE**
18¾ x 16½ in.
Collection of Mr. & Mrs. John O'Donnell
Courtesy James Corcoran Gallery

1989

**LANDSCAPE WITH FIGURES III**
20 x 30 in.
Private collection

1990

**GARDEN WALL**
15¼ x 23¼ in.
Private collection
Illustration, p. 117

1991

**UNTITLED**
19 x 23½ in.
Whereabouts unknown
Illustration, p. 66

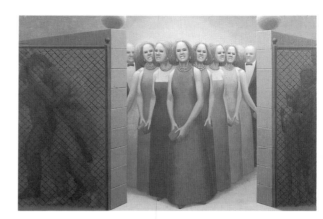

**LANDSCAPE WITH FIGURES III** 1989

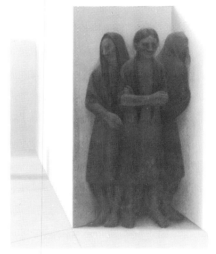

**WOMEN AT THE WALL** 1984

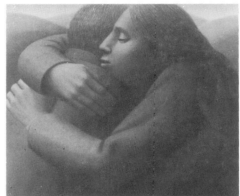

**EMBRACE IV** 1984

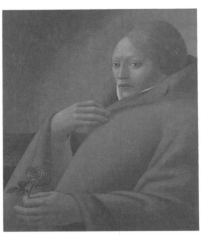

**WOMAN WITH ROSE** 1988

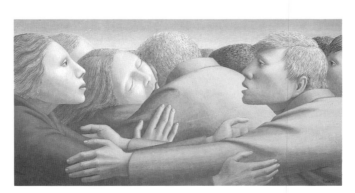

**EMBRACE OF PEACE II** 1988

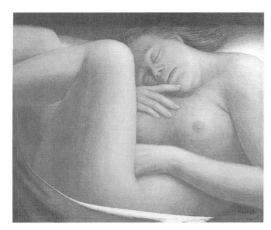

**SLEEPING WOMAN** 1998

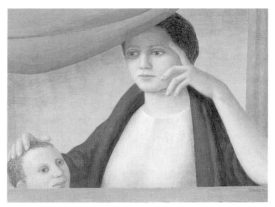

**WOMAN AND CHILD** 2000

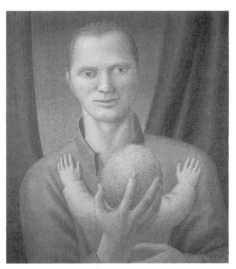

**FATHER AND CHILD** 2000

1992

**THE DREAM**
24 x 18 in.
Courtesy DC Moore Gallery, NYC
Illustration, p. 128

**WOMAN WITH A SPRIG OF LAUREL**
18 x 24 in.
Collection of Peter and Susan Tuteur
Illustration, p. 72

1993

**THE COUPLE**
18 x 17$3/4$ in.
Collection of Mr. & Mrs. Theodore Baum
Illustration, p. 138

1994

**SELF PORTRAIT**
14 x 12 in.
Private collection
Illustration, p. 136

1996

**DARK ANGEL**
24 x 19 in.
Courtesy DC Moore Gallery, NYC
Illustration, p. 140

1997

**MOON RISE**
17$1/4$ x 26 in.
Private collection
Illustration, p. 143

**POTTED ORANGE TREE**
18 x 16 in.
Private collection
Illustration, p. 142

1998

**MAN IN A TREE**
14 x 17 in.
Collection of James and Barbara Palmer
Illustration, p. 143

**SLEEPING WOMAN**
14 x 17 in.
Private collection

1999

**LANDSCAPE WITH FIGURES IV**
19$1/2$ x 29 $1/4$ in.
Private collection
Illustration, p. 139

**WINDOW XI**
24 x 20 in.
Courtesy DC Moore Gallery, NYC
Illustration, p. 141

2000

**WOMAN AND CHILD**
17$1/4$ x 23 in.
Private collection

**FATHER AND CHILD**
24 x 20 in.
Private collection

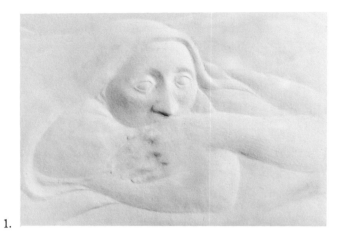

1.

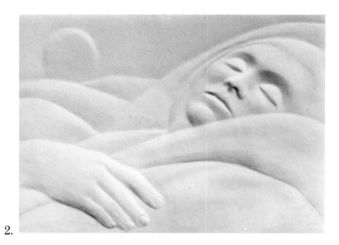

2.

## THE GRAPHIC WORK

**U**nlike his mentor, Reginald Marsh, Tooker resisted the idea of making prints, even though the print boom of the late 1960s and early '70s brought Tooker more and more requests from fine print publishers to consider making lithographs. At least one of these requests was accompanied by a handsome blandishment in the form of a substantial check. Tooker, rather than being seduced or flattered, was concerned. "What if what I make isn't worth what he has paid me?" The check was sent back with a polite but firm "No."

One of the reasons that the artist has resisted making prints his concern for the finesse of his draftsmanship. Tooker regards drawing as he has traditionally used it simply as a tool of translation, first in creating the study for a painting, then in transferring it in the simplest and most direct way to the panel. It is a medium necessary in the production of a painting but not much more. The prospect of drawing upon a stone, with every mark to be visible and preserved, was a bit overwhelming to him.

Yet the idea of the multiple image intrigued him, and in 1975, with little technical assistance, he sculpted a shallow relief in artist's wax. It was a version of *Night* and bore the same title. The wax original was cast into a negative mold of bronze. Moist paper was pressed into the mold, creating a blind embossing, a print without ink.

This first attempt at printmaking, which required remarkable finesse, was a surprising excursion for one as technically conservative as Tooker. The finished work, however, as is the case with Tooker's paintings, was not about line but about volume and the

1. NIGHT (*The Dreamer*), 1975.
   Intaglio, 7½ x 10¼ in.
   Edition of 100 embossed at Joel Meisner
   & Company, Inc., Foundry, Plainview,
   New York, on Arches buff paper, signed
   and numbered from 1/100 through
   100/100.

2. REPOSE (*Sleep*), 1976.
   Intaglio, 9¾ x 12½ in.
   Edition of 150 embossed at Joel Meisner
   & Company, Inc., Foundry, Plainview,
   New York, on Arches buff paper, signed
   and numbered 1/150 through 150/150.

3. VOICE, 1977.
   Lithograph, 11 x 9¾ in.
   Edition of 125 printed at Editions Press,
   San Francisco, on Rives BFK gray
   paper, 21½ x 18 in., signed and numbered
   from 1/125 through 125/125.
   Publisher: Editions Press, San Francisco

4. MIRROR, 1978.
   Lithograph, 20 x 16 in.
   Edition of 125 printed at Editions Press,
   San Francisco, on Arches Cover white
   paper, 27 x 22 in., in two colors (black
   over ivory), signed and numbered from
   1/125 through 125/125.
   Publisher: Editions Press, San Francisco

3.

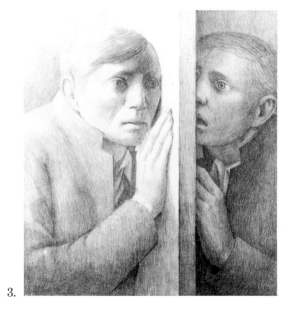

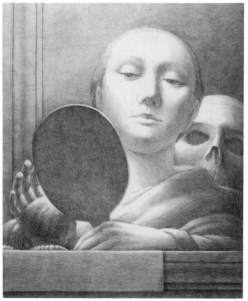

4.

evanescent influence of light. One is reminded of Tooker's great appreciation of early Italian Renaissance relief sculpture. Another relief print, *Repose*, quite similar in subject to *Night*, followed in 1979. This version, whose finish is somewhat smoother, showed a refinement of Tooker's wax-working technique.

In 1977, Tooker created the first of a small group of black-and-white lithographs that now number five. With one exception these lithographs – *Voice* (1977), *Mirror* (1978), *Lovers* (1982), *Embrace II* (1984) and *Self-Portrait* (1984) – reiterate themes of earlier paintings. *Self-Portrait* is an exception because Tooker has never painted his self-portrait in this manner. The lithographs show that Tooker's draftsmanship is simple, without artifice, and used directly in the service of the imagery, in order to form strong volumes and contrasts between light and dark. Even in black and white, Tooker delights in carving the image from the picture plane.

In 1982 Tooker was approached by a print publisher who was developing a series of prints and posters by artists to benefit the Metropolitan Opera. Each artist was asked to produce a color study that would then be translated by the chromiste (a lithographic artisan) onto lithographic plates. Tooker chose to illustrate a scene from Giuseppe Verdi's *Un Ballo in Maschera*, one that is remarkably reminiscent of two earlier paintings, *Entertainers* and *Sevillanas*. The illumination appears to come from footlights, lighting the three figures from below, throwing the eyes into shadow. The background is dominated by an overscaled egg-and-dart molding which presses the background close to the picture plane.

In the process of creating this print Tooker made a tempera painting on cardboard, then painted a black-and-white version as the key plate from which the chromiste developed the form, using the color study to closely duplicate the original colors. This print was produced in a limited edition and offset as a poster as well.

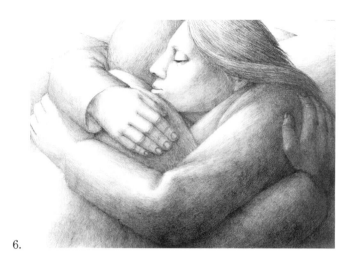

6.

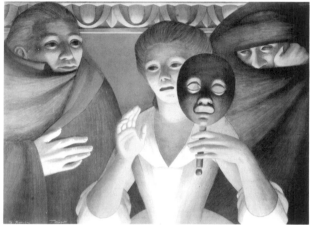

7.

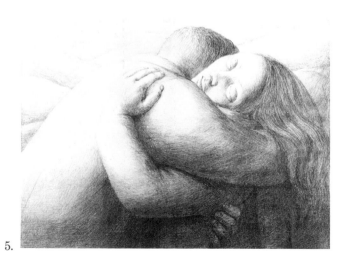

5.

5. LOVERS, 1982.
Lithograph, 12 x 16 in.
Edition of 175 printed at George C. Miller & Son, New York, on Rives BFK white paper, 16½ x 20 in., signed and numbered 1/175 through 175/175.
Publisher: Imago Imprint, New York

6. EMBRACE II, 1984
Lithograph, 13½ x 17½ in.
Edition of 175 printed at George C. Miller & Son, New York, on Rives BFK white paper, 16½ x 20 in., signed and numbered from 1/175 through 175/175.

7. UN BALLO IN MASCHERA, 1983
Twenty-six color lithographs, 22 x 30 in.
Edition of 250 printed at American Atelier, New York, on Somerset soft white paper, 22 x 30 in., signed and numbered from 1/250 through 250/250.
Deluxe edition of 25 printed at American Atelier, New York, on Inomachi nacre paper, 22 x 30 in., signed and numbered from I/XXV through XXV/XXV.
Publisher: Circle Fine Art Corporation, Chicago and New York

8. SELF-PORTRAIT I, 1984
Lithograph, 8½ x 7¾ in.
Edition of 75 printed at George C. Miller & Son, New York, on Rives BFK white paper, 18 x 14 in., signed and numbered I/LXXV through LXXV/LXXV.
Publisher: Imago Imprint, New York

9. SELF-PORTRAIT II, 1985. (not shown)
Lithograph, 8½ x 7¾ in.
Edition of 250 printed at George C. Miller & Son, New York, on Rives BFK white paper, 10⅝ x 9¼ in., signed and numbered 1/250 through 250/250.
Included in specially bound collector's edition in 1985.
Publisher: Imago Imprint, New York

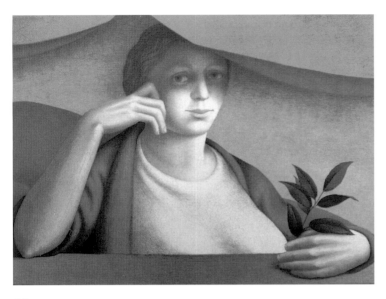

11.

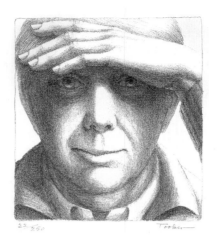

8.

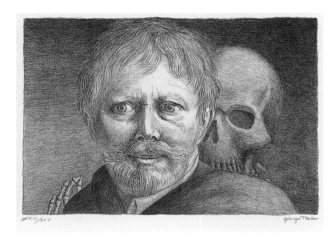

12.

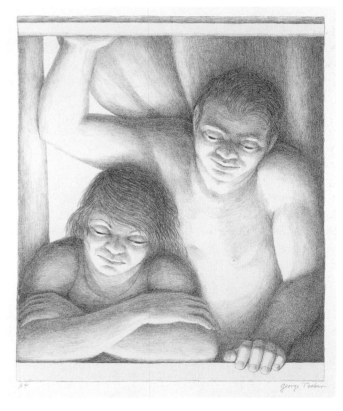

10.

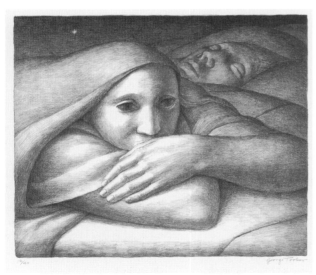

13.

10.  WINDOW, 1994.
     Lithograph, 23³/₄ x 19³/₄ in. Edition of
     175 printed in two colors; black on
     cream ground on 30¹/₄ x 25¹/₂ in.
     White Arches paper by George C. Miller
     & Son. Publisher: Chameleon Books,
     Inc., MA

11.  WOMAN WITH A SPRIG OF LAUREL,
     1992. Color lithograph, 17³/₄ x 23¹/₂ in.
     Edition of 125 printed on White Arches
     22¹/₂ x 28¹/₂ paper at George C. Miller
     & Son. Publisher: Marisa del Re
     Gallery, NY

12.  SELF-PORTRAIT, 1996
     Lithograph, Image, 12 x 18 in. Edition
     of 50 printed at Perry Tymeson,
     Petersburg Studios, Jersey City, NJ, on
     18 x 24 in. Somerset Soft White paper.
     Publisher: American Academy of Arts
     and Letters, New York, 1998

13.  NIGHT, 1998
     Lithograph, 14³/₄ x 18³/₄ inc. Edition
     of 40 printed at Perry Tymeson,
     Petersburg Studios, Jersey City, NJ, on
     21 x 24 in. Somerset Soft White paper.
     Publisher: George Tooker

## STAGE DESIGN
## THE SAINT OF BLEECKER STREET

In 1954, Tooker was approached by his friend Lincoln Kirstein, then managing director of the City Center of Music and Drama, to design the sets for *The Saint of Bleecker Street*, a new opera by Gian Carlo Menotti. The opera had been commissioned by the City Center, which ran an active program of musical and dramatic productions from its theater on West Fifty-fifth Street. Although commissioned by the City Center, the opera was not premiered there; for financial reasons it opened at the Broadway Theater in New York in December 1954.

The story was set on Bleecker Street (from which Tooker had only recently moved, and which was then as much a part of Manhattan's Little Italy as Greenwich Village). The two major protagonists were Michele and his sister, Annina. Michele was a person of this world, as passionate, angry, and unbelieving as Annina was saintly, trusting, and devoutly religious. The opera is fired by the conflict of temporal and spiritual sensibilities and of the struggle between the culture of "the old country" as it is subsumed by life in the new country. Menotti had seen Tooker's painting *Festa* at Kirstein's home and felt that it illustrated visually the spirit he was attempting to achieve in the opera.

Tooker accepted the commission to produce four sets for the opera. Tooker also agreed to an exhibition of the designs at his gallery following the premiere of the opera. Only one requirement remained to be fulfilled. To receive credit for his designs, Tooker had to become a member of the Scenic Designers' Union. The test for union membership was complex, and one part of it required the painting of a design on a large canvas stage flat. Tooker, who had crammed and practiced for the exam, overcompensated for his usual tight painting style and was flunked for painting the flat too broadly and without sufficient detail.

Thus, while Tooker did design the sets, credit went to others. The exhibition of the set designs, impossible now under his own name unless he was willing to see the theatrical unions picket the theater and close the production, was hastily transformed into a mini-survey exhibition of paintings from the previous seven years borrowed from museums and private collectors. For many years it was thought that the opera's producers had destroyed the original designs. Everyone, Tooker included, was told that this had been done to avoid any hint of conflict with the powerful theatrical unions. Recently, however, Menotti acknowledged to George Tooker that he spirited the designs away and had the producers claim that they had been destroyed. We are now told that they are safe – but no longer in the United States.

Lincoln Kirstein described *The Saint of Bleecker Street* as having "the smashing theatrical grip of a street accident," and he credited that to Menotti's understanding of "Cocteau's formula for poetry: the rehabilitation of the commonplace."[19] In addition, Kirstein noted one of Menotti's most important dramatic strengths – that "he has never failed to involve us in the commonality of intense experience."

Kirstein complimented Tooker's set designs, declaring that "Tooker had actually illustrated the whole of *The Saint of Bleecker Street* before he had met Menotti or before Menotti had written the opera. But when Menotti saw the pictures, . . . he knew immediately that Tooker's version was his own." Thus it may also be speculated that Tooker was not only selected to design the sets, but that his paintings exerted a strong a priori influence on the formation and composition of the opera itself. The style of the paintings, Kirstein recalled, conveyed "an airless dignity, an impersonal grandeur . . . The ordinary people in their workclothes are seen uniformed in a simple splendor. The forms are less generalized than enlarged. The pictures are never big, but they seem huge because the scale, the mastery of the achieved perspective in relation to the human figures, is so well realized."

The sets apparently functioned well, for Tooker had edited and selected the elements of each set carefully. They created a real sense of place and people and helped to give the drama its identity, but without extraneous details that might detract from the performers themselves.

Based on Tooker's prototype paintings, the four sets comprised the interior of Michele's and Annina's cold-water flat, an Italian religious street festival, the interior of a Neapolitan restaurant, and the first level of a subway station.

The flat is drawn from *The Chess Game*, although the view has been turned 90 degrees and one wall has been stripped away. The partition dividing the two rooms is indicated only vestigially by a bit of wall which shelters the stove. The living arrangements are also indicated schematically: a bed in the right corner, the stove at center stage, and a homely shrine (a small table covered with a cloth, surmounted by a chromolithograph of the Madonna and Child and festooned with ribbons and crepe paper) to the left. Light streams into the room from a glazed door that obviously opens onto the front room of the flat on the left, for the window at stage center looks out on an airshaft. The floors have been covered in those long-extinct linoleum rugs, and it is the abrupt shift of patterns on the floor rather than the fragment of wall that indicates the separation of the stage into two rooms.

The second scene was set at a street festival. The street has been adorned with lighted arches – "electric pearls," in Kirstein's evocative phrase – which march across the backstage and disappear down the street to the right. The area to the right of the stage is clearly a direct reference to *Festa*, but the position of the viewer in relation to the street is quite different. The perspective the audience sees is from the back of a vacant lot that fronts on the

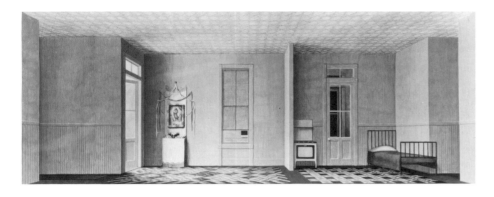

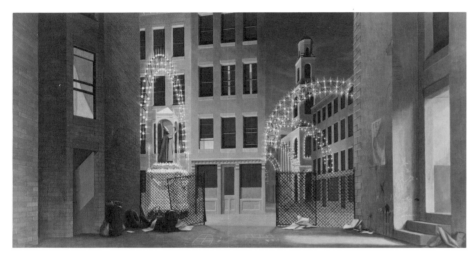

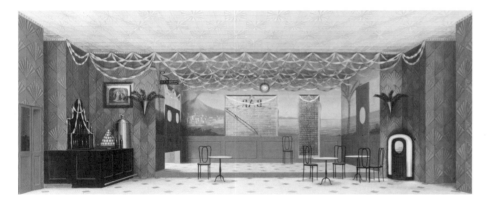

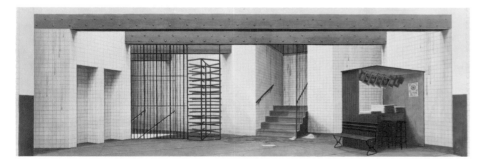

street. The action is set both in the street and the lot, which is separated from the street only by a disheveled woven-wire fence and sagging gate. It is not difficult to see this bit of dirty asphalt as a commonplace variant of the plaza that fronts the figures in *Audience*, and, indeed, there are the same sorts of openings here, though more recognizable as entrances to basements or back stairways, bits of everyday New York, which Tooker so transformed in *Audience*.

The second act is set in a little Neapolitan bar and restaurant. The jukebox of *Jukebox* stands to the right, and the room gives us a chance to consider – after having seen so many fragments – what a full "Tooker room" might have looked like. This room is an amalgam of styles, typical of such places, and the design has obviously been based on close observation, even as it has been subjected to Tooker's strong ordering sensibilities. The furniture is pure Tooker and drawn directly from *Gypsies*, as are the side wall and ceiling treatments of pressed tin (with the crepe paper hanging from the ceiling, courtesy of *Jukebox*). The most interesting aspect of this set is its back wall. A grand scene of the Bay of Naples with Vesuvius smoking in the left background is obviously a requirement of such establishments, although here a major part of the vista is broken by a doorway and window opening onto an alley stairway. Several levels of illusion are at work here. The Bay of Naples vista, clearly an illusion, is perforated by the doorway and window fronting on an almost blank brick wall, and, at least in the rendering, the image seems curiously suggestive of the paintings of René Magritte. The window filled with bricks is particularly provocative.

The major scene of the third act is played in the upper level of a subway station – in Kirstein's words, "a labyrinthine crossroads where the corridors lead down to the black cars or up to the bright sky." It is here that Michele and Annina have their final meeting. He is by then a wanted and hunted criminal, she an almost canonized saint. Menotti's score reconstructs the rumble of arriving and departing trains, while Tooker's design, replete with stained walls, steel beams, and the everpresent gridded tile walls, is a paradigm of depersonalized processing, a perfect foil for the emotional apogee of the opera.

It is unfortunate that the original designs are so far from view, for Tooker would seem to have captured so well the flavor of Little Italy in New York, of sanctity and brutality amid the rubbish that marks the city. They offered, Kirstein said, "an atmosphere of pregnant emptiness, the focusing on a site where incident is about to take place, similar to the clear, blank, imposing backgrounds of the predella panels of Sassetta and Botticelli, but painted as if Botticelli and Sassetta were living in New York today: that is what Menotti has hoped for, and that is what he has been given." Indeed it is a tribute to George Tooker that he could change the size and scale of his work so completely and in so doing transform it so well into a workable geometry for Menotti's opera.

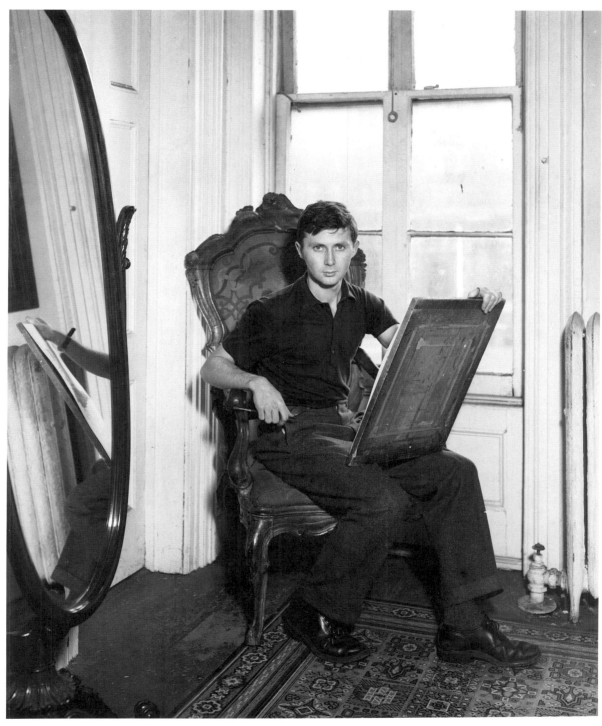

Photograph by George Platt Lynes, c. 1948.

# BIOGRAPHY

George Clair Tooker, Jr. was born in Brooklyn, New York on August 5, 1920, the first child of a municipal bond broker and his Cuban-American wife. (Tooker also has a younger sister, Mary.) Shortly after he was born, the family moved from Brooklyn to Bellport, on the south shore of Long Island. In the 1920s and '30s this area was much more rural than it is today and New York City was much more remote in its influence. Tooker's father worked for a group of small Long Island banks and the family lived comfortably.

At the age of seven, Tooker began two years of painting lessons with a family friend, Malcolm Fraser, a painter in the Barbizon tradition who lived nearby. Tooker remembers that Fraser tended to "finish" his students' paintings to insure that they would be favorably received, yet at an early age Tooker learned the rudiments of academic composition and paint handling.

Tooker attended high school in Bellport, but because his parents were concerned that their son was not receiving a solid academic education there, he spent his last two years at Phillips Academy, Andover, Massachusetts. Tooker disliked the school intensely. It was then rather straight-laced. Most of the students were oriented toward business and finance and he recalls that the school "trained them to hide their emotions." His only academic interest was English, but he spent a great deal of time in the school's art studio making landscape drawings and watercolors. The Phillips Academy experience also introduced him to the other side of American urban life, as he saw the effects of the Depression on the mill towns to the north of Andover. Tooker remembers that he was deeply angry at the social and economic imbalance that put people out of work, but at the same time he enjoyed the dances and parties hosted by those whom the system continued to support so well. He graduated from Phillips Academy in 1938 and attended Harvard College, majoring in English Literature. He spent much of his spare time at the Fogg Art Museum, and in Cambridge and the towns surrounding Boston making watercolor sketches of landscapes and buildings. At Harvard he became involved in several radical organizations but dropped them because he found their answers to social and economic problems to be too doctrinaire and ultimately "boring." He did, however, begin to sense the uses of art as a tool of social expression and social change. He was especially interested in the political and emotional content of the Mexican painters, particularly David Alferos Sequeiros and José Clemente Orozco.

Tooker graduated from Harvard in 1942 and immediately entered the Marine Corps Officers Candidate School, but an old stomach ailment developed into a serious problem and he was discharged after a few months. He had wanted to study art for some time and now his parents supported him in doing so. In the spring of 1943 he enrolled at the Art Students League in New York, which he attended for two years, studying with Reginald Marsh, Kenneth Hayes Miller, and Harry Sternberg.

Tooker met the painter Paul Cadmus in 1944 and later, through Cadmus, met Jared and Margaret French. With Cadmus's guidance Tooker began to paint in the traditional Renaissance tempera technique that marks his mature style.

In 1945 with a stipend of $90 a month from his family, Tooker moved to a cold-water flat on Bleecker Street in New York's Greenwich Village (rent $17 per month) where he was to live for five years. His friendship with Cadmus and the Frenches grew, and in 1949 Tooker and Cadmus spent six months traveling in Italy and France. It was later that year that he met the painter William Christopher with whom he shared his life until Christopher's death in 1973. In 1950 Tooker and Christopher moved to an illegal loft on West Eighteenth Street, where they made custom furniture to support themselves. Although his painting *The Subway* had been bought by the Whitney Museum that same year, the income from his artwork was not yet enough to live on. In 1953 they bought and renovated a brownstone on State Street in Brooklyn Heights.

Tooker's painting received increasing recognition with one-person exhibitions in New York City in 1951 and 1955 and the commission to design the sets for Gian Carlo Menotti's opera *The Saint of Bleecker Street* in 1954. In the late 1950s, inspired by the French's summer place in eastern Vermont, Tooker and Christopher acquired land north of Hartland and built a weekend house, which was subsequently expanded several times. They moved to Vermont permanently in 1960 and sold the house in Brooklyn Heights.

Four more one-person exhibitions in New York galleries followed in 1960, 1962, 1964, and 1967, and his work was included in numerous group exhibitions during this time. He taught at the Art Students League from 1965 to 1968. In 1968 William Christopher's health had deteriorated to the point where the Vermont winters were too rigorous, and they sought a location in Europe where they could spend the winter season. They finally settled in Malaga, Spain, on the Mediterranean coast, and Tooker maintained the apartment there until 1990.

William Christopher died in Spain in late 1973 and Tooker spent most of 1974 there settling his estate. That same year, the first major museum survey exhibition of Tooker's work was organized by the Fine Arts Museums of San Francisco at the California Palace of the Legion of Honor. The exhibition subsequently traveled to the Museum of Contemporary Art, Chicago; the Whitney Museum of American Art, New York; and the Indianapolis Museum of Art. In 1976 Tooker became a Roman Catholic and a parishioner of St. Francis of Assisi Church in Windsor, Vermont. In late 1977 the church burned and in 1979 while it was undergoing reconstruction Tooker agreed to create a major painting for it. That painting, *The Seven Sacraments*, was dedicated in January 1981.

George Tooker now lives and works in Hartland, Vermont.

T. H. G.

## SOLO EXHIBITIONS

2000
DC Moore Gallery, New York, NY

Hart Gallery at the Guild Art Center,
Northampton, MA

1998
DC Moore Gallery, New York, NY

1996
*Reality and Dream: The Art of George Tooker*,
Ogunquit Museum of American Art, ME

1994
*50 Years of Painting and Study Drawings*,
Addison Gallery of American Art, Andover, MA

1992
*Tooker's Women*, Marisa del Re Gallery,
New York, NY

1989
*George Tooker: Paintings and Drawings,
1946–1989*, Marsh Gallery, University of
Richmond, VA

1988
Marisa del Re Gallery, New York, NY

1987
*George Tooker: Working Drawings*,
Robert Hull Fleming Museum, University of
Vermont, Burlington

*The Paintings of George Tooker: Spoleto at the
Gibbes Art Gallery*, Gibbes Art Gallery (now
Gibbes Museum of Art), Charleston, SC

1985
*George Tooker: Paintings 1948–1985*, Marisa
del Re Gallery, New York, NY

1974
*George Tooker: Paintings 1947–1973*, Fine
Arts Museums of San Francisco, CA (traveled
to: Museum of Contemporary Art, Chicago,
IL; Whitney Museum of American Art, New
York, NY; Indianapolis Museum of Art, IN)

1967
Durlacher Brothers, New York, NY

*George Tooker: Paintings and Drawings*,
Jaffe-Friede Gallery, Hopkins Center,
Dartmouth College, Hanover, NH

1964
Durlacher Brothers, New York, NY

1962
Robert Isaacson Gallery, New York, NY

1960
Robert Isaacson Gallery, New York, NY

1955
Edwin Hewitt Gallery, New York, NY

1951
Edwin Hewitt Gallery, New York, NY

## GROUP EXHIBITIONS

2001
*American Tableaux*, Walker Art Center,
Minneapolis, MN

*Cadmus, French, Tooker*, Columbus Museum
of Art, Columbus, OH

*Interwoven Lives: George Platt Lynes and His
Friends*, DC Moore Gallery, New York, NY

*Magic Vision*, Arkansas Arts Center, Little
Rock, AR

*Re-presenting, Representation*, organized by
the Arnot Art Museum, Corning Gallery, New
York, NY

*Self Made Men*, curated by Alexi Worth,
DC Moore Gallery, New York, NY

2000
*Figures and Forms: Selections from the Terra
Foundation for the Arts*, Terra Museum of
American Art, Chicago, IL

*League Masters Then: A Selection of Works by
Artists Associated with the Art Students
League of New York*, Art Students League,
New York, NY

*Making Choices 1929–1955*, Museum of
Modern Art, New York, NY

*Twentieth-Century American Art: The
Ebsworth Collection*, National Gallery of Art,
Washington, DC (traveled to: Seattle Art
Museum, Seattle, WA)

1999
*The American Century 1900–1950*, Whitney
Museum of American Art, New York, NY

*Magic Realism: A Selection of Paintings,
1925–1998*, Beth Urdang Gallery, Boston, MA

*Magic Realism: America's Response to
Surrealism*, Southern Alleghenies Museum of
Art, Loretto, PA

*Men without Women, Paul Cadmus as Curator*,
National Academy of Design Museum, New
York, NY

*Modern American Realism: The Sara Roby
Foundation Collection from the National
Museum of American Art*, Everson Museum
of Art, Syracuse, NY

1997
*Civil Progress: Images of Black America*,
Mary Ryan Gallery, New York, NY

*Views from Abroad: European Perspectives on
American Art 3: American Realities*, curated
by Nicholas Serota and Sandy Nairne, Tate
Gallery, London, and Adam D. Weinberg,
Whitney Museum of American Art, New York,
NY

1996
*In the Eye of the Storm: An Art of Conscience,
1930–1970, Selections from the Collection of
Philip J. and Suzanne Schiller*, Parrish Art
Museum, Southampton, NY

1991
*Contemporary Surrealism*, New Jersey Center
for the Visual Arts, Summit, NJ

1990
*Art What Thou Eat: Images of Food in
American Art*, Edith C. Blum Art Institute,
Bard College, Annandale-on-Hudson, NY

*Cadmus, French and Tooker: The Early Years*,
Whitney Museum of American Art at Philip
Morris, New York, NY

*Close Encounters: The Art of Paul Cadmus,
Jared French and George Tooker*, Midtown
Galleries, New York, NY

1987
*Modern American Realism: The Sara Roby
Foundation Collection*, National Museum of
American Art, Washington, DC

1985
*Surreal City, 1930–1950*, Whitney Museum of
American Art at Philip Morris, New York, NY

1984
*Contemporary Artists in Vermont*, Robert Hull
Fleming Museum, University of Vermont,
Burlington

1983
*Born in Brooklyn*, Rotunda Gallery, Brooklyn,
NY

*Dreams and Nightmares, Utopian Visions in
Modern Art*, Hirshhorn Museum and
Sculpture Garden, Washington, DC

*1984 Preview*, Ronald Feldman Gallery, New
York, NY

1982
*Homo Sapiens, the Many Images*, Aldrich
Museum of Contemporary Art, Ridgefield, CT

*Realism and Realities: The Other Side of
American Painting, 1940–1960*, Rutgers
University Art Gallery, New Brunswick, NJ
(traveled to: Montgomery Museum of Fine
Arts, AL; Art Gallery, University of Maryland,
College Park)

*Selected Works on Paper*, Marisa del Re
Gallery, New York, NY

*Solitude: Inner Visions in American Art*,
Terra Museum of American Art, Evanston, IL

1971
*The Hydeman Collection*, Fuller Memorial,
Brockton Art Center, MA

1969
*Annual Exhibition of Contemporary American
Painting*, Whitney Museum of American Art,
New York, NY

*Human Concern, Personal Torment: The
Grotesque in American Art*, Whitney Museum
of American Art, New York, NY (traveled to:
University Art Museum, Berkeley, CA)

1967
*Annual Exhibition of Contemporary American
Painting*, Whitney Museum of American Art,
New York, NY

1966
*Annual Exhibition of Painting and Sculpture*,
Pennsylvania Academy of Fine Arts,
Philadelphia, PA

First Flint Invitational: An Exhibition of Contemporary Painting and Sculpture, Flint Institute of Arts, De Waters Art Center, MI

1965
Annual Exhibition of Contemporary American Painting, Whitney Museum of American Art, New York, NY

1964
Between the Fairs: 25 Years of American Art, 1939–1964, Whitney Museum of American Art, New York, NY

Realist Painting: Yesterday, Today, and Tomorrow, Silvermine Guild of Artists, New Canaan, CT

Trends in Painting, 11th Annual Exhibition of Contemporary American Painting, Bayonne Jewish Community Center, NJ

1963
Annual Exhibition of Contemporary American Painting, Whitney Museum of American Art, New York, NY

Painting and Drawing the Nude, Part II: The Female, Banfer Gallery, New York, NY

Paintings from the Museum of Modern Art, New York, National Gallery of Art, Washington, DC

1962
American Painting, 1962, Virginia Museum of Fine Arts, Richmond, VA

Art: USA: Now, Johnson Collection of Contemporary American Painting (traveled throughout the United States and abroad)

1961
Annual Exhibition of Contemporary American Painting, Whitney Museum of American Art, New York, NY

1960
An Exhibition of Works by Newly Elected Members and Recipients of Honors and Awards, National Institute of Arts and Letters, American Academy Art Gallery, New York, NY

Painting and Sculpture Acquisitions, Museum of Modern Art, New York, NY

1959
The Collection of the Sara Roby Foundation, Whitney Museum of American Art, New York, NY

69th Annual American Exhibition: Paintings and Sculpture, Art Institute of Chicago, IL

1958
Annual Exhibition of Contemporary American Painting, Whitney Museum of American Art, New York, NY

Festival of Two Worlds, Spoleto, Italy

1957
Annual Exhibition of Contemporary American Painting, Whitney Museum of American Art, New York, NY

Contemporary Directions: The Realist Painters, Silvermine Guild of Artists, New Canaan, CT

1956
American Artists Paint the City, 28th Biennale, Venice, Italy

Annual Exhibition, Nebraska Art Association, University of Nebraska Art Galleries, Lincoln, NE

Annual Exhibition of Contemporary American Painting, Whitney Museum of American Art, New York, NY

An Exhibition of Works by Candidates for Grants in Art, 1956, National Institute of Arts and Letters, American Academy Art Gallery, New York, NY

The First Annual Purchase Awards Exhibition for Contemporary American Painters, 1950–1955, Thomas Welton Stanford Art Gallery, Stanford University, CA

1955
Annual Exhibition of Contemporary American Painting, Whitney Museum of American Art, New York, NY

The New Decade: 35 American Painters and Sculptors, Whitney Museum of American Art, New York, NY (traveled to: San Francisco Museum of Art; University of California, Los Angeles; Colorado Springs Fine Arts Center, CO; City Art Museum of St. Louis, MO)

1954
American Painting, 1954, Virginia Museum of Fine Arts, Richmond, VA (traveled to: Des Moines Art Center, IA)

Reality and Fantasy, 1900–1954, Walker Art Center, Minneapolis, MN

64th Annual American Exhibition: Paintings and Sculpture, Art Institute of Chicago, IL

Third Annual Exhibition, Young America: Artists under Forty, Brandeis University, Waltham, MA

1953
Annual Exhibition of Contemporary American Painting, Whitney Museum of American Art, New York, NY

63rd Annual Exhibition, Nebraska Art Association, University of Nebraska Art Galleries, Lincoln, NE

1952
Annual Exhibition of Contemporary American Painting, Whitney Museum of American Art, New York, NY

Annual Exhibition of Contemporary American Sculpture, Whitney Museum of American Art, New York, NY

Contemporary Drawings from 12 Countries, 1945–1952, Art Institute of Chicago, IL

5th Annual Exhibition of Contemporary American Painting, California Legion of Honor, Fine Arts Museums of San Francisco, CA

147th Annual Exhibition of Painting and Sculpture, Pennsylvania Academy of Fine Arts, Philadelphia, PA

39th Annual Exhibition of Contemporary American Paintings, Toledo Museum of Art, OH

1951
The New Reality: Exhibition of Paintings, Edwin Hewitt Gallery, New York, NY

60th Annual American Exhibition: Paintings and Sculpture, Art Institute of Chicago, IL

22nd Biennial Exhibition of Contemporary American Oil Paintings, Corcoran Gallery of Art, Washington, DC

1950
Annual Exhibition of Contemporary American Sculpture, Watercolors, and Drawings, Whitney Museum of American Art, New York, NY

Nineteen Young Americans, Metropolitan Museum of Art, New York, NY

Painting in the United States, 1950, Museum of Art, Carnegie Institute, Pittsburgh, PA

Sixty Years of American Art, Whitney Museum of American Art, New York, NY

Symbolic Realism, Edwin Hewitt Gallery, New York, NY

Symbolic Realism in American Painting, 1940–1950, Institute of Contemporary Art, London, England

1949
Annual Exhibition of Contemporary American Painting, Whitney Museum of American Art, New York, NY

Painting in the United States, 1949, Museum of Art, Carnegie Institute, Pittsburgh, PA

1948
Annual Exhibition of Contemporary American Painting, Whitney Museum of American Art, New York, NY

Biennial Exhibition, Worcester Art Museum, MA

Painting in the United States, 1948, Museum of Art, Carnegie Institute, Pittsburgh, PA

1947
Annual Exhibition of Contemporary American Painting, Whitney Museum of American Art, New York, NY

Painting in the United States, 1947, Museum of Art, Carnegie Institute, Pittsburgh, PA

1946
Fifteen Americans, Museum of Modern Art, New York, NY

1944
28th Annual Exhibition: Brooklyn Society of Artists, Brooklyn Museum, Brooklyn, NY

# SELECTED BIBLIOGRAPHY

Allende, Isabel. *Afrodita: Cuentos, Recetas y Otros Afrodisiacos*. Barcelona, Spain: Plaza & Janes, 1997 (four reproductions).

Art Students League of New York. *92nd Regular Session*. New York: Art Students League, 1967.

*Artists in New York*. New York Board of Education and the Bureau of Radio and Television. Radio series.

Baigell, Matthew. *Dictionary of American Art*. New York: Harper & Row, 1979.

Baker, John. "Report from New Brunswick: Representational Painting in the U.S., 1940–1960." *Art in America* 70 (November 1982): 23.

Barr, Alfred H., Jr. "Painting and Sculpture Acquisitions." *Museum of Modern Art Bulletin* 28, nos. 2–4 (1961): 24.

Baur, John I. H. *Between the Fairs: 25 Years of American Art, 1939–1963*. New York: Whitney Museum of American Art, 1964.

———. *The New Decade: 35 American Painters and Sculptors*. New York: Whitney Museum of American Art, 1955.

Benedikt, Michael. "George Tooker." In *Art: USA: Now*, edited by Lee Nordness, vol. 2, 348–51. New York: Viking Press, 1963.

Berman, Greta, and Jeffrey Wechsler. *Realism and Realities: The Other Side of American Painting, 1940–1960*. New Brunswick, NJ: Rutgers University Press, 1982.

Bolin, A. "Bilden: det Formedvetna" (The picture: The conscious form). *Paletten* (Sweden), no. 3 (1976): 27–29.

*Britannica Encyclopedia of American Art*. Chicago, IL: Encyclopaedia Britannica Education Corporation, 1973.

Candee, Marjorie Dent, ed. "George Tooker." *Current Biography* 19 (March 1958): 38–39.

Cohen, George M. *A History of American Art*. New York: Dell, 1971.

Cummings, Paul. *A Dictionary of Contemporary American Artists*. 2d ed. New York: St. Martin's Press, 1971.

Dartmouth College, Hopkins Center. *George Tooker*. Hanover, NH: Dartmouth College, 1967.

Davidson, Marshall B. *The American Heritage History of the Artist's America*. New York: American Heritage, 1973.

De Micheli, Mario. "L'Arte d'Inspirazione Sociale e d'Impegno Civile in America dal 1900 al 1945." *L'Arte Moderna* 8, no. 71 (1967): 306, 311.

Fletcher, Valerie J. *Dreams and Nightmares: Utopian Visions in Modern Art*. Washington, DC: Smithsonian Institution, Joseph H. Hirshhorn Museum, 1983.

Freegood, Lillian. *An Enduring Image: American Painting from 1665*. New York: Crowell, 1970.

Garver, Thomas H. *George Tooker*. San Francisco, CA: Fine Arts Museum of San Francisco, 1974.

———. *George Tooker*. New York: Clarkson N. Potter, 1985.

———. *George Tooker—1988*. New York: Marisa del Re Gallery, 1988.

———. *A Silent Theater: The Paintings of George Tooker*. Charleston, SC: Gibbes Art Gallery, 1987 (reprinted in the souvenir program of the Spoleto Festival, USA, 1987).

Gear, Josephine. *Cadmus, French and Tooker: The Early Years*. New York: Whitney Museum of American Art at Philip Morris, 1990.

Good, Joan. *Contemporary Surrealism*. Summit, NJ: New Jersey Center for the Visual Arts, 1991.

Goodrich, Lloyd, and John I. H. Baur. *American Art of Our Century*. New York: Whitney Museum of American Art, 1961.

Green, Samuel M. *American Art: A Historical Survey*. New York: Ronald Press, 1966.

Gustafson, Donna, Nan Rothschild, Kendall Taylor, Gilbert T. Vincent, and Linda Weintraub. *Art What Thou Eat*. Annandale-on-Hudson, NY: Edith C. Blum Art Institute, Bard College, 1990.

Harvard College. *Class of 1942: 15th Anniversary Report*. Cambridge, MA: Harvard, 1957.

Hefferman, Ildiko. *George Tooker: Working Drawings*. Burlington, VT: Robert Hull Fleming Art Museum, University of Vermont, 1987.

Huyghe, Rene, ed. *Larousse Encyclopedia of Modern Art*. New York: Phaidon, 1973.

Kirstein, Lincoln. *Symbolic Realism in American Painting, 1940–1950*. London, England: Institute for Contemporary Art, 1950.

Kirwin, Linda. "Visual Thinking." Journal of the Archives of American Art 27 (1987): 24.

Kloss, William. *Modern American Realism*. Washington, DC: Smithsonian Institution, National Museum of American Art, 1987.

Kramer, Hilton. "The Whitney's New Ambition." *Art and Antiques*, October 1996.

Kuh, Katherine. *American Artists Paint the City*. Venice: 28th Biennale, 1956.

Levin, Gail. "The Office Image in the Visual Arts." *Arts Magazine* 59 (summer 1984): 102.

Mendelowitz, Daniel M. *A History of American Art*. New York: Holt, Rinehart & Winston, 1970.

Munro, Isabel Stevenson, and Kate M. Munro. *Index to Reproductions of American Paintings: First Supplement*. New York: H. W. Wilson, 1964.

Myers, Bernard S., ed. *Encyclopedia of Painting*. 3d ed. New York: Crown, 1970.

———. *McGraw Hill Dictionary of Art*. Vol. 3. New York: McGraw Hill, 1969.

Newmeyer, Sarah. *Enjoying Modern Art*. New York: Reinhold, 1955.

Osborne, Harold, ed. *The Oxford Companion to Twentieth-Century Art*. Oxford, England: Clarendon Press, 1970.

Pacheco, P. "Point Counterpoint: Five American Painters Discuss the Relevance and Influence of George Seurat's Work Today." *Art and Antiques* 8 (October 1991): 75.

*Phaidon Dictionary of Twentieth-Century Art*. New York: Phaidon, 1973.

*Phaidon Encyclopedia of Art and Artists*. New York: E. P. Dutton, 1978.

Pierson, William H., Jr., and Martha Davidson, eds. *Arts of the United States: A Pictorial Survey*. Athens, GA: University of Georgia Press, 1960.

Pomeroy, Ralph. "A Master of Modern Dismay." *New Lugano Review* (Switzerland), nos. 8–9 (1976): 38–41.

———. "Tooker, Really." *Art and Artists* 2 (April 1967): 24–27.

Preston, Stuart. "Painting in the United States, 1885–1957." In *Modern Art: A Pictorial Anthology*, edited by Charles McCurdey, 146. New York: Macmillan, 1958.

Robertson, Bruce. *Twentieth-Century American Art: The Ebsworth Collection* (exhibition catalogue), 263–65. Washington, DC: National Gallery of Art, 2000.

Rodman, Selden. *Conversations with Artists*. New York: Devin-Adair, 1957.

Rose, Barbara. *American Painting: The 20th Century*. Geneva, Switzerland: Skira, 1970.

Sokol, David M. *Solitude: Inner Visions in American Art*. Evanston, IL: Terra Museum of American Art, 1982.

"The Strange World of George Tooker." *Avant-Garde*, September 1968, 36–45.

Sultan, Altoon. *The Illuminous Brush: Painting with Egg Tempera*, 18, 19, 20, 27, 107–8, 121. New York: Watson-Guptill Publications, 1999.

Taubes, Frederic. "Egg Tempera Painting." *American Artist*, May 1957, 20–25, 69.

*Time*. 7 September 1962, 36.

Time-Life Books, ed. *American Painting 1900–1970*. New York: Time-Life Books, 1970.

## SELECTED REVIEWS

Tomor, Michael A. "Magic Realism: An American Response to Surrealism." *American Art Review* 11, no. 4 (1999).

Von Blum, Paul. *The Art of Social Conscience.* New York: Universe Books, 1976.

Wechsler, J. "Magic Realism: Defining the Indefinite." *Art Journal* 45 (winter 1985): 294.

Weinberg, Adam D., Nicholas Serota, and Sandy Nairne. *Views from Abroad: European Perspectives on American Art 3: American Realities.* New York: Whitney Museum of American Art and Harry N. Abrams, 1997.

Weller, Allen S. *The Joys and Sorrows of Recent American Art.* Urbana, IL: University of Illinois Press, 1968.

*Art Digest* 25 (March 1951): 24.

*Art News* 50 (March 1951): 50.

*Arts Digest* 29 (January 1955).

*Arts Magazine* 4 (April 1967): 16.

Bagg, Mary. "Artistic Tempera-ment." *Valley Advocate,* June 2000.

Butler, Joseph T. "Surrealism of George Tooker." *Connoisseur* 187 (October 1974): 135.

Derfner, Phyllis. *Art International* 19 (March 1975): 38–40.

Edgar, Natalie. *Art News* 61 (April 1962): 60–61.

Gablik, Suzi. *Art News* 63 (May 1964): 16.

Glueck, Grace. "Art: A Nostalgic Visit to 'The Surreal City.'" *The New York Times*, 31 May 1985.

———. "George Tooker at DC Moore." *The New York Times*, 22 December 2000.

Grimes, Nancy. [Exhibition: Cadmus, French and Tooker, Whitney Museum of American Art at Philip Morris]. *Art News* 89 (summer 1989): 159.

———. "George Tooker at DC Moore." *Art in America*, July 1998.

Johnson, Ken. "Interwoven Lives: George Platt Lynes and His Friends." *The New York Times*, 12 October 2001.

McQuid, Cate. "The Magic That Lies Beyond Reality." *Boston Globe*, 18 February 1999.

Mitchell, Phoebe "Simply Luminous." *Daily Hampshire Gazette*, 6 June 2000.

Moorman, M. *Art News* 84 (May 1985): 117.

———. *The New Yorker*, 11 December 2000, 26.

*New York Herald Tribune*, February 25, 1951.

Noh, David. *New York Blade News,* December 2000, 20.

Preston, Stuart. *Burlington Magazine* 102 (May 1960): 229.

Raynor, Vivien. *Art News* 59 (April 1960): 55.

———. *Art Magazine* 36 (May 1962): 101.

———. *The New York Times*, 22 February 1985.

Risatti, H. [Exhibition: Marsh Gallery, University of Richmond, VA]. *New Art Examiner* 17 (December 1989): 42.

Tyler, Parker. *Art News* 53 (January 1955): 56.

Zucker, Barbara. *Art News* 74 (March 1975): 109–10.

*George Tooker Papers*, on deposit at the Archives of American Art, Smithsonian Institution, Washington, DC. (Papers are microfilmed and are available only on a restricted basis. Access requires permission from the artist.)

## AWARDS

1983
Governor's Award for Excellence in the Arts, Vermont Council on the Arts

Member, American Academy and Institute of Arts and Letters

1970
Member, National Academy of Design

1960
Grant, National Institute of Letters

## PUBLIC COLLECTIONS

Addison Gallery of American Art, Phillips Academy, Andover, MA

Arizona State University Art Museum, Tempe, AZ

Brooklyn Museum of Art, Brooklyn, NY

Columbus Museum of Art, Columbus, OH

Delaware Art Museum, Wilmington, DE

Hirshhorn Museum, Washington, DC

Hood Museum of Art, Dartmouth College, Hanover, NH

Metropolitan Museum of Art, New York, NY

Muscarelle Museum of Art, College of William and Mary, Williamsburg, VA

Museum of Contemporary Art, Chicago, IL

Museum of Modern Art, New York, NY

National Academy of Design, New York, NY

National Museum of American Art, Smithsonian Institution, Washington, DC

New Britain Museum of American Art, New Britain, CT

New York Historical Society, New York, NY

Terra Museum of American Art, Chicago, IL

Virginia Museum of Fine Arts, Richmond, VA

Walker Art Center, Minneapolis, MN

Wayne County Public Library, Goldsboro, NC

Whitney Museum of American Art, New York, NY

# INDEX